99BB

Carnegie Commission on Higher Education

Sponsored Research Studies

ACADEMIC TRANSFORMATION:
SEVENTEEN INSTITUTIONS UNDER PRESSURE
David Riesman and Verne A. Stadtman (eds.)

WHERE COLLEGES ARE AND WHO ATTENDS:
EFFECTS OF ACCESSIBILITY ON COLLEGE
ATTENDANCE
C. Arnold Anderson, Mary Jean Bowman, and
Vincent Tinto

NEW DIRECTIONS IN LEGAL EDUCATION
Herbert L. Packer and Thomas Ehrlich
abridged and unabridged editions

THE UNIVERSITY AS AN ORGANIZATION
James A. Perkins (ed.)

THE EMERGING TECHNOLOGY:
INSTRUCTIONAL USES OF THE COMPUTER
IN HIGHER EDUCATION
Roger E. Levien

A STATISTICAL PORTRAIT OF HIGHER
EDUCATION
Seymour E. Harris

THE HOME OF SCIENCE:
THE ROLE OF THE UNIVERSITY
Dael Wolfle

EDUCATION AND EVANGELISM:
A PROFILE OF PROTESTANT COLLEGES
C. Robert Pace

PROFESSIONAL EDUCATION:
SOME NEW DIRECTIONS
Edgar H. Schein

THE NONPROFIT RESEARCH INSTITUTE:
ITS ORIGIN, OPERATION, PROBLEMS, AND
PROSPECTS
Harold Orlans

THE INVISIBLE COLLEGES:
A PROFILE OF SMALL, PRIVATE COLLEGES
WITH LIMITED RESOURCES
Alexander W. Astin and Calvin B. T. Lee

AMERICAN HIGHER EDUCATION:
DIRECTIONS OLD AND NEW
Joseph Ben-David

A DEGREE AND WHAT ELSE?
CORRELATES AND CONSEQUENCES OF A
COLLEGE EDUCATION
Stephen B. Withey, Jo Anne Coble, Gerald
Gurin, John P. Robinson, Burkhard Strumpel,
Elizabeth Keogh Taylor, and Arthur C. Wolfe

THE MULTICAMPUS UNIVERSITY:
A STUDY OF ACADEMIC GOVERNANCE
Eugene C. Lee and Frank M. Bowen

INSTITUTIONS IN TRANSITION:
A PROFILE OF CHANGE IN HIGHER
EDUCATION
(INCORPORATING THE 1970 STATISTICAL
REPORT)
Harold L. Hodgkinson

EFFICIENCY IN LIBERAL EDUCATION:
A STUDY OF COMPARATIVE INSTRUCTIONAL
COSTS FOR DIFFERENT WAYS OF ORGANIZ-
ING TEACHING-LEARNING IN A LIBERAL
ARTS COLLEGE
Howard R. Bowen and Gordon K. Douglass

CREDIT FOR COLLEGE:
PUBLIC POLICY FOR STUDENT LOANS
Robert W. Hartman

MODELS AND MAVERICKS:
A PROFILE OF PRIVATE LIBERAL ARTS
COLLEGES
Morris T. Keeton

BETWEEN TWO WORLDS:
A PROFILE OF NEGRO HIGHER EDUCATION
Frank Bowles and Frank A. DeCosta

BREAKING THE ACCESS BARRIERS:
A PROFILE OF TWO-YEAR COLLEGES
Leland L. Medsker and Dale Tillery

ANY PERSON, ANY STUDY:
AN ESSAY ON HIGHER EDUCATION IN THE
UNITED STATES
Eric Ashby

THE NEW DEPRESSION IN HIGHER
EDUCATION:
A STUDY OF FINANCIAL CONDITIONS AT 41
COLLEGES AND UNIVERSITIES
Earl F. Cheit

FINANCING MEDICAL EDUCATION:
AN ANALYSIS OF ALTERNATIVE POLICIES
AND MECHANISMS
Rashi Fein and Gerald I. Weber

HIGHER EDUCATION IN NINE COUNTRIES:
A COMPARATIVE STUDY OF COLLEGES AND
UNIVERSITIES ABROAD
*Barbara B. Burn, Philip G. Altbach, Clark Kerr,
and James A. Perkins*

BRIDGES TO UNDERSTANDING:
INTERNATIONAL PROGRAMS OF AMERICAN
COLLEGES AND UNIVERSITIES
Irwin T. Sanders and Jennifer C. Ward

GRADUATE AND PROFESSIONAL EDUCATION,
1980:
A SURVEY OF INSTITUTIONAL PLANS
Lewis B. Mayhew

THE AMERICAN COLLEGE AND AMERICAN
CULTURE:
SOCIALIZATION AS A FUNCTION OF HIGHER
EDUCATION
Oscar Handlin and Mary F. Handlin

RECENT ALUMNI AND HIGHER EDUCATION:
A SURVEY OF COLLEGE GRADUATES
Joe L. Spaeth and Andrew M. Greeley

CHANGE IN EDUCATIONAL POLICY:
SELF-STUDIES IN SELECTED COLLEGES AND
UNIVERSITIES
Dwight R. Ladd

STATE OFFICIALS AND HIGHER EDUCATION:
A SURVEY OF THE OPINIONS AND
EXPECTATIONS OF POLICY MAKERS IN NINE
STATES
Heinz Eulau and Harold Quinley

ACADEMIC DEGREE STRUCTURES,
INNOVATIVE APPROACHES:
PRINCIPLES OF REFORM IN DEGREE
STRUCTURES IN THE UNITED STATES
Stephen H. Spurr

COLLEGES OF THE FORGOTTEN AMERICANS:
A PROFILE OF STATE COLLEGES AND
REGIONAL UNIVERSITIES
E. Alden Dunham

FROM BACKWATER TO MAINSTREAM:
A PROFILE OF CATHOLIC HIGHER
EDUCATION
Andrew M. Greeley

THE ECONOMICS OF THE MAJOR PRIVATE
UNIVERSITIES
William G. Bowen
(Out of print, but available from University Microfilms.)

THE FINANCE OF HIGHER EDUCATION
Howard R. Bowen
(Out of print, but available from University Microfilms.)

ALTERNATIVE METHODS OF FEDERAL
FUNDING FOR HIGHER EDUCATION
Ron Wolk
(Out of print, but available from University Microfilms.)

INVENTORY OF CURRENT RESEARCH ON
HIGHER EDUCATION 1968
Dale M. Heckman and Warren Bryan Martin
(Out of print, but available from University Microfilms.)

*The following technical reports are available from the Carnegie Commission on Higher Education, 2150 Shattuck
Ave., Berkeley, California 94704.*

RESOURCE USE IN HIGHER EDUCATION:
TRENDS IN OUTPUT AND INPUTS, 1930–1967
June O'Neill

TRENDS AND PROJECTIONS OF PHYSICIANS
IN THE UNITED STATES 1967–2002
Mark S. Blumberg

The following reprints are available from the Carnegie Commission on Higher Education, 2150 Shattuck Ave., Berkeley, California 94704.

ACCELERATED PROGRAMS OF MEDICAL EDUCATION, by Mark S. Blumberg, reprinted from JOURNAL OF MEDICAL EDUCATION, vol. 46, no. 8, August 1971.*

SCIENTIFIC MANPOWER FOR 1970–1985, by Allan M. Cartter, reprinted from SCIENCE, vol. 172, no. 3979, pp. 132–140, April 9, 1971.

A NEW METHOD OF MEASURING STATES' HIGHER EDUCATION BURDEN, by Neil Timm, reprinted from THE JOURNAL OF HIGHER EDUCATION, vol. 42, no. 1, pp. 27–33, January 1971.*

REGENT WATCHING, by Earl F. Cheit, reprinted from AGB REPORTS, vol. 13, no. 6, pp. 4–13, March 1971.*

COLLEGE GENERATIONS—FROM THE 1930S TO THE 1960S, by Seymour M. Lipset and Everett C. Ladd, Jr., reprinted from THE PUBLIC INTEREST, no. 25, Summer 1971.

*The Commission's stock of this reprint has been exhausted.

AMERICAN SOCIAL SCIENTISTS AND THE GROWTH OF CAMPUS POLITICAL ACTIVISM IN THE 1960s, by Everett C. Ladd, Jr., and Seymour M. Lipset, reprinted from SOCIAL SCIENCES INFORMATION, vol. 10, no. 2, April 1971.

THE POLITICS OF AMERICAN POLITICAL SCIENTISTS, by Everett C. Ladd, Jr., and Seymour M. Lipset, reprinted from PS, vol. 4, no. 2, Spring 1971.*

THE DIVIDED PROFESSORIATE, by Seymour M. Lipset and Everett C. Ladd, Jr., reprinted from CHANGE, vol. 3, no. 3, pp. 54–60, May 1971.*

JEWISH ACADEMICS IN THE UNITED STATES: THEIR ACHIEVEMENTS, CULTURE AND POLITICS, by Seymour M. Lipset and Everett C. Ladd, Jr., reprinted from AMERICAN JEWISH YEAR BOOK, 1971.

THE UNHOLY ALLIANCE AGAINST THE CAMPUS, by Kenneth Keniston and Michael Lerner, reprinted from NEW YORK TIMES MAGAZINE, November 8, 1970.

PRECARIOUS PROFESSORS: NEW PATTERNS OF REPRESENTATION, by Joseph W. Garbarino, reprinted from INDUSTRIAL RELATIONS, vol. 10, no. 1, February 1971.*

. . . AND WHAT PROFESSORS THINK: ABOUT STUDENT PROTEST AND MANNERS, MORALS, POLITICS, AND CHAOS ON THE CAMPUS, by Seymour Martin Lipset and Everett C. Ladd, Jr., reprinted from PSYCHOLOGY TODAY, November 1970.*

DEMAND AND SUPPLY IN U.S. HIGHER EDUCATION: A PROGRESS REPORT, by Roy Radner and Leonard S. Miller, reprinted from AMERICAN ECONOMIC REVIEW, May 1970.*

RESOURCES FOR HIGHER EDUCATION: AN ECONOMIST'S VIEW, by Theodore W. Schultz, reprinted from JOURNAL OF POLITICAL ECONOMY, vol. 76, no. 3, University of Chicago, May/June 1968.*

INDUSTRIAL RELATIONS AND UNIVERSITY RELATIONS, by Clark Kerr, reprinted from PROCEEDINGS OF THE 21ST ANNUAL WINTER MEETING OF THE INDUSTRIAL RELATIONS RESEARCH ASSOCIATION, pp. 15–25.*

NEW CHALLENGES TO THE COLLEGE AND UNIVERSITY, by Clark Kerr, reprinted from Kermit Gordon (ed.), AGENDA FOR THE NATION, The Brookings Institution, Washington, D.C., 1968.*

PRESIDENTIAL DISCONTENT, by Clark Kerr, reprinted from David C. Nichols (ed.), PERSPECTIVES ON CAMPUS TENSIONS: PAPERS PREPARED FOR THE SPECIAL COMMITTEE ON CAMPUS TENSIONS, American Council on Education, Washington, D.C., September 1970.*

STUDENT PROTEST—AN INSTITUTIONAL AND NATIONAL PROFILE, by Harold Hodgkinson, reprinted from THE RECORD, vol. 71, no. 4, May 1970.*

*The Commission's stock of this reprint has been exhausted.

WHAT'S BUGGING THE STUDENTS?, *by Kenneth Keniston, reprinted from* EDUCATIONAL RECORD, *American Council on Education, Washington, D.C., Spring 1970.**

THE POLITICS OF ACADEMIA, *by Seymour Martin Lipset, reprinted from David C. Nichols (ed.),* PERSPECTIVES ON CAMPUS TENSIONS: PAPERS PREPARED FOR THE SPECIAL COMMITTEE ON CAMPUS TENSIONS, *American Council on Education, Washington, D.C., September 1970.**

INTERNATIONAL PROGRAMS OF U.S. COLLEGES AND UNIVERSITIES: PRIORITIES FOR THE SEVENTIES, *by James A. Perkins, reprinted by permission of the International Council for Educational Development, Occasional Paper no. 1, July 1971.*

FACULTY UNIONISM: FROM THEORY TO PRACTICE, *by Joseph W. Garbarino, reprinted from* INDUSTRIAL RELATIONS, *vol. 11, no. 1, pp. 1–17, February 1972.*

MORE FOR LESS: HIGHER EDUCATION'S NEW PRIORITY, *by Virginia B. Smith, reprinted from* UNIVERSAL HIGHER EDUCATION: COSTS AND BENEFITS, *American Council on Education, Washington, D.C., 1971.*

ACADEMIA AND POLITICS IN AMERICA, *by Seymour M. Lipset, reprinted from Thomas I. Nossiter (ed.),* IMAGINATION AND PRECISION IN THE SOCIAL SCIENCES, *pp. 211–289, Faber and Faber, London, 1972.*

POLITICS OF ACADEMIC NATURAL SCIENTISTS AND ENGINEERS, *by Everett C. Ladd, Jr., and Seymour M. Lipset, reprinted from* SCIENCE, *vol. 176, no. 4039, pp. 1091–1100, June 9, 1972.*

THE INTELLECTUAL AS CRITIC AND REBEL, WITH SPECIAL REFERENCE TO THE UNITED STATES AND THE SOVIET UNION, *by Seymour M. Lipset and Richard B. Dobson, reprinted from* DAEDALUS, *vol. 101, no. 3, pp. 137–198, Summer 1972.*

THE POLITICS OF AMERICAN SOCIOLOGISTS, *by Seymour M. Lipset and Everett C. Ladd, Jr., reprinted from* THE AMERICAN JOURNAL OF SOCIOLOGY, *vol. 78, no. 1, July 1972.*

THE DISTRIBUTION OF ACADEMIC TENURE IN AMERICAN HIGHER EDUCATION, *by Martin Trow, reprinted from* THE TENURE DEBATE, *Bardwell Smith (ed.), Jossey-Bass, San Francisco, 1972.*

THE NATURE AND ORIGINS OF THE CARNEGIE COMMISSION ON HIGHER EDUCATION, *by Alan Pifer, based on a speech delivered to the Pennsylvania Association of Colleges and Universities, Oct. 16, 1972, reprinted by permission of the Carnegie Foundation for the Advancement of Teaching.*

COMING OF MIDDLE AGE IN HIGHER EDUCATION, *by Earl F. Cheit, address delivered to American Association of State Colleges and Universities and National Association of State Universities and Land-Grant Colleges, Nov. 13, 1972.*

MEASURING FACULTY UNIONISM: QUANTITY AND QUALITY, *by Bill Aussieker and J. W. Garbarino, reprinted from* INDUSTRIAL RELATIONS, *vol. 12, no. 2, May 1973.*

PROBLEMS IN THE TRANSITION FROM ELITE TO MASS HIGHER EDUCATION, *by Martin Trow, paper prepared for a conference on mass higher education sponsored by the Organization for Economic Co-operation and Development, June 1973.*

This book was set in Palatino by B. Handelman Associates, Inc. It was printed and bound by The Maple Press Company. The designer was Elliot Epstein. The editors were Nancy Tressel and Janine Parson for McGraw-Hill Book Company and Verne A. Stadtman and Karen Seriguchi for the Carnegie Commission on Higher Education. Audre Hanneman supervised preparation of the index. Milton J. Heiberg supervised the production.

Higher Education
and Earnings

Higher Education and Earnings

COLLEGE AS AN INVESTMENT AND A SCREENING DEVICE

by **Paul Taubman**

Professor of Economics
University of Pennsylvania

and **Terence Wales**

Associate Professor of Economics
University of British Columbia

A Report Prepared for
The Carnegie Commission on Higher Education
and the
National Bureau of Economic Research
General Series 101

MCGRAW-HILL BOOK COMPANY

New York St. Louis San Francisco
Düsseldorf Johannesburg Kuala Lumpur London Mexico
Montreal New Delhi Panama Paris São Paulo
Singapore Sydney Tokyo Toronto

The Carnegie Commission on Higher Education,
2150 Shattuck Avenue, Berkeley, California 94704
and the National Bureau of Economic Research,
261 Madison Avenue, New York, New York 10016,
have sponsored preparation of this report as part
of a continuing effort to obtain and present
significant information for public discussion.
The views expressed are those of the authors.

HIGHER EDUCATION AND EARNINGS
College as an Investment and a Screening Device

Library of Congress Cataloging in Publication Data

Taubman, Paul, date
Higher education and earnings.

(National Bureau of Economic Research. General
series 101)
"A report prepared for the Carnegie Commission on
Higher Education."
Bibliography: p.
1. College graduates—Employment—United States.
2. High school graduates—Employment—United States.
3. Wages—United States. 4. Education—Economic
aspects—United States. I. Wales, Terence, joint
author. II. Carnegie Commission on Higher Education.
III. Title. IV. Series.
HD6278.U5T38   331.2'973   74-9941
ISBN 0-07-010121-3

1 2 3 4 5 6 7 8 9 MAMM 7 9 8 7 6 5 4

Contents

List of Figures

List of Tables

Foreword

by Clark Kerr
Chairman, Carnegie Commission on Higher Education

This is the third volume resulting from studies conducted by the National Bureau of Economic Research for the Carnegie Commission. It presents the full report by Taubman and Wales of their detailed analysis of the results of a 1969 follow-up survey of a large sample of men who were accepted for a special Army Air Corps volunteer program in 1943. A brief summary of the findings was also included in the recently published volume of essays edited by Juster (*Education, Income, and Human Behavior*).

The Taubman and Wales study is based on what is in some ways the most valuable source of data that has as yet been available for human-capital analysis. Most earlier studies of the rate of return from education have been based on decennial census data that have yielded information on educational attainment and earnings, but not on individual ability. Thus, it has not been possible to determine how much of the variation in earnings associated with education might be attributable to differences in ability, although some analysts have devised methods for attempting to measure the influence of ability. But the Army Air Corps volunteers included in the Taubman-Wales study had all participated in a battery of 17 tests designed to measure various aspects of physical and mental ability. The results of these tests were available for analysis, along with the information on earnings and work histories provided by the respondents.

Another valuable feature of the data is their longitudinal character, in contrast with the cross-sectional data used by most human-capital analysts. The men included in the 1969 follow-up survey had also been respondents in an earlier study conducted by Thorndike and Hagen in 1955. Thus, Taubman and

Wales were able to analyze how education, ability, and other factors affected actual changes in earnings of these men between 1955 and 1969, rather than having to rely on variations in earnings at a given point in time to draw inferences about the interaction between age and other influences on income.

The study owes its importance, also, to the high degree of technical skill the authors have brought to the analysis.

The findings indicate that there was an upward bias of about 25 percent in their measures of the impact of education on earnings in 1955, if the influence of ability was omitted. The bias was somewhat smaller in 1969, reflecting the fact that differences in earnings associated with ability did not increase as rapidly as those associated with education between 1955, when the men were aged about 33, on the average, and 1969, when their average age was 47. Variations attributable to ability did not differ greatly according to educational attainment, with the important and interesting exception that by 1969 differentials associated with high ability were relatively large for men with graduate training.

An important qualification, however, is that it was only the results of the mathematical aptitude test that were reflected in these impacts of ability—none of the other tests had a significant effect on earnings differences. This is at variance with the findings of Hause (based on the same data and reported in the Juster volume), who used a composite measure of ability and found it had a significant effect on earnings. In evaluating the ability results, it is also important to keep in mind the fact that the average ability of the men in this sample was high—they all had to pass an initial aptitude test with a score equivalent to the median for high school graduates before qualifying for the battery of 17 special tests. Clearly, we need more experimentation with alternative measures of ability and with samples representing a broader spectrum of the population before achieving definitive results on the relative impact of ability and other influences.

In other respects, the Taubman-Wales results will add "grist to the mill" of both the supporters and the critics of human-capital theory—probably especially the latter. On the one hand, if allowance is made for differences in methodology and for the special characteristics of their sample, their rates of return to investment in education do not appear to differ strikingly from those of earlier investigators. On the other hand, their findings lend support to those who argue that education accounts for only a relatively small proportion of variations in earnings. Yet Taubman and Wales provide some evidence that casts doubt on the implication of Christopher Jencks and his coauthors that much of the variance is attributable to "luck."[1] For example, they find that the difference between excellent and poor health in 1969 was worth about $7,000 a year. They also made use of a composite "background" variable that had a significant effect on earnings differences.

Potentially even more damaging to human-capital theory is the Taubman-Wales finding that, for those with some college or a B.A., a substantial part of the earnings advantage associated with education was attributable to "screening," that is, the requirements or preferences of employers for those with a college education. But their method of measuring the effect of screening is crude, as they admit. Even so, the issue of screening and of its relationship to employment discrimination is becoming increasingly important and calls for much more research.

We are also approaching a stage in the evolution of human-capital research, I believe, when more attention needs to be paid to occupational differences in rates of return, as Eckaus has shown. Perhaps even more fundamental is the need to look less exclusively at money income as *the* measure of the economic results of education. Virtually all human-capital theorists pay lip service to the role of the consumption benefits of education and then ignore them as not susceptible of measurement. Similarly, most researchers, including Taubman and Wales, admit that there are social benefits that cannot be measured by the usual conventional methods, but then proceed to confine their efforts to measurement in the coventional manner. Finally, there is accumulating evidence that job satisfaction is often an extremely important component of the benefits of higher education. It would be a great step forward if someone were to devise a method of adjusting measures of pecuniary benefits to allow for the contribution of nonpecuniary rewards.

---

[1]C. Jencks and others: *Inequality: A Reassessment of the Effect of Family and Schooling in America*, Basic Books, New York, 1972, p. 8.

Foreword

by John R. Meyer
President, National Bureau of Economic Research

In this volume Taubman and Wales report on their study of the determinants of earnings. This work was supported by the Carnegie Commission on Higher Education as a part of the National Bureau of Economic Research's study of the benefits of higher education. The larger study was directed by F. Thomas Juster, and much of the research is summarized in the CCHE-NBER volume *Education, Income, and Human Behavior*, edited by Juster.

In their study Taubman and Wales make extensive use of the NBER-TH data set, a longitudinal sample of some 5,000 men born in the decade 1916–1926, surveyed in 1943 (by the U.S. Army), in 1955 (by Thorndike and Hagen), and in 1969 (by NBER). The sample consists of men who volunteered for certain Army Air Corps training programs during World War II. The data set, which is described in detail in Chapter 4, is a unique and important one. The authors of this volume were instrumental in bringing its potential availability to the attention of the National Bureau. They participated in planning the 1969 survey, and this volume contains much of their analysis of these data. (The sample was again surveyed in 1970 and 1971, and Taubman, as well as others within and outside NBER, are continuing to study the behavior of these men.) Here, Taubman and Wales use single-equation regression techniques to investigate the influence of formal schooling, measured ability, age, family background, and personal characteristics on the level of observed earnings in 1955 and in 1969, and on the growth in earnings over the working life through 1969.

This volume complements other recently completed and ongoing studies at NBER. It is one of several projects which contribute to an understanding of the relationship between formal schooling and measured ability as determinants of the level of and lifetime growth in earnings, of the influence of family background variables on earnings, and of the mechanisms through which schooling affects earnings.

This question of mechanisms, of how schooling affects earnings, is a difficult and complex one. It is also one on which those subscribing to human-capital theories and those skeptical of such theories are likely to differ. For adherents of the human-capital approach, many of the "other" influences on income often cited by critics as contradicting or undermining their theory are seen as easily incorporated into the human-capital model. To the critics, such incorporations often seem artificial, or at least unnecessary if one starts with a broader, less constricting set of relationships among income and human qualities, institutions, and environments. These differences are discernible at several points in this manuscript, but perhaps most noticeably in the discussion of the possible use of colleges as a "screening" device by employers.

The larger issue, though, in determining the benefits of education remains that of measuring social and nonpecuniary returns rather than just the private monetary returns. On this point, both those who adopt and those who criticize the human-capital approach agree. As a consequence, an ever-increasing portion of our human-capital studies at the National Bureau are devoted to these issues—the relationships between education and household's consumption behavior; the relationships between the preschool environment and the later school performance and the extent to which this preschool environment is conditioned by the income and education of the parents; the relationship between education and the taste for leisure (or, its obverse, labor force participation); the relationships between education and health; and the relationships between education and demographic behavior. Some of the preliminary findings of this research is to be found in the recent volume *Education, Income, and Human Behavior*, published jointly by the National Bureau and the Carnegie Commission; the rest has, or will emerge, in formal publications of the National Bureau itself.

Nevertheless, the unanswered questions about the value of education beyond the purely pecuniary remain and loom large. I am sure that they will challenge scholars at the National Bureau and elsewhere for years to come.

Acknowledgments

The research delineated in this book has benefited greatly from the assistance of many individuals at different institutions over the past few years. To achieve the goals of this study, it was necessary to have much better data than those previously available. Fortunately, Robert L. Thorndike at the Teachers College of Columbia University retained much of the data that he and Elizabeth Hagen had used in the fifties and made them available to us. Similarly, Dael W. Wolfle at the University of Washington allowed us to use the data that he and Joseph Smith employed in their analysis of earnings, also in the fifties. We wish to express our gratitude and to acknowledge our debt to both men for permitting us to share their data and for providing us with useful comments and warm encouragement.

We are greatly indebted to F. Thomas Juster and John R. Meyer at the National Bureau of Economic Research for providing overall guidance for our research effort and for helpful comments and insights. In addition, we have benefited from general discussions with the others at the Bureau engaged in closely related research—Jacob Mincer, Lewis C. Solmon, and Finis R. Welch. Suggestions of the Bureau's reading committee, Gary S. Becker, John C. Hause, Christopher Sims, and Melvin Reder, resulted in a number of changes that improved the manuscript considerably.

We had many helpful discussions with our colleagues at the University of Pennsylvania and at the University of British Columbia, and are especially grateful for the extensive time given by Robert Summers. Several individuals in addition to those mentioned above, to whom we sent preliminary copies of the manuscript, responded with very thoughtful and useful suggestions for improvement. In this connection, we are indebted to Carl Kaysen of the Institute for Advanced Study, who originally suggested this research topic; to Edward F. Denison of the Brookings Institution; and to Margaret S. Gordon, an associate director of the Carnegie Commission on Higher Education.

A study such as this relies heavily on the ability of research assistants to implement empirically the various hypotheses of interest. Consequently, we are deeply indebted to a number of excellent assistants, including Marc Freiman, Peter Gottschalk, Abe Haspel, Edward Villani, Keith Wales, and Janet Young. We also wish to thank Florence Barrow, Shelley Orloff, Patricia Purvin Good, Marie Resanovic, Machilla Roberts, Catherine Grant, and Diane Haspel for typing the many drafts of this volume. The services of the computer centers at both the University of British Columbia and the University of Pennsylvania were used extensively in carrying on the empirical analysis. At the National Bureau of Economic Research, Ruth Ridler did the editing and H. Irving Forman was the chartist.

The research in this study was financed in part by the Carnegie Commisson on Higher Education.

Paul Taubman
Terence Wales

Relation of the Directors to the Work and Publications of the National Bureau of Economic Research

1   The object of the National Bureau of Economic Research is to ascertain and to present to the public important economic facts and their interpretation in a scientific and impartial manner. The Board of Directors is charged with the responsibility of ensuring that the work of the National Bureau is carried on in strict conformity with this object.

2   The President of the National Bureau shall submit to the Board of Directors, or to its Executive Committee, for their formal adoption all specific proposals for research to be instituted.

3   No research report shall be published until the President shall have submitted to each member of the Board the manuscript proposed for publication, and such information as will, in his opinion and in the opinion of the author, serve to determine the suitability of the report for publication in accordance with the principles of the National Bureau. Each manuscript shall contain a summary drawing attention to the nature and treatment of the problem studied, the character of the data and their utilization in the report, and the main conclusions reached.

4   For each manuscript so submitted, a special committee of the Directors (including Directors Emeriti) shall be appointed by majority agreement of the President and Vice-Presidents (or by the Executive Committee in case of inability to decide on the part of the President and Vice-Presidents), consisting of three Directors selected as nearly as may be one from each general division of the Board. The names of the special manuscript committee shall be stated to each Director when the manuscript is submitted to him. It shall be the duty of each member of the special manuscript committee to read the manuscript. If each member of the manuscript committee signifies his approval within thirty days of the transmittal of the manuscript, the report may be published. If at the end of that period any member of the manuscript committee withholds his approval, the President shall then notify each member of the Board, requesting approval or disapproval of publication, and thirty days additional shall be granted for this purpose. The manuscript shall then not be published unless at least a majority of the entire Board who shall have voted on the proposal within the time fixed for the receipt of votes shall have approved.

5   No manuscript may be published, though approved by each member of the special manuscript committee, until forty-five days have elapsed

from the transmittal of the report in manuscript form. The interval is allowed for the receipt of any memorandum of dissent or reservation, together with a brief statement of his reasons, that any member may wish to express; and such memorandum of dissent or reservation shall be published with the manuscript if he so desires. Publication does not, however, imply that each member of the Board has read the manuscript, or that either members of the Board in general or the special committee have passed on its validity in every detail.

6   Publications of the National Bureau issued for informational purposes concerning the work of the Bureau and its staff, or issued to inform the public of activities of Bureau staff, and volumes issued as a result of various conferences involving the National Bureau shall contain a specific disclaimer noting that such publication has not passed through the normal review procedures required in this resolution. The Executive Committee of the Board is charged with review of all such publications from time to time to ensure that they do not take on the character of formal research reports of the National Bureau, requiring formal Board approval.

7   Unless otherwise determined by the Board or exempted by the terms of paragraph 6, a copy of this resolution shall be printed in each National Bureau publication.

(Resolution adopted October 25, 1926, and revised February 8, 1933, February 24, 1941, April 20, 1968, and September 17, 1973)

1. Earnings: Higher Education, Mental Ability, and Screening

A cursory examination of census data and studies based thereon reveals that earnings increase with education and that the rate of return to education is at least equal to the return available to society on other investments (Becker, 1964; and Miller, 1960). The proposition that education can be treated as an investment in human capital has proved to be powerful and illuminating in its own right and a major ingredient in studies of the sources of economic growth and the distribution of income (see Becker, 1964; Denison, 1964; Miller, 1960; and Schultz, 1963). Central to these studies are two concepts. First, the (observed or adjusted) differences in earnings by education level represent the net effect of education, rather than some other personal characteristics that have not been held constant. Second, these observed differences in earnings represent increases in productivity produced by education.

The fact that differences in earnings may not be due solely to differences in educational attainment has long been recognized (Becker, 1964; and Wolfle & Smith, 1956). Also, as is well known, omission of a variable that is positively correlated with education and that has a separate influence on earnings biases the education coefficient upward. Many people have hypothesized that the omission of mental ability and family background, in particular, will result in such a bias. Although in a number of studies attempts have been made to standardize for family background and other relevant determinants of earnings, there are no studies of higher education based on large samples that contain the relevant earnings, ability, and education information.[1] One of our goals is to obtain good estimates of the rate of return to higher education at various ability and education levels.

Most studies of the rate of return to education are based on the premise that differences in earnings at different education levels arise because of the various cognitive and affective skills produced by education. The existence of income differences need not imply that education has produced such skills, however; instead, differentials might arise because lack of education is a barrier to entry into high-paying occupations. As shown more rigorously below, if people are denied entry into an occupation because they lack education *credentials*, the private rate of return to education differs from, and may be higher than, the social rate.

Although many people have suggested that a primary role of education is to serve as a screening, certification, or licensing device, we are aware of no research in which an attempt has been made to separate differences in earnings due to productivity gains from those due to screening. Thus, our second goal is to examine the hypothesis that education adds to income by screening people with low education out of high-paying occupations.

We make use of a new and extremely rich data source to obtain substantially improved estimates of the private and social returns to higher educational attainment and crude estimates of the effect of screening on earnings differentials. Our findings, all of which are subject to qualifications as given in the text, can be briefly summarized as follows. First, the realized (real) rate of return—ignoring consumption and nonmonetary benefits—to the college dropout or college graduate is $7\frac{1}{2}$ to 9 per-

---

[1]Studies for the United States include Ashenfelter and Mooney (1968); Becker (1964); Bridgman (1930); Cutright (1969); Duncan, Featherman, and Duncan (1968); Griliches and Mason (1972); Hansen, Weisbrod, and Scanlon (1970); Hause (1972); Hunt (1963); Morgan and David (1963); Rogers (1967); Weisbrod and Karpoff (1968); and Wolfle and Smith (1956). Except for one segment of Hause (1972), each of these studies suffers from one or more of these serious problems: poor measures of education and ability; small and inadequate sample size; improper statistical technique; or too specialized a sample from which to form generalizations. In addition, only the Rogers study contains enough data to permit estimation of a rate of return as opposed to simply studying income differentials at a given age. The portion of the Hause study that is based on our sample is discussed below.

cent and does not vary with the level of mental ability. Ignoring the screening argument, the private and social rates of return are approximately the same. Second, certain types of mental ability and various personal characteristics are as important as education in determining earnings, and omission of these variables biases education coefficients by up to 35 percent. Finally, and more tentatively, there is evidence consistent with the hypothesis that education is used as a screening device and that up to one-half of (net) earnings differentials are due to such screening.

An important caveat is in order. This study is based primarily on a population that is much brighter and better educated than the United States population as a whole and is probably less averse to risk. Our results need not be capable of generalization to the population at large.

THE NBER-TH SAMPLE In this study we analyze hitherto unpublished details of the Wolfle-Smith sample and a new body of data that goes under the unpronounceable acronym of NBER-TH (National Bureau of Economic Research–Thorndike-Hagen). Most of our detailed conclusions are based on the NBER-TH sample, although comparisons are made between this sample and Wolfle-Smith. Since this study represents the first use of what we consider to be a major body of data, and because of the special characteristics of the population from which it is drawn, we will discuss the NBER-TH sample at this point, although more details are given in Chapter 4. During World War II, the Army Air Corps accepted volunteers for the pilot, navigator, and bombardier training programs. The volunteers, of whom there were some 500,000, had to pass the Aviation Cadet Qualifying Test with a score equivalent to that of the median of high school graduates.[2] These people were then given a battery of 17 tests that measured such abilities as mathematical and reasoning skills, physical coordination, reaction to stress, and spatial perception. While the tests were changed during the war, a given set of tests was used for 75,000 men in the period July to December 1943. In 1955, Robert L. Thorndike and Elizabeth Hagen undertook a study to determine how well these tests predicted the sub-

---

[2] This was about equivalent to the person's being able to complete two years of college. See Thorndike and Hagen (1959, p. 52).

sequent vocational success of a random sample of 17,000 of these 75,000 individuals. A large fraction of the 17,000 people responded to the questionnaire.[3]

Thorndike and Hagen have shown that there was no significant difference between the test scores of the civilian respondents in 1955 and those of the 75,000 tested on the same battery. But compared to the United States male population aged 18 through 26 in 1943, the air cadet group was more highly educated and brighter; all had at least a high school diploma, and a score equivalent to the average for college sophomores was used as a preliminary screening level.[4] Also, the tested group consisted of people willing to volunteer for the various programs. While the differences between the sample and the United States population complicate the extrapolation of our results, a substantial benefit in having a sample more homogeneous than that in a census is that many earnings determinants are held constant by sample design.

In 1968 we contacted Professor Thorndike and learned that he had retained much of the information collected for most people in the sample. The information thus resurrected is extremely valuable, because the sample is one of the largest known (of people with at least a high school diploma) that contains detailed measures of earnings, ability, education, and family background. In 1969, the NBER decided to conduct an additional survey of the people who responded in 1955. At the time our study was undertaken, there were 4,400 respondents to the follow-up, but subsequently there have been another 600.

Since the people were surveyed in 1955 and 1969, we have "direct" reports of earnings in those years and "recalled" reports of earnings for their initial jobs and jobs at other specific points in time. We concentrate our attention on the 1955 and

---

[3]The high response rate occurred in part because many veterans maintained contact with the Veterans Administration through life insurance policies and disability claims. The authors were able to increase the response rate by hiring the Retail Credit Bureau to find various individuals. About 1,500 people had died since 1943.

The questionnaire is reproduced in Thorndike and Hagen (1959, p. 86). The 2,000 people who were still in the military in 1955 were eliminated from the sample.

[4]Some rough comparisons with the population as a whole can be found in Thorndike and Hagen (1959, pp. 110–111).

1969 earnings because we expect them to be more accurate. The NBER-TH average earnings are consistent with data by education and age in the 1955 and 1968 *Current Population Reports* (CPR) and, although the 1969 respondents are more heavily concentrated in the higher education and ability levels, there is no success bias in reported earnings within ability and education groups. Because the sample is drawn from a special population, a few results may not be applicable to the population as a whole.

REGRESSION ANALYSIS OF THE NBER-TH DATA In our regressions, we relate earnings in a particular year to a large set of explanatory variables, nearly all of which are zero-one dummy variables. By breaking up the independent variables into discrete categories—for example, eight education levels—we allow for nonlinear effects, and by combining dummies we allow for interactions.[5] As noted earlier, there are scores on 17 ability tests for each person. Factor analysis conducted by A. Beaton indicates that four orthogonal factors could be extracted from these scores; two quite clearly represent spatial perception and physical coordination; the other two we treat as measuring mathematical and verbal ability.[6] A description of the tests and the factor loadings are given in Chapter 4. We divide the factors into fifths and use a separate dummy for each interval because the effect of any ability need not be linear, and because the test-score information is an ordinal rather than cardinal measure of ability. The main regression equations for both 1955 and 1969—including such measures as t statistics, $\bar{R}^2$, and standard errors—appear in Chapter 5.[7] The equations, estimated by ordinary least squares, include measures of education, mathematical ability, personal biography, health, marital status, father's education, and age—and, to account for non-

---

[5] Thus, our functional form incorporates the one advocated by Mincer (1970). The use of log of earnings, however, could still be justified to eliminate heteroscedasticity.

[6] As discussed in Chapter 4, Thorndike believes that our mathematical factor is close to IQ but that the verbal factor contains too heavy a mechanical component to be identified.

[7] To save space, we have not included the one containing the significant interaction between graduate education and the top two ability fifths.

pecuniary rewards, a dummy variable for precollege teachers.[8]
Nearly all these variables are significant at the 5 percent level in
both years studied, although a few are only significant in one of
the two years.

The net earnings differentials due to education can be
calculated from these equations for two points in the life cycle
and appear in Table 1-1. In 1955, when the average age in the
sample was 33, annual earnings of those attending college were
generally 10 to 15 percent higher than they were at the high
school level, although the differential was 70 percent for M.D.'s,
2 percent for Ph.D.'s, and 20 percent for LL.B.'s.[9] In 1969, those
with some college received about 17 percent more income than
high school graduates, while those with an undergraduate
degree, some graduate work, or a master's degree received 25 to
30 percent more. Ph.D.'s, LL.B.'s, and M.D.'s received about 25,
85, and 105 percent more income, respectively, than high school
graduates of the same ability level.[10] From 1955 to 1969, the differentials increased at all education levels, with the greatest percentage increase occurring for the most highly educated. As
explained in more detail below, these differentials are independent of ability level except for graduate students. In some ver-
sions of the 1969 equations, we replaced the college-dropout
category with the three categories of those who finished one,
two, and three years of college. The coefficient for completing
one year of college is essentially equal to that of the some-
college variable, and the coefficients for completing the second
and third years of college indicate no further increase in income.

[8]Father's education is included as a proxy for family background, but it may
also incorporate other abilities that are inheritable. The personal-biography
variable is a weighted average of the two indexes labeled "pilot and navigator
biography" by Thorndike and Hagen. These indexes are, in turn, weighted
averages of information collected in 1943 on hobbies, prior school studies, and
family background. The weights used in constructing these indexes depend on
how well the item predicted success in pilot school and in navigator school.

[9]Although not shown here, the returns to B.A. and B.S. holders are the same.

[10]These returns correspond to those of wage rates since average hours worked are
the same at all education levels except for the combination of Ph.D., LL.B., and
M.D., in which hours are 8 percent greater than that of the lowest category.
When, as in 1969, a dummy variable is included for business owners (but not
self-employed professionals), the income differential for non-business owners
with a bachelor's degree is raised by 25 percent, while the some-college differential is unchanged.

TABLE 1-1
Percentages
by which
earnings of those
with higher levels
of educational
attainment
exceed those
of the average
high school
graduate,
1955 and 1969

	Percentage increases in	
Education	1955	1969
Some college	11	17
Undergraduate degree*	12	31
Some graduate work*	15	26
Master's*	10	32
Ph.D.	2†	27
M.D.	72	106
LL.B.	19	84

* For those not teaching elementary or high school.

† All table entries are significant at the 5 percent level except for this one. See Chapter 5 for the underlying equations.

Mincer (1970) has suggested that the more educated also invest more in on-the-job training and, as a consequence, have an age-income profile that could lie below the profile of the less educated for a period of time (after leaving school) that is less than the reciprocal of the rate of return on education. Our analysis of initial salary by education level (not presented here) is consistent with part of this explanation. We find that in 1946, 1947, and 1948 the starting salary of high school graduates is nearly the same as that of college graduates, graduate students receive less than college graduates, and, finally, those with some college may earn more than those with a college degree.[11] Since in any year the more educated among the initial job applicants will tend to be older and since experience adds to income, these results do imply that the age-earnings profile of the less educated initially lies above that of the more educated. On the other hand, the growth rates in income of those with a college degree, some graduate work, and a master's degree were essentially the same from 1955 to 1969 (although there was still a tendency for faster growth at higher education levels), which suggests that the difference in investment in on-the-job training was not very large at these levels.

[11]Of course, all the people in the sample received some vocational training in the Air Force. If this training is more important for people with no college, comparisons of starting salary would not be appropriate for the civilian population. However, some of the vocational training would also benefit those who went to college. Most of the high school graduates began work in 1946, but a few were discharged from the military at a later date.

THE ROLE OF MENTAL ABILITY We have analyzed extensively the role of ability in the rate of return to education, using the factors mentioned above that represent mathematical ability, coordination, verbal ability, and spatial perception.[12] To allow for nonlinear effects, we divided each factor into fifths, which may be closer to population tenths for the verbal factor and for the mathematical factor, since only those in the top half of the mental-ability distribution were allowed into the test program. We find that, of these ability measures, only mathematical ability—which is based primarily on numerical fluency and only secondarily on problem-solving techniques—is a significant determinant of earnings.[13] The score a person achieves on the mathematical tests used here, or on IQ tests in general, can be determined by a combination of inherited skills (or capacities) and skills acquired through schooling, home environment, and so on. As described in detail in Chapter 5, however, the pretest variation in quantity and quality of schooling had little effect on test scores or earnings. Also, family environment is controlled for directly (though by a crude proxy). Thus, the ability coefficients should be closer to measures of the effect on earnings of inherited mathematical ability than anything else and should not incorporate part of the effect of the quantity and quality of education.

We also have estimated earnings equations within several different occupations. While these equations are discussed later in more detail, it is worth noting here that none of the ability measures were significant in the white- and blue-collar occupations, but mathematical ability was significant in the managerial, professional, technical, and sales groups.

In light of some recent literature on the distribution of income (Lydall, 1969), it is interesting to consider the relative importance of the effects of education and ability over time. In Table 1-2 we present estimates of the extent to which earnings of a high school graduate in each of the five ability levels differ

---

[12]The verbal measure is a weighted average of tests entitled (in order of importance in factor): Mechanical Principles, Reading Comprehension, General Information–Pilot, General Information–Navigator, Math B, and Spatial Orientation II. As described in Thorndike and Hagen (1959), these tests contain such elements as verbal fluency, reasoning, and mathematical skills. Knowledge of mechanical principles is contained in the General Information–Pilot and Reading Comprehension tests, as well as in the first item.

[13] The second fifth was not significant, but the other three were.

TABLE 1-2		
Percentages by		
which earnings		

Ability fifth	1955	1969
1	− 7.6	− 10.0
2	− 3.0	− 3.9
3	− 1.0	− 0.4
4	2.4	2.9
5	9.2	15.0

TABLE 1-2
Percentages by which earnings of high school graduates of a given ability exceed those of the average high school graduate, 1955 and 1969

NOTE: The top quality fifth is 5.

from the earnings of the average high school graduate. In 1955, those in the top fifth earned about 9 percent more, and those in the bottom fifth 8 percent less, than the average; in 1969, the corresponding figures are 15 percent and −10 percent.[14] Thus, over time, income of those in the top fifth has risen faster than the income of those at the low end of the ability scale; for those in the middle fifths, the growth rate has been about the same as that of the average high school graduate in this sample. In 1955, the 17 percent differential between the top and bottom ability fifths is greater than the differentials attributable to education, except for the M.D. and LL.B. categories (see Table 1-1). In 1969, the 25 percent differential is greater than the differential for some college and is quite close to the differentials at all education levels except LL.B. and M.D. Since our sample was drawn only from the top half of the ability distribution, it is almost certain that, for those in this cohort who are at least high school graduates, ability is a more important determinant of the range of the income distribution than is education.[15]

As far as interaction between ability and education is concerned, we find practically no evidence of any difference in the effect of ability at the various education levels in 1955, although we find some evidence in 1969 that those in the fourth and, to some extent, fifth ability groups who had graduate training received more income from ability than those at lower educa-

[14]The dollar effect of ability on education is the same at each education level (except in 1969 for high-ability people who attended graduate school); hence, these percentage figures would be lower at higher education levels.

[15]This comparison assumes that the bias from all omitted variables affects the education and ability coefficients in the same proportion. This assumption may be inappropriate for college quality, which is highly correlated with mental ability, as discussed below.

tion levels. However, we also find ability to be an important determinant of earnings even for high school graduates. Finally, in our study of initial salaries, we find that mental ability had no effect on income except for those with graduate training. Together with the results in Table 1-2, this indicates that ability initially has little effect on earnings, but that the effect grows over time, and perhaps grows more rapidly for those with graduate training and high ability.

Hause (1972) finds a significant interaction between IQ and education in the NBER-TH sample, and because this finding is at odds with ours, it is appropriate to compare the two studies. Hause began his work after we had finished this portion of our study; in the interval A. Beaton created the variable used by Hause, which was labeled IQ and which differs from any of our factors.[16] Tests we have conducted with our full sample indicate that if the test scores are entered linearly, the IQ variable yields a higher $\bar{R}^2$ in the earnings equation than does our first factor, but if the test scores are entered in the general nonlinear dummy-variable fashion, the reverse is true. Since the test scores are an ordinal index, it is appropriate that an allowance be made for general nonlinear effects. Hause did not allow for such effects, but instead specified a double-logarithmic earnings function. We conclude that the finding by Hause of an "interaction" between ability and education is attributable to his selection of a restrictive functional form.

These conclusions on ability and education suggest the following type of model for the labor market. For most jobs, firms either have little or no idea of what determines success or have to engage in so much training and testing that the initial output of all employees without previous experience is similar. In either case, firms pay all those in comparable positions the same amount initially and then monitor performances, basing promotions and income on accomplishment. Because the highly educated and able perform better and win promotions sooner, the model can be described as one of upward filtration. Such a model is consistent with the human-capital concept, but it suggests a somewhat different interpretation of empirical results and somewhat different directions for research. That is,

---

[16]In addition to this different ability measure, Hause's study differs from ours in that he excludes self-employed and certain other people from his analysis and does not include all the variables that we found significant.

it provides an explanation other than learning by doing for the shape of the age-income profile, while a natural extension of the model in which firms try to minimize information costs leads to the screening model discussed below.

A criticism that has been made of many education studies is that the education coefficients are biased upward because relevant abilities and other characteristics have not been held constant. We can obtain an estimate of this bias by observing the change in the education coefficients that results when our equations are estimated with ability omitted. We have calculated the bias assuming, first, that each factor was the only type of ability that should be included and, second, that all abilities should be included.[17] In both instances we find that only the omission of mathematical ability leads to a bias of any magnitude. In 1955, the bias on the education coefficients from omitting mathematical ability is about 25 percent, varying from a low of 15 percent for some college to a high of 31 percent for a master's degree; in 1969, the biases are somewhat smaller, averaging about 15 percent and ranging from 10 to 19 percent.[18] The decline in the bias over time occurs because the coefficients on ability did not grow as rapidly between 1955 and 1969 as did those on education.[19] In some studies, rates of return have been calculated using differences in average income between education groups at various ages. In this sample, such a procedure would overstate the earnings differentials from higher education by 35 and 30 percent in 1955 and 1969, respectively. Because of the (contrary) effects of the GI Bill and pressing family responsibility on post-World War II educational attainment by ability level, these bias results need not apply to other groups in the population.

[17] One of our important variables, however, is a mixture of background and ability; thus we can calculate only the upper and lower bounds of the bias resulting from omitting ability. For simplicity in this summary, we use the average of these bounds.

The bias is expressed below as the ratio of the difference in the education coefficients when ability is excluded and included to the education coefficient when ability is excluded.

[18] The 15 percent bias for the some-college category is higher than in other studies and may be due to our use of mathematical ability rather than IQ.

[19] The bias may also be expressed in terms of the coefficient on education in an equation relating ability to education, but since this equation would involve the same people in 1955 as in 1969, and since their education changed only slightly, the coefficient would be virtually unchanged in the two years.

OTHER VARIABLES Several sociodemographic and background variables are statistically significant and are important determinants of income. For example, the difference between excellent and poor health in 1969 was worth $7,000 a year, and the 100 individuals who were single earned about $3,000 a year less than the others.[20] Those whose father's educational attainment was at least the ninth grade earned about $1,200 more in 1969 and $300 more in 1955 than those whose fathers had not entered high school. (In the format of Table 1-1, a bachelor's degree added $700 and $4,000 in 1955 and 1969, respectively.) Other background information is contained in a biography variable constructed by Thorndike and Hagen from data on hobbies, family income, education prior to 1943, and mathematical ability. We find the fourth and fifth and either the second or third fifths of the biography variable to be significant and of about the same magnitude as mathematical ability, thus being as important as differences in education in explaining the range of earnings. In 1955 the age variable was significant and numerically large, and in 1969 its effect was negative and insignificant, thus consistent with the common notion of a rising age-income profile reaching a peak after the age of 40.

Although the results discussed above were obtained from analyzing separate cross sections, it is possible to develop a combined measure of motivation, drive, personality, and whatever other characteristics persist over long periods of time by using the residuals generated in one cross section, denoted by Q, as a variable in the equations in another cross section. In each year, the inclusion of Q raised the $\bar{R}^2$ from about .10 to .33 and reduced the standard error of estimate by 15 percent, while leaving the other coefficients unchanged.[21] Thus, we conclude that about two-thirds of the variation in earnings in any year

[20]In 1969, the respondents were asked to indicate the state of their health as being poor, fair, good, or excellent. The effects of health were statistically significant and approximately linear in 1969 and, interestingly, also in 1955, although the 1955 *t* value is lower.

[21]The relatively low $\bar{R}^2$ occurs partly because of the very limited range of education in our sample and of age in each cross section. For example, merging the two data sets but allowing for separate coefficients in each would raise the $\bar{R}^2$ to about .30.

The other coefficients are the same because Q is necessarily orthogonal to the other independent variables in 1955, and these are essentially the same as the variables used in 1969.

represents either random events, such as luck, or changes in underlying characteristics (or both). Further examination of the residuals from the regression equation leads to the following conclusions. First, although the equations do not explain well the very high incomes of the most successful, the estimates of extra income arising from education are only slightly altered if the very successful are excluded. Second, when the sample is divided up by education and ability, a test for constancy of the residual variance is rejected at the 5 percent level.[22] However, when the equation is estimated weighting each observation by the reciprocal of the standard error of its ability-education cell, the coefficients and conclusions reached above are changed very little.

QUALITY OF SCHOOLING   We have also explored briefly the effects of including an educational-quality variable in the NBER-TH regressions.[23] We used the Gourman academic rating, the intent of which is to measure the quality of undergraduate departments, in the form of fifths of the sample distribution.[24] At the some-college and B.A. levels, only the highest quality fifth affects earnings significantly; for graduates this is true for the top two undergraduate school fifths and the top graduate school fifth. The 1969 results, summarized in Table 1-3, indicate that differences in income at a given educational level attributable to college quality effects are very large. For example, the college dropout in the top quality fifth receives more income than anyone not in the top fifth except for those with a three-year graduate degree.[25] Similarly, the three-year-graduate-degree holder earns anywhere from 53 to 98 percent more than the average high school student, depending on school quality.

The quality variable may be important for several reasons. First, high-quality schools can impart different or additional in-

---

[22]Even when we use the log of earnings as our dependent variable or include Q in our equations, we reject the hypotheses of constant variance and of normally distributed errors.

[23]Since the quality data became available to us at a much later date than the other data, we have not attempted to incorporate the quality implications in the rate-of-return calculations. Of course, the direction of the effect is obvious. L. Solmon is currently examining the quality question in great detail.

[24]This rating is defined in Gourman (1956).

[25]This group includes Ph.D.'s, lawyers, and M.D.'s.

	Amount	Percent*
Education		
Some college		
Undergraduate quality 1–4	161	14
Undergraduate quality 5†	442	37
Undergraduate degree		
Undergraduate quality 1–4	340	29
Undergraduate quality 5†	457	39
Some graduate work‡	166	14
Master's‡	194	16
Ph.D. and LL.B.‡	633	53
Additional income to graduate as a function of educational quality		
Undergraduate quality 4†	182	15
Undergraduate quality 5†	268	23
Graduate quality 5†	257	22

TABLE 1-3 Amount by which monthly earnings of those with higher levels of educational attainment exceed those of the average high school graduate, 1969 (in dollars)

* Expressed as a percentage of the average income of high school graduates.

† Significantly different from earnings of comparable people who attended schools in the bottom quality fifths.

‡ For those at an undergraduate school in the bottom three quality fifths and a graduate school in the bottom four fifths.

NOTE: These regression results are based on a sample of 5,000 individuals. The top quality fifth is 5.

come-earning skills compared with low-quality schools. Second, as described below, the quality as well as the quantity of education may be used as a screening device.[26] Finally, one of Gourman's stated objectives in providing the quality ratings is to permit students to match their capabilities, as reflected by Scholastic Aptitude Test (SAT) ratings, with schools. If individuals' SAT ratings and school quality ratings were *perfectly* correlated, then the quality rating would reflect mental-ability differences rather than differences in the quality of education provided by the school. Evidence in Wolfle (1954) and Solmon (1969) indicates that school quality and the average IQ of those

[26]Some of the schools included in the top undergraduate quality fifth are Berkeley, Brown, Chicago, Columbia, Harvard, Michigan, Minnesota, MIT, Princeton, Stanford, Wisconsin, and Yale.

attending are positively correlated, but that within schools there is a wide range in individual abilities. In addition, evidence in Astin (1968) indicates that schools are differentiated by characteristics of their students other than mental ability and that schools have different attitudes toward various forms of social and psychological behavior. Thus, the quality variable may reflect individual mental-ability differences not captured in our personal-ability measures, other personality differences, or quality-of-schooling differences.

THE RATE OF RETURN TO EDUCATION The data for 1955 and 1969, as well as data on initial-job earnings, yield information at three points on the age-earnings profile for those in our sample. It is possible to interpolate for the intervening years on the basis of various data collected by the census and to extrapolate beyond 1969 (when the people in our sample averaged 47 years of age) to obtain "realized," or ex post age-earnings profiles by education level.[27] We have constructed such profiles for a person with the characteristics of the average high school graduate in the sample. The differences between those profiles, together with information on the costs of education, are used to estimate rates of return to education.[28]

Private rates of return may differ from social rates because some benefits accrue to individuals other than those who are educated, or because of market imperfections based on education. Ignoring the latter group of problems, which are discussed below, differences between our estimates of private and social rates of return occur because the private benefits are calculated after deducting income taxes from earnings, and because social costs include the total (per student) expenditures on higher education rather than just average tuition.[29] However, our estimated social and private rates are very similar because the before-tax income streams are the same, and because the largest

---

[27]For details, see Appendix J.

[28]Earnings provide an inadequate measure of benefits from education if there are nonpecuniary returns that vary by education level. In our estimates, we in effect add to the incomes of elementary and high school teachers a large nonpecuniary return. Without this adjustment, the rates of return would be smaller at the undergraduate and master's levels. No other adjustments are made for nonmonetary returns or for consumption benefits.

[29]The details in constructing the cost estimates can be found in Appendix L. The forgone earnings are estimated from the sample.

cost component in each instance is forgone earnings.[30] In this discussion, therefore, we concentrate on estimates of the social rates of return calculated from nominal profiles and after deflation by the Consumer Price Index (CPI). These are presented in Table 1-4 along with nominal private rates.

Compared with those of a high school graduate with the same abilities and background, the social rates of return realized in our sample (before deflation) are 14, 10, 7, 8, and 4 percent for two years of college only, an undergraduate degree, some graduate work, a master's degree, and a Ph.D., respectively.[31] The most striking aspect of these results is the general decrease in the rate of return with increases in education, which holds even though we have adjusted for the large nonpecuniary reward to precollege teachers, who are concentrated in the B.A., some-graduate-work, and master's degree categories. On the other hand, nonpecuniary returns may be contributing to the low return in the Ph.D. category, which includes professors. Rates of return calculated without standardizing for ability and background, although not presented here, are generally about 20 percent higher; for example, the some-college return rises from 14 to 18 percent. These rates of return, based on current-dollar profiles, differ from those based on constant-dollar profiles because inflation increases the absolute differences between the profiles and alters the purchasing power of the investment "costs" and "dividends." Estimates of real rates of return, obtained by deflating by the CPI, are two to three percentage points lower.

A surprising result is that the rate of return to a college dropout exceeds that to a college graduate. This result might, in part, be attributed to the heavy concentration in the some-college category of self-employed individuals, whose earnings probably include a return to financial capital.[32] Including a

---

[30]These returns, which are not very sensitive to small changes in the data, are calculated under the following assumptions. First, we do not include GI education benefits as offsets to forgone earnings, since we want rate-of-return estimates applicable to the population as a whole. Second, we assume that, as in our sample, the average age of people about to undertake higher education in 1946 was 24. We also calculate a rate of return for people identical to those in the sample but who were 18 in 1946; but since these rates are about the same, we ignore this distinction in our discussion.

[31]The Ph.D. category does not include self-employed professionals.

[32]The questionnaire did not specify that "earnings" included profits, but it seems reasonable that some owners included some profits in their answers.

	Private (before taxes)	Social (before taxes)	
Education	Not deflated	Not deflated	Deflated
High school to:			
Some college	15	14	11
B.A.	11	10	8
Some graduate work	8	7	5
Master's	8	8	6
Ph.D.	4	4	2
LL.B.	12	11	9
Some college to B.A.	7	7	5
B.A. to LL.B.	13	12	10

TABLE 1-4 Realized rates of return to education, NBER-TH sample, for people entering college in 1946 (in percentages)

dummy variable for people who were business owners in 1969, we find that the earnings-differential percentage, compared to that for the average high school graduate, is unchanged for college dropouts but is increased by 25 percent for college graduates who are not business owners. Hence, if this 25 percent adjustment is appropriate (and holds at all ages), the rate of return to obtaining a B.A. but not becoming a business owner is about the same as for a college dropout.[33] Of course, even the finding that college dropouts receive as high a rate of return as bachelor's degree holders is not in accord with findings by such others as Becker (1964). This difference may be due partly to the fact that in other studies ability is not held constant, whereas many of those who drop out of college do so because they do not have the intelligence, drive, or other attributes to handle the work. That is, much of the earnings differential between the some-college and bachelor's degree levels may, in fact, be due to these characteristics and not to the education difference. The college dropouts in our sample, however, were in their mid-twenties in 1946 and about a year older than the college graduates. Also, those who were married before 1949 tended to have a half year less education. Thus, the dropouts probably had a family to support and could not afford (in the short run) a

---

[33]This dummy-variable procedure understates the true return to some college if obtaining that education level increases the likelihood that the individual will become a businessman. On the other hand, our sample information about the self-employed obviously does not include data on those who failed earlier in life; thus, the dummy-variable coefficient overstates the average return to being self-employed and may overstate the return to education.

college degree. This suggests that, in our sample, dropouts may be more like college graduates than is true in the population as a whole and that our result is the more reliable. In other words, dropouts may have been pulled out of college by their children and by attractive alternatives to education, rather than pushed out by lack of drive and motivation.

As explained earlier, except for those with graduate training, there is no evidence of an interaction between ability and education in determining earnings. Further, since the data on initial earnings—although they are "recalled" estimates and hence less accurate—indicate that ability does not affect initial earnings, forgone earnings do not vary by ability level. Therefore, except for those with graduate training, the rates of return discussed above apply to individuals at all ability levels in our sample. For those with graduate training, differences in the rates of return between those in the top two and those in the bottom mathematical-ability fifths are approximately two percentage points (centered about the average).[34]

Is it reasonable to expect the results from this sample to generalize to the population as a whole and to other time periods? While the sample is drawn from a rather special population, we see no reason why most results from our equations in which special characteristics of the people are held constant would not generalize. (This is not so true of the previous bias calculations, since these involve the relationship between education and the special characteristics.) Moreover, as just shown, one special characteristic of our sample probably aids us in obtaining generalizable results.

If the economy were on a balanced growth path, information over time for the people in our sample would yield an estimate of the rate of return for all cohorts. We doubt that the huge changes in educational attainment are consistent with a balanced growth path and would suspect that cohorts currently being educated will, on the average, do no better than the people in the NBER-TH sample.

---

[34]In this report we also calculate rates of return using data from the 1949 census and from 1946 in Miller (1960), but with adjustments for the omission of ability and other variables. The bachelor's rate of return in both of these cross sections and the some-college rate in the 1946 sample are close to the realized real rates given above. For the some-college group, the 1949 cross section yields a much smaller estimate than the time-series data.

Are investments in education worthwhile? From a social point of view this involves comparing social rates of return with alternative returns available to society. Assuming a fixed amount of saving and investment in society, the appropriate alternative rate is that obtainable on physical investment, usually thought to be about 13 to 15 percent in real terms (Phelps, 1962; Taubman & Wales, 1969). Thus, ignoring consumption benefits and externalities, there is overinvestment in the education of males from society's viewpoint except, perhaps, for the some-college category and college graduates who are not self-employed. If society were to raise the funds through taxation or debt issues without affecting private investment, the risk-free discount rate (probably about 4 percent) would be the appropriate alternative marginal time-preference rate (Arrow & Lind, 1970). On these grounds, investments in education are worthwhile from society's viewpoint, especially since we have not allowed for either externalities or the consumption value of education.

From a private viewpoint, the appropriate alternative return is best represented by an after-tax, or ex post, rate of return on common stocks—say about 10 percent. Since the private after-tax rates differ from the before-tax rates by less than one percentage point, we conclude that (in addition to some college) obtaining a B.A. or LL.B. degree is a profitable investment, although—subject to the earlier qualifications on the college-dropout results—it would be better to drop out after two years of college. The private return to education is more profitable relative to alternative assets than is the social return because of the various subsidies given to higher education.

THE WOLFLE-SMITH SAMPLE In the mid-1950s, Dael Wolfle and Joseph Smith collected information on a large group of people who had graduated from high school between 1933 and 1938. In their analysis, they generated about one thousand pages of detailed cross tabulations, but their well-known and extensively quoted article published only about ten tables. Professor Wolfle has graciously provided us with all his tabulations, enabling us to redo and to extend his analysis. Because of the form in which the information was retained, however, we could use only the Minnesota data. This sample was drawn from all high school graduates of 1938. The mental-ability test used was given to these students in high school and does not reflect the influence of further education.

According to Wolfle and Smith, there may have been a response-success bias in this sample, in which case we might expect the returns to education to be understated. However, the analysis of the 1953 earnings indicates greater net effects of education than those found in the NBER-TH sample for people of the same age. Part of the difference may arise from the fact that in the Wolfle-Smith sample the ability measure is the combined scores on the American College Entrance Examination (ACE), whereas in the NBER-TH study only the mathematical measure was important. More significantly, it was not possible in the Wolfle-Smith sample to eliminate the effects of family background and other variables that are significant determinants of earnings and correlated with education in the NBER-TH sample. The differences in type of test may also explain why a strong interaction between high ability and education is found in this sample but not in the NBER-TH. Another interesting finding is that the Wolfle-Smith mental-ability measure is a more important determinant of earnings than high school rank.

EDUCATION AS A SCREENING DEVICE Our analysis of earning differentials and rates of return to education was conducted without considering how education increases income. Becker and others have shown that if education produces additions to an individual's skills (cognitive or affective), his income will increase. A number of people, however, have asserted that a primary role of education is to serve as a credential, particularly in the highly paid managerial and professional occupations (Griliches & Mason, 1972; Hansen, Weisbrod, & Scanlon, 1970; and Thurow & Lucas, 1972).[35]

If education is used to screen people, then the extra earnings a person receives from education are due both to the skills produced by his schooling and to any income-redistribution effects resulting from supply limitations. Since income redistribution need not be a gain to society, the social return may be less than the private return to education. This conclusion, however, overlooks one particularly important component of the problem, which can best be considered by asking why firms use education as a screening device. There are several possible an-

---

[35]For lower-paying occupations, such as skilled laborer, the required credential may be a high school diploma.

swers, including snobbery and a mistaken belief in the true importance of education. On the other hand, the use of such credentials may be motivated by profit-maximizing behavior. Consider jobs in which a person is not paid on a piece-rate basis, but rather on a fixed wage and salary per period of time, and suppose that on these jobs successful performance depends upon a complex set of talents, skills, and motives only some of which can be measured easily by direct tests. Clearly, firms could attempt to develop and use tests in selecting employees with the necessary skills for particular occupations. But developing tests, examining recruits, and incurring performance errors can be expensive. Alternatively, in order to save on hiring costs and to reduce mistakes made on the job, firms might decide to use information on educational attainment, available at near-zero cost, as a preliminary screening device, if they either knew (from past experience) or believed that a significantly larger percentage of college graduates had the desired complex of skills.[36]

The implications for the social rate of return are clear—if educational screening were not permitted, additional resources would have to be used in order to sort people. Hence, any sorting costs saved by using education as a screen are a benefit to society and must be taken into account when comparing the social and private rates of return. In this volume, we do not attempt to estimate the magnitude of these costs, but we do obtain a rough estimate of the contribution of screening to income differentials, based on the logic outlined in Chapter 9.

Briefly, to test for the existence of screening, we compare the actual occupational distribution of individuals at various education levels with the "expected" free-entry distribution. The basic assumption made in estimating the expected distribution is that each individual selects the (broad) occupational category in which his income will be highest. To estimate earnings in other occupations, we make use of the estimated occupational regressions based on the NBER-TH sample presented and discussed in Chapter 8. The coefficients on the various ability and education variables can be thought of as the valuations of the extra skills produced by ability and schooling.

Using the occupation equations, we can estimate an individ-

---

[36]Note that the larger percentage could occur either because education produces skills or because the more talented receive the education.

ual's income in the *m*th occupation as the mean income of persons with the same education, ability, and other characteristics as this individual, but currently in the *m*th occupation. Since we do not have measures of all individual characteristics, the potential earnings for each individual will be distributed about this mean. We assume that the distribution of the residuals in our occupational regressions would also hold for people with any given set of personal characteristics currently in any other occupation. Finally, we assume that for any individual the earnings distributions about the mean in various occupations are independent. If residuals are positively correlated, the latter is a conservative assumption that biases our results against accepting the screening hypothesis; that is, if the distributions about the means are positively correlated, people who earn more in one occupation would do so in all others. Hence, fewer people would pick the occupation with the lower mean income.

Table 9-1, (page 164) contains the expected and actual occupational distributions for the high school, some-college, and B.A. categories, together with the means and standard deviations of the corresponding existing income levels for 1969.[37] The most striking result is that, for the high school group, the actual fractions of people in the three lowest-paying occupations are considerably greater than the expected fractions. In the some-college group this result holds but is less pronounced, and for the undergraduate-degree holders the actual and expected distributions are essentially the same in the lowest-paying occupations. In general, then, if there were free entry into all occupations, very few people at any education level included in our sample would choose the blue-collar, white-collar, or service occupations. In practice, however, a substantial fraction (39 percent) of high school graduates, a smaller fraction (17 percent) of the some-college group, and only 4 percent of the B.A. holders enter these occupations. Since the discrepancy between the expected and actual distributions is directly related to education, we conclude that education itself is being used as a screening device to prevent those with low educational attainment from entering high-paying occupations.[38]

---

[37]There is almost no one with graduate training in the blue-collar, white-collar, or service occupations.

[38]Although not presented here, the same general pattern holds for 1955.

We can also attempt to estimate what the rates of return to education would have been if there had been no screening.[39] These returns are of interest since they represent the extent to which those presented earlier reflect increases in productivity rather than discrimination in the job market. To calculate returns to education, we weight the income differences due to education in various occupations by the expected distribution of people across occupations. These returns are upper bounds to those that would actually occur, since they do not allow for income levels to adjust as the occupational distributions change. Also, they are unadjusted estimates in that they do not allow for differences in ability, background, age, and the like. They can, however, be compared with estimates obtained using the actual distributions, and the percentage differences between these two sets of estimates will probably be reasonable approximations to differences in returns, adjusted for relevant factors.

We have calculated the percentages by which income in the some-college and B.A. categories exceeds the income of high school graduates for the actual and expected distributions for 1955 and 1969. In 1955 the earnings differentials due to education under the assumption of no entry barriers are only about one-half to one-third as large as actual returns, and in 1969 they are about one-half as large. This suggests that the effect of screening on the returns to education is, in fact, substantial at these education levels and that, without screening, the returns might be 50 percent below those presented earlier.[40]

CONCLUSIONS Our results are helpful in determining whether society has over- or underinvested in education. Since none of the deflated social rates of return presented in Table 1-4 exceeds 11 percent and very few exceed even 8 percent, and since the before-tax return on physical capital is generally thought to be about 13 to 15 percent, it appears that society has invested too many resources in education if the supply of savings is fixed. Further, the rates are lower the higher the education level (excluding lawyers and

---

[39]As explained above, calculation of the social rate requires information on the sorting costs saved by screening. Since we are assuming these costs to be zero, the social (but not the private) rates will be underestimated.

[40]Moreover, if there were no screening, the forgone earnings of those at the high school level would have been greater.

M.D.'s), suggesting that the overinvestment is more severe at the higher levels.[41] However, we have not included in our analysis allowances for externalities or consumption benefits which, if they yield large enough returns, could justify expenditures on education. Further, we find that the rates of return at the some-college and B.A. levels are higher than they would be if there were free entry into the high-paying occupations; that is, since the part of the return to education that reflects the income redistribution due to the credential aspect of education does not benefit society, its effect should be subtracted from actual rates when studying the question of whether there has been overinvestment in education.[42] Since we find screening to be important quantitatively, our conclusion that overinvestment in education has occurred is strengthened.

Perhaps the best way to indicate what we consider to be the overall limitations of this study is to list the areas into which future research should be channeled. As noted earlier, we are worried by some of the differences in results between the Wolfle-Smith and NBER-TH samples. One reason for the result may be the differences in the conceptual and measurement bases of IQ. Thus, it is appropriate for research to determine what types of ability affect earnings and what are the best measures of these abilities. Second, in this study we have not tried to determine what affective or cognitive skills higher education augments or how education produces such changes. Many issues in education can only be resolved by looking into the black box called education. It would also be best for the NBER-TH results to be retested on samples with a wider spectrum of ability, education, and other characteristics, and on different cohorts to see if our results can be generalized to the population as a whole. Finally, the tests for screening are crude and would benefit from more detail on occupations and the different types of skills that influence earnings.

---

[41]To the extent that lower rates at high education levels reflect nonpecuniary returns, the overinvestment is diminished somewhat.

[42]However, as mentioned above, if screening were not practiced, the costs to firms (and society) of finding suitable employees would increase. These costs are therefore one of the benefits of the existing educational system and should be included when the income-redistribution aspects due strictly to screening are excluded.

2. The Human-Capital Approach to Higher Education

The major purpose of this study is to determine the extent to which education increases an individual's lifetime income and why the increase occurs. By focusing on the monetary benefits we do not mean to imply that the consumption benefits of education are unimportant but only that their analysis is beyond the scope of the present study. The most complete and elegant model relating education to income was constructed by Becker (1964). At the risk of doing him an injustice, we present a simplified version of his model and indicate how it will be implemented empirically. We then discuss some alternative models based on different assumptions.[1]

THE HUMAN-CAPITAL APPROACH TO EDUCATION Items purchased currently that produce benefits in the future are defined as "investments" by economists. For reasons to be spelled out shortly, education produces monetary and, perhaps, nonmonetary benefits and qualifies as investment in human capital. As the phrase "human capital" suggests, individuals have certain capacities or skills of a cognitive, physical, social, or psychological nature with which they earn a living. The level of any one skill possessed by an individual is partly determined by genetic inheritances and is partly acquired in the family, from friends, from formal education, and so on. The type of education in which we are primarily interested increases inherited skill levels by developing a person's cognitive and/or affective attainment levels. For example, higher education is capable of teaching a person general facts, the use of specific

[1]Thus, we indicate how different theoretical frameworks may yield divergent estimates of the return to education when used to interpret a given set of regression coefficients.

tools, and general problem-solving techniques. In addition, it can influence a person's behavior by making him more tolerant of diversity, better able to stand stress, a better leader, and more disciplined mentally. All these aspects of cognitive and affective behavior could make a person a more productive and effective worker.[2]

The skill function can be represented for the jth person as

$$\text{Skill}_j = f(A_j, ED_j, P_j, X_j) \tag{2-1}$$

where A_j represents various types of innate mental abilities; P_j represents other innate characteristics such as personality, drive, and motivation; ED_j measures the extent of the individual's formal education; and X_j represents all other determinants of skill. Thus, provided people are paid for the skills they exhibit and provided education augments skills, increases in education will lead to higher income.[3] In principle it would be possible to estimate Eq. (2-1) for all skills that determine earnings, though we would still need to attach price tags to each skill. But we do not know what constitutes all the relevant skills, nor do we have measures of all of them. There are, however, indirect ways to estimate the effect of education on earnings. One method is to combine the human-capital approach with the theories of marginal productivity and perfect competition.

THE MARGINAL-PRODUCTIVITY THEORY OF INCOME DETERMINATION UNDER PERFECT COMPETITION According to the marginal-productivity theory, perfectly competitive firms will hire any individual, provided the real wage rate paid to him (w) is less than, or equal to, his marginal product. By equating marginal productivity (MP) to all the skills described by Eq. (2-1) we have

$$w_j = MP_j = g(A_j, ED_j, P_j, X_j) \tag{2-2}$$

Since earned income is equal to the hourly wage rate times the number of hours worked per year (H), income can be used to

---

[2] Although we do not try to distinguish between the affective and cognitive aspects of education in this study, we acknowledge that this is an extremely important question.

[3] For a thorough summary of research on affective development of college students, see Feldman and Newcomb (1969). A shorter summary is available in Simon and Ellison (1973).

measure the effect of education on skills, provided H is assumed constant as education varies.[4]

The effect of education on a person's lifetime income can be measured by examining the income earned in every year by two individuals who are alike in all characteristics (that produce skills) except for education.[5] However, since differences in income arising from education need not be the same in every year, it is customary to compute either the discounted value of the extra lifetime earnings from education or the rate of return earned over a person's lifetime on his educational investment.[6] Since these calculations involve the amounts of income earned by an individual, they are called individual, or private, rates of return.

The benefits that accrue to the individual from his education need not be restricted to extra earnings, but will also include nonpecuniary benefits. These might include, for example, the status or degree of risk in particular occupations.[7] When nonmonetary rewards differ by occupation, wage rates will be a poor guide to total benefits from education, especially if wages adjust to offset the nonpecuniary rewards.

The total benefits accruing to all members of society from an individual's actions are called the social benefits. Since the increased education of only one person will not cause a readjustment of wages, society's income increases by the same amount as an individual's income. There may, however, be other monetary social benefits, such as inventions that are not patentable, or nonmonetary benefits, such as a better-functioning democracy, that an individual does not fully capture.[8] An examination of such benefits is beyond the scope of this book.

---

[4]If hours vary with education, then other adjustments must be made. Also, increases in education may reduce the likelihood of later unemployment. See the discussion in Becker (1964).

[5]These characteristics should include any on-the-job investments. Mincer (1970) has argued that such investments explain most of the variation in age-earnings profiles by education level.

[6]Both these concepts incorporate the costs of obtaining education as well as the extra income attributable to education.

[7]There are many other nonmonetary returns from education that an individual may receive, and the interested reader is referred to the recent survey by Simon and Ellison (1973) and the discussion in Hartman (1973).

[8]The interested reader should consult the papers of Hartman and Mundell in Solmon and Taubman (1973) for a recent discussion of the subject.

But as discussed and examined below, differences between the private and social returns may arise if education is used as a screening device.

EDUCATION AS A MONOPOLY DEVICE

Since very few markets are perfectly competitive, the question of how various types of noncompetitive behavior affect our analysis and conclusions naturally arises. We consider first a model in which education is a prerequisite to entry into a particular occupation and in which entry is restricted. The medical profession is an example of such a model. To become a qualified M.D., it is necessary to attend medical school (which, in turn, requires some undergraduate training). Since the 1930s, however, the American Medical Association (AMA) has restricted medical school enrollments and has reduced the supply of medical doctors per patient.[9] Suppose that in the absence of these restrictions the supply curve of doctors would be SS^* in Figure 2-1, while the demand curve was DD with an equilibrium income per doctor of Y_0. Suppose that this earnings level were such that the rate of return was equal to that available on other assets, and thus that the supply curve was stable over time. If we limit college enrollment, and hence the number of doctors, to S_1, the supply curve becomes SAS_1 and income per doctor Y_1. The income level of Y_1 offers a rate of return on the costs involved in attending medical school above that on other assets, so that more people would like to enter the medical profession, but because of control over education the supply remains SAS_1.

Notice that because doctors have a college education and a high income, a sample of people that includes doctors would indicate a substantial return to a college education, even if all other college graduates received a rate of return that only equaled the interest rate on other assets. Imperfections such as are involved in the case of doctors do not introduce complications into calculations of the return to education; that is, since doctors are assumed to earn their marginal products (even though these are very high due to artificial supply restrictions), a comparison of earnings of individuals with various levels of education provides a basis for calculating the return to any individual.

[9]See, for example, the discussion in Lynch (1968).

FIGURE 2-1
*Supply and
demand
for doctors*

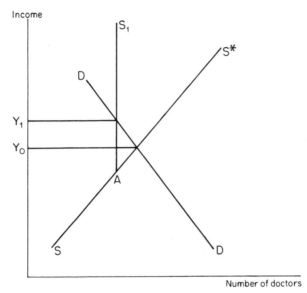

Number of doctors

Although this analysis was applied to doctors, it clearly applies to any other occupation in which education is a prerequisite for entrance and in which the current members can control the number of people who obtain the required education. Of course, there are relatively few occupations in which education has been an absolute prerequisite for entrance over a long period of time. In addition, very few professions have had the AMA's power to limit the number of people obtaining the necessary education. Thus, this type of imperfection is not widespread.

**EDUCATION AS
A SCREENING
DEVICE** A model that does not satisfy the assumptions of competition but that is probably more widespread than the case of doctors is one in which education is used as a preliminary screening device. Because a formal discussion of screening appears in Chapter 9, the following treatment is primarily intended to indicate that different implications may be drawn from education-income data when the standard marginal-productivity and perfect-competition assumptions are dropped.

Individuals, who possess different levels of different types of skills, are more productive at some jobs than at others. If there were no nonpecuniary rewards for such factors as status or risk attached to various occupations, then in a perfectly competitive world each person would end up in the occupation in which his productivity was highest. For such a market to function, however, it is necessary for the employer and employee to evaluate a person's productivity and to be able to determine his appropriate job slot. If the labor market functioned on a piece-rate basis, an employer could let the employee take any job he wanted, and then pay him by performance.[10] But only relatively small sections of the labor market are so organized. Instead, people are generally paid by the hour, week, month, or year and are hired for a relatively lengthy period—subject to certain conditions—because of the substantial costs of hiring and firing.

Firms must do some sorting to match persons and jobs, but subjecting people to prejob tests may be an expensive way to gain such information, especially if the tests are not particularly accurate. Even short probationary periods on the job can be expensive and uninformative if a breaking-in period is needed. Thus, suppose that for certain jobs, such as executive, engineer, and researcher, firms need people with a high level of cognitive and affective skills—especially for advanced positions.[11] If firms believe that college graduates are *more likely* than high school graduates to have the skills necessary for the advanced positions, then by excluding all people with a high school education only, they will not have to interview as many candidates. This screening process will, however, exclude some high school graduates who have the skills necessary for the position.

Firms do not have to know that, on the average, college graduates are better; they must merely believe this to be so. Even if education added nothing to a person's talents, the fact that it correlates with mental ability would mean that education is an indicator of relevant skills.[12] Firms in certain occupations may therefore decide to try to recruit solely from higher educational groups. However, to the extent that the number of people with a college degree desiring to work in an occupation is less than

[10]However, on an assembly line where one worker's productivity depends on the number of acceptable pieces supplied to him by workers earlier in the line, an employer cannot let anyone chosen at random work at a job even when a piece-rate system is in effect.

[11]Of course, the firms hire many people at the trainee and junior levels. For these positions not as much skill is required, but firms may fill these positions primarily to find talented individuals to promote.

[12]For evidence that they are correlated see Chapter 5.

the number of positions the firms wish to fill,[13] some hiring will have to take place from less educated groups. This represents an important difference between the screening and the M.D. exclusion models.

Both secular and cyclical developments on the supply and demand side can affect the level of education used as a screen. If in any time period studied the screen excluded everyone with less than a given amount of education, then the outcome would be very similar to, and indistinguishable from, an M.D. exclusion model. But if some people with less education get by the screen, it is possible to observe their wage payments and to calculate what other people with the same education and abilities would have earned if employed in this occupation.

Such a calculation is the heart of our test for screening, which is explained in detail in Chapter 9. At this point we merely note that screening implies that some people have been excluded from occupations in which they would have a higher productivity. On the other hand, any individual obtaining the requisite education can pass the screen; hence, observed earnings differences do represent the private return to education even though only a portion of the difference represents productivity augmented by education. From a social viewpoint, only the productivity gain is a benefit, but the social rate of return from education could still exceed the private return if alternative sorting systems were more expensive to operate.

It should be noted that if persons are excluded from earning a level of income commensurate with their skills, then in some sense the marginal-productivity theory is being violated. Although a person with education below the screening level is restricted to a lower-paying occupation, he is still paid his marginal product in this occupation, and thus the model is one not of exploitation, but of discrimination.[14]

The previous discussion has indicated that private returns to education can be calculated by relating earnings to measures of innate abilities, education, and other elements that produce

[13]Both the supply of and demand for jobs, of course, can depend on the wage rate being paid in the occupation.

[14]"Discrimination" is probably too strong a term, because it implies that firms pay a person less than they know he is worth. In our model, firms exclude people from certain occupations because of the high sorting costs associated with lower education levels.

skills.[15] There are, however, certain statistical problems that must be discussed before the empirical results are presented.

ESTIMATION PROBLEMS   While marginal productivity has been measured directly in a few instances (for example, Berg, 1971), nearly all existing implementation of the human-capital model has been based on the indirect method of income differences. As mentioned above, we can estimate the effect of education on earnings if we compute a regression of the form of Eq. (2-2). Suppose for the moment that all the assumptions made earlier in deriving this equation are actually met in the population from which our sample is drawn. If all the variables in Eq. (2-2) can be measured and the functional form specified properly, then the estimated coefficients can be used to calculate the extra income due to education. However, no existing samples contain measures of all the relevant variables. Thus, one explanation of the finding of many researchers that income is related to education may be that variables that should have been included in the regression were excluded because of the unavailability of data.

Since the effect on the other coefficients of omitting a variable has been extensively analyzed by others (see, for example, Theil, 1961), we present only a brief summary. To simplify matters, suppose that we abstract from all but the ability and education variables, thus giving an equation of the form

$$Y_j = \alpha + \beta ED_j + \gamma A_j + u_j \qquad (2\text{-}3)$$

where u is a random error. If we use the ordinary-least-squares estimating technique but omit A_j, it can be shown that as an estimate of β we obtain b, which satisfies

$$E(b) = \beta + \gamma d \qquad (2\text{-}4)$$

where d is defined as the least-square estimate of δ in

$$A_j = \delta_o + \delta ED_j + v_j \qquad (2\text{-}5)$$

---

[15]It would also be possible to relate earnings to measures of skills obtained after education was completed. To find the effects of education, we would then have to find the net effect of education on these abilities.

The one exception occurs when wages have adjusted to offset nonpecuniary rewards, but this problem can be solved by including a dummy variable for those occupations for which nonpecuniary rewards are suspected to exist.

and E denotes the expected value of a statistic. From Eq. (2-4), we observe that if A_j is omitted, then our coefficient on education will be a biased estimate of β unless either γ or d is zero.[16] If γ is zero, then ability does not influence income (or skills), while if d is zero, then ability and education are not linearly related to each other. In other words, unless either γ or d is zero, our estimate of the coefficient on education attributes to education the combined effect of ability and education.

While the above example was conducted in terms of the two variables ED and A, it is easy to demonstrate that if ED represents all the included variables and A represents all the omitted variables, the same general conclusions are reached. Thus, in assessing the reliability of various estimates of the returns to education, it is necessary to consider what variables have been omitted that are related to income and education.

Of course, the set of omitted variables differs from study to study. At this point, therefore, we will list the types of variables that in previous research have either been suggested to be or found to be significantly related to earnings.[17] The reader will note that the list of variables has been divided into those that have been included in our analysis of the NBER-TH sample and those that have not.

The determinants of earnings wholly or partially included in our analysis are

1 Educational attainment[18]
2 Quality of schools[19]
3 Various types of mental ability
4 Physical health
5 Age and on-the-job experience

[16]Bias is a statistical concept defined as follows. We are interested in estimating a coefficient whose true value is β. From any sample, a particular estimating formula will yield an estimate b of β. We could apply the same technique to other samples of the same size and obtain a b from each sample. We say technique is unbiased if the mean of the b_i's, $[E(b_i)]$, equals β.

[17]For there to be a bias it is also necessary for the omitted variable to be related to education.

[18]In Appendix A we discuss various possible measures of attainment.

[19]For a more thorough analysis of measures of the quality of colleges, see Solmon (1969) or Wales (1973).

6 Family background

7 Marital status

8 Nonpecuniary rewards

9 Sex and race (by sample design)

Some other variables that may determine income but have not been allowed for in our analysis or in the design of the sample include

10 Personality traits such as motivation, drive, and risk aversion[20]

11 Religious preference

12 Mental health

13 Migration

Of all the variables omitted in our analysis, we would judge personality traits to be the most likely to bias our education co-efficients. This bias may in fact be fairly small, since, as discussed in Chapter 4, the population from which the sample is drawn is probably more homogeneous than the United States population as a whole. Further, while people with more motivation and drive may be better able to complete college, they may also be more impatient to drop out and begin earning income. In any event, we do present evidence suggesting the existence of a set of omitted variables that affect income and whose effects persist over time.

The above discussion was based on an equation in which the effects of education and ability were both linear and independent of each other. In many instances it is important to determine if, or how much, the effects of education vary with educational attainment and/or ability level. In this study we allow for nonlinear effects of education and ability and for interactions between these two variables. It is worth noting that if, for example, the effect of ability is nonlinear and if the relationship between schooling and ability is also nonlinear, omitting ability from our equation will cause a differential bias at the various education levels. Moreover, if the effects of education are

---

[20]The sample design may have minimized differences in traits.

nonlinear but no allowance is made for this in the estimation, then it would be possible to conclude that the effects of education varied with ability when, in fact, this is not the case.[21] With this background we are ready to consider some empirical results.

---

[21] That is, the more able would be more concentrated in the high education groups in which the nonlinear effects of education would be observed.

3. Effects of Education and Mental Ability on Income: The Evidence from the Wolfle-Smith Data

As discussed in the preceding chapter, in order to estimate the net effect of education on earnings, it is necessary to standardize for all other determinants of earnings that are correlated with education. This is not an easy task, since innate ability, which is correlated with educational attainment and probably is a determinant of earnings, is not available in most samples. In this chapter we make use of a sample whose members span the entire IQ range to study the effects of education and the comparative usefulness of high school rank and the American College Entrance Examination. The results of this study are of limited applicability for the following reasons: only grouped data are used; the sample is drawn only from Minnesota; the respondents may be more successful than the nonrespondents, given education and ability; the individuals' educations and lives were interrupted by World War II; and earnings for only one year are available.

SUMMARY AND CONCLUSIONS

We use hitherto unpublished details of data collected by Wolfle and Smith (1956) on Minnesota high school graduates of 1938 to estimate the effect of education and ability on wages and salaries earned in 1953. Using a general nonlinear functional form, we find that, for a person with the same IQ as the average high school graduate, the extra earnings from vocational training are less than 7 percent; from attending college for less than two years, 18 percent; from attending college for more than two years but not graduating, 36 percent; from earning one degree, 47 percent for those in the first nine IQ tenths and 100 percent for those in the top tenth; and from earning two degrees, 58 percent for those in the first nine IQ tenths and 111 percent for those in the top tenth.[1] Except for the people in the top IQ tenth, the percentage increase in income falls as education grows. For those in the top IQ tenth, one college degree represents a huge 50 percent increase over not graduating.

An important feature of the sample is that because the IQ test (the ACE) was administered to all the students in their senior year in high school, subsequent differences in schooling would not affect students' scores. Besides reflecting differences in innate ability, the test scores could also depend on the quality of previous schooling and home environment. By holding constant such elements, the test scores should improve the education estimates but will overstate the effects of innate ability. We find that mental ability adds to earnings but that education is a more important determinant than IQ. The effect of mental ability on income differs for three groups: those in the lowest four IQ tenths, those in the next five tenths, and those in the top tenth.[2] While we find that high ability and high educational attainment interact strongly to produce very large income differences, ability affects income even for high school graduates.

Two important questions concern the types of mental ability that determine earnings and the best measure of a particular type of ability. In this chapter we use a general innate-mental-ability concept, two measures of which are an IQ-type test and high school rank in class.[3] For this body of data it is clear that the IQ scores are the superior measure, since they have the expected signs and are significant determinants of income differences. Coefficients on the rank-in-class variables are neither significant nor large, and do not increase with higher rank.[4] Our explanation for the poor performance of the rank-in-class measure is that, because the quality of the student body varies between schools, it is not legitimate to call all students in the

---

[1] The sample is Minnesota male high school graduates of 1938. The average annual salary in 1953 of those with no additional education was $4,500.

[2] Within each of these groups, variations in ability have no effect on income.

[3] Of course, both measures could also incorporate other attributes.

[4] In interpreting both measures, it must be remembered that there was a response bias on the sample, with the more educated and more able much more likely to respond. In addition, there may have been a success bias, which could have been more extreme at the lower ability and education levels.

top ranks of different schools equal or to assume that they are more able than those in the lower ranks.

For any ability measure, it is useful to calculate the bias that could be expected in samples that relate income to education without holding ability constant. We find that the bias is quite small—no more than 4 percent at the various education levels. The peculiarities of the sample used heighten the importance of this result. As indicated in our earlier paper (Taubman & Wales, 1972), the coefficient on education in the regression between ability and the percentage of students entering college is higher in the Wolfle-Smith sample than in any other studied. Thus, as long as the estimates of the effects of ability and education on income are similar in other samples, the bias from omitting ability would be larger in this sample than in any other.[5] In our analysis of the NBER-TH sample, however, we find the bias to be larger than in the Wolfle-Smith sample, especially when a different concept of ability is used.

After dividing the data into groups involving the three highest-paying (on the average) occupations and the other five, we computed our regressions within each of the two groups. For the high-paying group of professionals, semiprofessionals, and sales, we find that the education coefficients are very small and statistically insignificant as long as ability is held constant.[6] Ability, however, is statistically significant and quite large, with those in the top tenth earning 20 percent more than those in the fifth and sixth tenths and about 30 percent more than those in the bottom four tenths. For the other occupations, which have lower average wage and salary levels, we find that neither education nor ability is a significant determinant of income.[7]

---

[5] In samples such as the census, in which people in different age groups are studied simultaneously, the problem is more complex because the ability-education relationship shifts for different age groups. See our earlier paper (Taubman & Wales, 1972).

[6] This conclusion holds if we use the six possible education categories; if we combine the data into the three groups of no college, college dropout, college graduate; if we use the two categories of college graduate and all others; or if we use the two categories of no college and all others.

[7] See, however, the discussion in Chapter 6 on the position, steepness, and intersection of age-income profiles at various education levels.

The above regression results could occur if there were no variations in education and ability within the two occupational groups. But as shown in Appendix B, Table B-9, there are wide ranges of education and ability in the various occupations. For example, 34 percent of the people with just a high school education in the bottom four tenths of IQ are in professional, semi-professional, and sales occupations, while more than 30 percent of high school graduates in the top six tenths are in the other occupations. However, over 90 percent of people with one or more college degrees are in the professional, semiprofessional, and sales categories in each of the bottom four tenths, middle three tenths, and top three tenths of ability.

The occupation regressions indicate that people with less education can earn the same income as more educated people with the same ability when they are given the opportunity. But there is a disproportionately low percentage of people with low education in the high-paying occupations. (In Chapter 9, we indicate a method to calculate the "proper" percentage.)

For females, we find that ability is not significant, but that one or more college degrees add substantially to income, although by lesser absolute amounts than for males.[8] Housewives are included in these data; hence, the results are partly determined by the fact that a smaller proportion of college graduates are married and/or not working full time.

While we believe the above conclusions to be important, they are subject to some qualifications. First of all, Wolfle and Smith (1956) report that there was a tendency for a greater proportion of those high school students who did not enter college not to respond to the questionnaire. It may also be true that the less successful, in terms of income, did not respond.[9]

Of more concern is the date at which the sample was taken. While chronologically the sample refers to a period 15 years after high school graduation, the interval includes World War II. Thus, lawyers and those with Ph.D.'s would have had fewer

---

[8] College dropouts among females may make their return through better selection of husbands.

[9] There is some evidence that the nonrespondents were those with lower scores; hence, our results with IQ held constant could be valid, although the bias calculation need not be. For the NBER-TH sample we show that there is a response bias but no success bias (see Chapter 4).

than five years in their primary occupation and M.D.'s only one or two years. Graduates with one degree who entered college in 1938 would have been on the job for as long as seven years if they were in the service; hence, their income figures should reflect promotions and phenomena other than starting salaries. However, as reported in Anderson and Berning (1941), the percentage of Minnesota high school graduates of 1938 who entered college in 1939 was one-half as large as the corresponding group who had entered by 1953, as recorded by Wolfle and Smith (1956).[10] While some of this difference reflects the response bias previously discussed, part also reflects post-World War II education. If we assume their earlier work experience to be irrelevant after college, the veterans who entered college after the war and who graduated would have been on the job about four or five years.

Besides these technical problems, there is the obvious qualification that our results apply to only one year out of an individual's lifetime experience. It is conceivable that the high school graduates who are professionals and who were making more income in 1953 than their counterparts in other jobs will have the same lifetime income as their counterparts. We doubt it, however, since census data indicate the same hierarchy of average income in all age brackets. It is also possible that the lifetime income of the more educated will be greater, even though this is not observed in this sample, because it takes time for them to overcome the advantages derived from experience on the job by their less well-educated coworkers. Both these possibilities can be tested by examining data for individuals over long time periods, as is done in Chapter 5.

The final qualification is that there may be other individual characteristics that determine income *and* are correlated with education, ability, or occupational choice, but that we have not held constant.[11] Since our sample incorporates only Minnesota high school graduates of 1938, some of these factors have been accounted for. However, such personal characteristics as drive,

---

[10] Wolfle has informed us that his sample was a reinterview of the people dealt with in Anderson and Berning (1941).

[11] These characteristics must be correlated with education, ability, or occupational choice in order to cause a bias.

motivation, personality, and the like have not been held constant. If these attributes determine income and are correlated with education, then the calculations of the individual return are biased because part of the credit apportioned to education belongs to these attributes. In Chapter 5, we test for the relative importance of some of these omitted variables using the NBER-TH sample.

DATA The body of data collected by Wolfle and Smith (1956) is described in detail in Taubman and Wales (1972). Summarizing briefly, the population from which the samples were drawn consists of (1) the top 20 percent of Rochester, New York, high school graduates of 1933–1938; (2) the top 60 percent of Illinois high school graduates of 1935 (excluding Chicago); and (3) all Minnesota high school graduates of 1938. Information on an individual's income in 1953, occupation in 1953, post-high school education, father's occupation, and many other sociological and economic items were collected as part of the study.

We have not been able to locate the original questionnaires or the cards on which the data were punched. However, Dr. Wolfle retained a file of extensive cross tabulations, which he graciously made available to us. Included in his files are such tables as the distribution of Minnesota males for each of ten high school class ranks, for eight classes of post-high school education, and for each of nine occupational groups.[12] Another table presents, for each tenth in class rank, the data on the distribution of wage and salary income by occupation for Minnesota males. Comparable tables for males in the other two areas and for females are available, as well as cross tabulations using IQ in place of rank in class.

Although the Wolfle-Smith sample has been extensively analyzed in the literature on the returns to education, very few of the basic data have been published. The three tables published in the original Wolfle and Smith article are presented in Appendix B, Tables B-1, B-2, and B-3. While the data contained in these tables are useful for some purposes, in general

---

[12] There is a misprint in the original Wolfle and Smith article in the labeling for the ability classes for the Minnesota ACE tenths. The correct classifications are given in Appendix B, Table B-2.

we believe that the information is to some extent either misleading or inadequate.[13]

Wolfle's extensive cross tabulations permit us to rectify many of the problems detailed in footnote 13 and to provide comparable information for females. Since the data are basic to the analysis and since we consider the available tables to be deficient, we present in Appendix B a more comprehensive set of tables.

RETURN TO EDUCATION: MINNESOTA MALES For reasons given earlier, it is desirable to analyze the information for each state separately. Unfortunately, although rank-in-class data are available by tenths for all states, the IQ data are available in sufficient detail only for Minnesota. We have estimated separate equations for males and females because females may have been discriminated against in job markets and because many females in the sample were married and had dropped out of the labor force.

Using the data in Appendix B, Table B-6 (in which the measure of mental ability is the ACE score), we find[14]

---

[13] Specifically, the published data are deficient in the following respects:

(1) No useful mathematical operations, such as averaging, can be carried out properly using the medians available. For analysis of variance techniques or regressions, the appropriate measure of central tendency is the mean, though one problem with the mean is that an average income must be assigned to those people in the open-ended class.

(2) The published tables are not extensive enough to permit use of regression analysis, which allows other variables to be held constant and can utilize different weights for sample points with different numbers of observations.

(3) The most detailed table combines all Rochester, N.Y., Minnesota, and Illinois graduates who ranked in a given tenth of their high school class. Using combined rank-in-class data for the three states is misleading on several accounts. First, the quality of the schools or student body may differ substantially in these three areas. Second, the years in which the students graduated from high school differed in these three areas: 1933–1938 in Rochester, 1935 in Illinois, and 1938 in Minnesota. Abundant evidence exists that wages and salaries are related to time on the job. Because of this or for other reasons, the average income received in any educational and rank-in-class cell was higher in the other two states than in Minnesota. Finally, due to the design of the sample, nearly all the people in the lower ranks come from Minnesota, while most of those from the other two areas are in the top ranks.

(4) The other two tables based on IQ are more revealing, but the Rochester data do not indicate the average IQ in either of the two groups.

[14] These data have not been grouped by occupation.

$$Y = 4.259 + .302E_V + .814E_1 + 1.612E_3 + 2.107E_G + 2.658E_{GM}$$

$$\quad (10.3) \qquad (.6) \qquad (1.6) \qquad (3.4) \qquad (4.8) \qquad (5.5)$$

$$+ .483A_{5-9} + 1.283A_{10} \qquad\qquad\qquad \bar{R}^2 = .93 \quad (3\text{-}1)$$

$$\quad (2.3) \qquad\quad (2.9)$$

where Y = wage and salary income in thousands of dollars

E_V = a dummy variable that equals 1 if the person attended vocational, military, or other noncollege school

E_1 = a dummy variable that equals 1 if the person attended college, but for less than two years

E_3 = a dummy variable that equals 1 if the person attended college for two or more years but did not graduate

E_G = a dummy variable that equals 1 if the person had an undergraduate degree but no graduate degree

E_{GM} = a dummy variable that equals 1 if the person had more than one degree

A_{5-9} = a dummy variable that equals 1 if the person was in the fifth through ninth IQ tenths

A_{10} = a dummy variable that equals 1 if the person was in the tenth IQ tenth (the most able students are in this tenth)

$\bar{R}^2$ = the coefficient of determination adjusted for degrees of freedom

The equations are weighted regressions in which each weight is the square root of the number of observations in the IQ group.[15]

We first tried an equation with a separate dummy variable for each possible education and ability category, which is the greatest detail available. The individual coefficients on A_2 through A_4 were practically zero, while the coefficients on A_5 through A_8 were nonzero and very similar. For some reason, the coefficient of A_9 is very low, but for convenience we combined this category with A_5 through A_8. Finally, the coefficient of A_{10} was very large, a result consistent with earlier studies on the effect

---

[15] Eq. (3-1) has also been estimated using $20,000 instead of $25,000 as the mean of the open-ended class. The coefficients of the variables in the same order as in Eq. (3-1) are 4.270, .250, .810, 1.475, 1.906, 2.319, .477, and 1.015.

of mental ability on income.[16] To reduce collinearity, we combined the ability variables into three groups. This aggregation does not greatly change the education coefficient.

Since the categories for no post-high school education and for the bottom IQ decile have been excluded, the coefficient on a dummy variable indicates the average additional amount of income for people in the particular category compared with those in the lowest ability tenth who had no post-high school education (the reference group). Thus in Eq. (3-1), a person in the lowest IQ tenth but with zero to two years of college earned, on the average, approximately $800 more than a person in the reference group.

Consider the magnitudes of the education dummy variables. The coefficients increase continuously with education. For any IQ level, vocational training added about $300 to earnings 15 years (including World War II) after graduation from high school. Using the *t* statistic in parenthesis, this increase—about 7 percent—is not significantly different from the earnings of a comparable person with no post-high school training.[17] A person who attended college for less than two years received $800 more than a person with no post-high school education. The $800 figure is nearly statistically significant, and the remaining education coefficients are significant and are successively larger. In terms of percentages, the first two years of college add about 18 percent to income; the next two years add about 36 percent; one degree adds about 45 percent; and more than one degree adds roughly 57 percent (as compared with no post-high school education). While the increments in these percentages decrease as we move to higher education levels, it must be kept in mind that the mean years of college education in the various categories are approximately 1, 3, 4.5, and perhaps 6.[18] Thus, while it seems clear that the largest gain in income occurs for the first year in college, the absolute differences per year for the other categories may be about the same. Even this would mean that the percentage increase in income for each additional

---

[16] See, for example, Becker (1964).

[17] The 7 percent figure is for a person with the ability level of the average person with a high school degree only. For people with higher ability, the percentage would be smaller.

[18] We do not know how many Ph.D.'s and M.D.'s are in the sample.

school year was falling, because the constant absolute differences would be divided by a continually growing base. Thus, there is some evidence that there are diminishing (percentage) returns to education for an individual.

The ability variables indicate that those in the fifth through ninth tenths earn $480 more each year, and those in the top decile $1,300 more than persons in the bottom four deciles. When the discrete variables for each ability class are replaced with a continuous variable that takes on a value equal to the particular IQ tenth (1 through 10), the coefficient on the variable is approximately .1, while the coefficients of the education variables are unchanged. Although statistically significant and numerically important, ability explains much less of the range of income differences than does education. The income difference between the top and bottom ability group is less than the income difference between those with two and four years of college.

There is one other aspect of this equation that merits discussion. Unlike most other studies of the determinants of income, our equations do not contain an age or time-on-the-job variable. An age variable is not needed because all the people in our sample graduated from high school at the same time and would have been about the same age. Time on the job, however, would vary between individuals in part because of differences of time spent in the military and in college. We do not know the military experience of each individual. However, there should be little variation in length of service after averaging to obtain our grouped data.

Length of time in education obviously varies by amount of educational attainment. Suppose we write time on the job as equal to age minus years of education (S). Further, suppose that S is the proper measure of education in the income equation

$$y = aS + b(\text{age} - S)$$

This can be written as

$$y = (a - b)\, S + (b \times \text{age})$$

The last equation is the type we have estimated, though we have omitted age because it is constant, and we have partitioned S in a set of dummy variables. From this equation we see that the coefficients on the education variables represent the net effects of two different mechanisms. That is, a gives the impact of education on income for people with a given amount of time on the job, while b gives the effect of changes in time on the job for people with a given amount of education. Obtaining additional education automatically alters both variables; hence, the net impact is given by $a - b$. With this sample we cannot estimate b, whose magnitude is of some interest. For many purposes, however, the net impact $a - b$ is the required piece of information. It is worth noting that b could vary by education level; hence, the relative size of the various education coefficients could change with age.[19]

INTERACTION OF ABILITY AND EDUCATION   In the above equations it is assumed that the effect of education on income is the same regardless of the level of ability. Many people, however, have hypothesized that education is more important, or only important, for the most able students. This possibility can be tested by including various ability-education product terms in the regression equations. For example, to test the effect of high ability, we use variables defined as $A_{10}(E_G + E_{GM})$, $A_{10}(E_1 + E_3)$, and $A_{10}(E_V + E_H)$, where E_H is high school education only. To test the effect of higher education, we use variables defined as $A_{10}(E_G + E_{GM})$, $A_{5-9}(E_G + E_{GM})$, and $A_{1-4}(E_G + E_{GM})$, and for low education, we replace $E_G + E_{GM}$ by $E_V + E_H$. The only interaction term that appears to be significantly related to earnings is the product of A_{10} and $E_G + E_{GM}$. This variable represents high ability together with high educational attainment. The following equation is the same as Eq. (3-1) except that it contains this additional term.[20]

$$Y = 4.307 + .276E_V + .786E_1 + 1.642E_3 + 2.017E_G + 2.494E_{GM}$$
$$(11)(.6)(1.7)(3.6)(4.8)(5.4)$$

$$+ .499A_{5-9} - .593A_{10} + 2.460A_{10}(E_G + E_{GM}) \quad \bar{R}^2 = .93 \quad (3\text{-}2)$$
$$(2.5)\phantom{A_{5-9}}(.7)(2.6)$$

---

[19] See Chapters 5 and 6.

[20] Eq. (3-2) has also been estimated with an open-end mean of $20,000. The corresponding coefficients are 4.307, .228, .788, 1.499, 1.834, 2.185, .490, −.509, and 2.000.

The result may be interpreted in the following ways. First, the additional income attributable to one college degree is $2,017 for those in the first nine ability classes but is $4,477 ($2,017 + $2,460) for those in the top tenth. For more than one degree, the corresponding values are approximately $2,500 and $4,900. An alternative interpretation suggests that no additional income accrues to individuals in the top tenth without a college degree, since the coefficient of A_{10} is insignificant. This result should be treated with caution, since there are only 15 people without college degrees in the top tenth. Individuals in the fifth through ninth tenths, on the other hand, earn a modest amount of added income—about $500—regardless of their education.[21]

Another proposition that we have tested is that ability differences have no effect on income for those with just high school or vocational training.[22] This was tested by including in Eq. (3-3) a set of additional variables defined as $A_{1-4}(E_{H+V})$, $A_{5-9}(E_{H+V})$, and $A_{10}(E_{H+V})$, where E_{H+V} is a dummy variable representing all those with just high school or vocational training. In order to interpret the results of including these variables, it should be noted that the ability variables also appear separately, that A_{5-9} is significant, and that (when interactions are used) A_{10} is not significant except when included as an interaction with $E_G + E_{GM}$. Consequently, if it were true that ability had no effect at low education levels, the coefficient of $A_{5-9}(E_{H+V})$ would have to be significant and negative, and of a magnitude sufficient to negate the effect of the separate ability variable A_{5-9}. This is not the case, as all three variables are insignificant, with t values less than .5. These data therefore do not support the hypothesis that ability differences contribute to income differences only for those with high educational attainment.[23]

THE BIAS FROM OMITTING IQ   Many previous studies of the returns to education have been based on census or other data sources that contain no ability

---

[21] We tested a variable defined as $A_{5-9}(E_G + E_{GM})$, and although the coefficient was positive (.304), its t value was less than 1.

[22] Becker (1964) reaches this conclusion.

[23] Evidence given below strongly suggests that ability adds to income only if people are employed as professionals, semiprofessionals, or salesmen. Since most high school graduates are not in these professions, there is some truth to the proposition.

measure. As the authors of those studies and others have noted, if ability and education are positively related, then the omission of ability will result in attributing too much of the earnings differential to education. To observe the extent of this bias when IQ is the measure of ability, we have reestimated the equation omitting the ability variables.[24]

$$Y = 4.493 + .273E_V + .808E_1 + 1.673E_3 + 2.218E_G$$
$$(10) \qquad (.5) \qquad (1.5) \qquad (3.3) \qquad (5.8)$$
$$+ 2.914E_{GM} \qquad\qquad\qquad \bar{R}^2 = .92 \quad (3\text{-}3)$$
$$(5.8)$$

For the significant education variables in Eq. (3-2), we calculate the extent to which each coefficient in Eq. (3-3) exceeds the corresponding one in Eq. (3-2) and express this as a percentage of the latter. This is a measure of the upward bias in Eq. (3-3) attributable to omitting the ability measure. For E_3 this value is approximately 2 percent. The additional income due to one college degree from Eq. (3-3) is $2,017 for the first nine ability classes, and $4,477 for the top ability class. The weighted average of these two values (with weights equal to the numbers in the two groups) is $2,151. The difference between this and the value of $2,218 from Eq. (3-3) is approximately 3 percent. The corresponding estimate for those with more than one degree is −1 percent.

Since these percentages are all very small (less than 4 percent), the additional income from education can, with these data, be estimated fairly accurately without including an ability measure. This result is of great interest in view of our discussion in Taubman and Wales (1972), in which we traced the pattern of the relationship between ability and educational attainment for various samples. The conclusion reached there was that the slope of such a relation for Minnesota males, using the ACE decile measure, was *steeper* than in any other time period. The implication of these two results taken together is that the bias in the education coefficients due to omitting IQ will in general be very small *provided* the relative importance of the education and ability coefficients in determining income is as in

[24] The corresponding coefficients of Eq. (3-3) using an open-end mean of $20,000 are 4.493, .225, .808, 1.531, 2.009, and 2.532.

this sample.[25] (However, in Chapter 5, in which the NBER-TH sample is discussed, the bias based on a different ability measure is larger.)

The relatively small bias due to omitting ability is also of interest, because it is derived from the data source that was used in summary form by Becker (1964) and Denison (1964) in attempts to answer the same question. Becker concluded that an increase in ability has a negligible effect on the earnings of high school graduates and a 15 to 20 percent effect among college graduates. Denison concluded that about one-third of the income differentials between individuals with different educational attainment was not due to education. Our estimate of this differential is about 4 percent.[26] This does not imply that ability differences are unimportant, since as mentioned above, college graduates in the top decile earn approximately 30 percent more income than college graduates in the bottom four deciles. But as indicated in footnote 25, the relative bias on the education coefficient α is equal to $\beta\gamma/\alpha$, where β is the effect of income on education and γ is the *reciprocal* of the marginal effect of IQ on educational attainment. While both β and α vary by ability and educational level, their ratio would be no smaller than one-fourth. Hence, the relative bias is less than 4 percent because (in the units used in this study) γ is small. However, a small γ implies that the marginal effect of IQ on educational attainment is large.

RANK IN CLASS The above equations use IQ as a measure of mental ability. It has been suggested that high school rank in class is a more appropriate measure. The arguments for rank in class are that it is a more accurate measure of mental ability and that it accounts for such factors as drive and motivation, which are important in determining income. On the other hand, as suggested earlier, the rank-in-class data can be deficient because the quality of the

---

[25] Of course, the only data we have here are for individuals 15 years (including World War II) out of high school. The bias could be greater at different ages. This aspect is discussed in more detail in Chapter 5.

If the true equation is $y = \alpha S + \beta A$, then the bias from omitting A is equal to $\beta\gamma$ where γ is found by estimating the equation $A = \gamma S$. In Taubman and Wales (1972), we show that γ has varied.

[26] However, Denison's one-third also allowed for differences in family background (Denison, 1964).

student body varies from one school to the next. Since data are available for rank in class as well as IQ, it is interesting to compare the effect upon income of these two ability measures.

The following equation, in which the ability measure is rank in class (R), can be compared with Eq. (3-2).

$$Y = 4.545 + .227E_V + .793E_1 + 1.565E_3 + 2.034E_G + 2.565E_{GM}$$
$$\quad (10.5) \quad\quad (.5) \quad\quad\quad (1.7) \quad\quad\quad (3.5) \quad\quad\quad (4.9) \quad\quad\quad (5.6)$$

$$\quad - .112R_{5-9} + .352R_{10} \quad\quad\quad\quad\quad\quad \bar{R}^2 = .92 \quad (3\text{-}4)$$
$$\quad\quad (.4) \quad\quad\quad (1.1)$$

The most noticeable difference between the two equations is that in Eq. (3-4) the ability variables are no longer significant. In addition, the point estimates here are much lower; in fact, the coefficient of R_{5-9} is negative. For the equation in which R_1 through R_{10} are included separately, no ability t value exceeds 1.5 and there is no apparent pattern in magnitude or sign to the coefficients. Clearly, the rank-in-class ability variable is inferior to the IQ ability variable, in that the latter measures an attribute that is significantly related to income and the former does not. If data were available on the quality of the various schools, inclusion of such a variable would yield more meaningful results.

OCCUPATIONAL REGRESSIONS According to the material to be discussed in Chapter 9, it is possible to test the hypothesis that education is used as a screening device by determining if a disproportionately lower percentage of people at lower education levels are in the high-paying occupations open to them.[27] The test requires that we estimate the income that could be earned in each occupation by a person with a given set of characteristics. To accomplish this, we estimate equations within occupation groups. Such equations are also of interest for other reasons.

The Wolfle-Smith data are available by the nine broad census occupational categories.[28] However, we have only the cross tabulations of the basic data and at most ten observations (corresponding to the ability measure) on income and education

---

[27] See pp. 158–163

[28] These are professional (1), semiprofessional-managerial (2), clerical (3), sales (4), service (5), skilled (6), farm (7), unskilled (8), and housewife (9).

within any occupation. The possibility, therefore, of testing various education and ability variables is severely limited. For example, the six educational categories and ten ability categories would have to be combined into fewer than ten variables in order to estimate the equation. In order to preserve degrees of freedom, we first combined the data for the professional, semiprofessional, and sales occupations.[29] In these equations we included a dummy intercept variable for two of the occupations. This method constrains the slope coefficients to be the same, while permitting the average income levels to vary among the three occupations. The number of observations in this group of occupations (30) permits estimation of the type of income-education-ability relationship discussed above. The other occupations (3, 5, 6, 7, and 8) were combined in the same way and estimated as a group with dummy constant terms for some or all of the occupations.

Examples of the types of relationships with which we have experimented are:

Occupations 1, 2, 4

$$Y = -.377E_{V+1+3} - .373E_G - .725E_{GM} + .693A_{5-9}$$
$$\quad\quad (.1) \quad\quad\quad (.1) \quad\quad\quad (.2) \quad\quad\quad (2.8)$$

$$+ 1.895A_{10} - .797D_{2+4} + 6.582 \quad\quad \bar{R}^2 = .97 \quad (3\text{-}5)$$
$$\quad (2.7) \quad\quad\quad (1.6) \quad\quad\quad (1.9)$$

Occupations 3, 5, 6, 7, 8

$$Y = .594E_{V+1+3} + 2.037E_G + 1.279E_{GM} + .049A_{5-9} - .199A_{10}$$
$$\quad\quad (.7) \quad\quad\quad (1.6) \quad\quad\quad (.7) \quad\quad\quad (.2) \quad\quad\quad (.3)$$

$$+ .182D_{3+5} + .942D_6 + 3.194 \quad\quad \bar{R}^2 = .91 \quad (3\text{-}6)$$
$$\quad (.5) \quad\quad\quad (2.6) \quad\quad\quad (4.8)$$

where E_{V+1+3} is a dummy variable with a value of 1 if the individual has either vocational training or any college education short of a degree, and D_i is an occupational dummy with a value of 1 for those in occupation i, and a value of zero otherwise.

In no case does the *t* statistic for an education variable

---

[29] This division was made on the basis of preliminary equations using all the occupations. In these equations we allowed the constant term to vary by using a dummy variable. These equations consistently pointed to this division which, moreover, is in accord with intuitive impressions and census data rankings.

suggest a coefficient significantly different from zero at the 5 percent level.[30] The point estimates of the education parameters from Eq. (3-5) are negative, whereas those from Eq. (3-6), although positive, are not significant, nor do they increase with educational attainment. The ability variables have significant effect on income in the former case but not the latter. Regressions with different education and ability groupings yielded similar results—in no case did education appear to influence income in a systematic manner.[31] From these regressions we reach the somewhat surprising conclusions that, at an average age of 33, there is no (determinable) significant effect of education on income within occupations.

The two equations also reveal some other interesting information. In Eq. (3-5), those in the semiprofessional and sales occupations earn about $800 a year less than those in the professional occupations.[32] This difference amounts to about $7^1/_2$ percent of the professional income. Ability is statistically significant and numerically important, with those in the tenth ability class earning nearly $1,900 more than those in the bottom four tenths. Indeed, the ability coefficients in Eq. (3-5) are larger than those in Eq. (3-1). Thus it appears that within the professional occupations, income is determined by the suboccupation that a person enters and by his IQ score, but not by his education.

In Eq. (3-6), the only significant variables are the constant term and the dummy variable for skilled workers. Thus, for unskilled, clerical, farm, skilled, and service workers, neither higher education nor mental ability significantly determines income. It certainly is not surprising to find that higher education is not important here, since such education is not generally focused toward the skills used in these areas. Similar arguments probably also apply to mental ability.

In summary, it is not astonishing to find that mental ability is only important in certain types of occupations, but it is surprising to find that education is not all important in either of the

---

[30] The high-ability–high-education interaction term is also insignificant when included in the equations.

[31] As noted earlier, these results, which differ from those in census data, may represent the particular set of ages involved.

[32] We tried separate dummy variables for occupations 2 and 4, but the coefficients were nearly identical.

two occupational groups. There is, however, a possible technical explanation for this result, which we consider now. If, in fact, there is little or no variation in education within occupations, then the finding that income is not affected by education is of little importance, since it follows necessarily from the data. But the fraction of people in each occupation at each IQ and education level—given in Appendix B, Tables B-9 and B-12—indicates a wide range of education and ability within the various occupations. In Table B-9 it can be seen that, at all ability levels, substantial numbers of persons with either high school or some college education are working in all the occupational groups. Those with one or more degrees are mainly employed in occupations 1, 2, and 4 (and especially 1). For any level of education, the occupational distribution of people is almost the same at various ability levels.[33]

We consider now the difference between these results and those from similar regressions using census data. In general, the latter yield significant education coefficients (particularly for college graduates versus noncollege graduates) after standardizing for such influences as age, race, weeks worked in the year, and so on. Of course, there is no standardization for ability in the equations from census data. One suspects, therefore, that the education variables in equations such as Eq. (3-5) and Eq. (3-6) might be significant if the ability variable were omitted. We have estimated the following equations to test this hypothesis; the first is for occupations 1, 2, and 4, and the second is for occupations 3, 5, 6, 7, and 8.

$$Y = 4.637 + 2.831(E_G + E_{GM}) + .249D_{2+4} \qquad \bar{R}^2 = .96 \quad (3\text{-}7)$$
$$\underset{(6.2)}{} \quad \underset{(2.7)}{} \quad \phantom{+ .249D_{2+4}}\underset{(.5)}{}$$

[33] Another question that arises in connection with these results concerns the occupational breakdown. Admittedly, the nine occupations are rather broad and, consequently, heterogeneous. Even if a finer classification were used, however, it seems unlikely that the results would differ, although it is conceivable. For example, if the professionals were divided into four or five groups, then it would be possible to have education and income positively related in one group and to have, in the others, either education and income negatively related (which is unlikely) or virtually no variation in education *within* them, but variation *between* them, with income higher in the occupation with lower average education. It seems unlikely, however, that these relationships would be such as to cancel out when the data were combined. In addition, an obvious difficulty in defining occupations less broadly is that the variation in education within any ability class is likely to be smaller.

$$Y = 3.607 + 1.301(E_G + E_{GM}) + .296D_{3+5} + 1.065D_6$$
$$\quad (12.4) \qquad (1.7) \qquad\qquad\qquad (.9) \qquad\qquad (3.3)$$

$$\bar{R}^2 = .92 \quad (3\text{-}8)$$

These equations differ from Eq. (3-5) and Eq. (3-6) in that the ability variables are omitted and the education coefficients have been collapsed to represent college graduates and all others (with at least a high school education).[34] Eq. (3-7), for the professional, semiprofessional, and sales occupations, is in accord with general census results in which college graduates are found to have a significantly higher income. The Wolfle-Smith data suggest, however, that this higher income, once entrance into any of these occupations is achieved, is entirely due to ability. For the remaining occupations, on the other hand, education appears to be more important than ability in determining income, although the education variable is not significant even when ability is omitted.[35]

One final comment is in order. We showed earlier that the education coefficient we estimate is net of the value of work experience forgone while obtaining education. Making allowance for time spent in the military, the people in the sample with a college degree had a maximum of seven years' experience. At an older age, greater impacts of education might be found. Indeed, this is the case with the NBER-TH sample as analyzed in Chapter 9.

MINNESOTA FEMALES We have also used the Wolfle-Smith data on females ranked by ACE decile. The following equation is analogous to Eq. (3-1) for males.

$$Y = 2.138 + .108E_V + .175E_1 + .158E_3 + .777E_G + 2.184E_{GM}$$
$$\quad (17.8) \qquad (.7) \qquad (1.0) \qquad (1.0) \qquad (4.9) \qquad (7.0)$$

$$+ .124A_{5-9} - .171A_{10} \qquad\qquad \bar{R}^2 = .83 \quad (3\text{-}9)$$
$$\quad (1.2) \qquad\quad (1.2)$$

---

[34] With the ability variables included in Eq. (3-7), the coefficient of $(E_G + E_{GM})$ has a *t* value of .2, while inclusion in Eq. (3-8) yields a *t* value on the education variable of 1.5.

[35] Morgan and David (1963) find that education is significant when dummy variables for five occupations are included. Their ability measure, however, does not seem to be very appropriate.

The income measure here is average earnings of all females in the sample regardless of whether they were working. Approximately 70 percent of the females in the sample listed their occupation as housewife, although some also worked part time.

There are several interesting conclusions to be drawn from Eq. (3-9). First, the ability variables are not significant, nor were they significant when included in continuous form, as 10 decile tenths, or as part of a high-ability–high-education interaction term. Second, only the education variables representing one college degree and post-bachelor's education are significant—and these are highly significant. On the other hand, the magnitudes differ considerably from those for males—particularly the coefficient of E_G. One college degree adds only $777 to the average female's income, but $2,100 to the average male's income; the corresponding values for more than one degree are $2,184 and $2,658. The relatively better performance for women with more than one degree and the lack of significance of ability may be because teachers, who are not necessarily drawn from the high IQ groups but who plan to be in the labor force, obtain master's degrees for certification and higher pay. Thus, people who are not in the labor force—and who did not plan to be—would have less education.

FINAL COMMENT Unfortunately, without the original observations, we cannot proceed much further with this data set in exploring questions that need to be answered. Much additional information is available in another body of data, which regrettably contains people from the top half of the IQ distribution only. Most of this book will be concerned with this latter data set.

4. The NBER-TH Sample: A Description

Most of the empirical analysis in this study is based on a new and extremely important body of data, the NBER-TH sample. This sample is important both because of its size and because of its detailed information on such items as earnings, family background, education, and ability. While this sample is superior to the Wolfle-Smith sample in terms of size and information, it is less representative, having been drawn from the top half of the IQ distribution only and from a population probably less risk-averse and more specialized in other ways than the United States population as a whole. Thus, the results described in the previous chapter are in some ways complementary to those obtained with the NBER-TH data.

Since the sample is not representative of the entire population, it is necessary to ask to what extent its results are appropriate for generalization to the population as a whole. To answer this and other related questions, assume that the true relationships between earnings (Y), education (ED), and ability (A) can be represented by

$$Y = \alpha ED + \beta A \qquad (4\text{-}1)$$

The distribution of earnings will depend on the distribution of education and ability and on the coefficients α and β. Suppose for the moment that β equals zero and that ED is distributed normally. Then Y would also have a normal distribution, but with a mean and standard deviation α times as large as in the education distribution. Next, suppose that a study is undertaken in which only people above a certain education level are included and that a random sample is drawn from this truncated population. Since ED in the sample is no longer distributed normally, we would not expect the distribution of earnings in the sample to be distributed normally. In other words, we could not use such a sample to draw inferences about the distribution of earnings in the population. We can, however, use the information to estimate α. Suppose, for example, that Figure 4-1 illustrates the relationship between education and income in the population and in the sample. The relationship is more realistic than that of Eq. (4-1) because all the points do not lie on a line; that is, there is an error term, which we assume is distributed normally at every level of education. Thus a random sample including only people with a high school education or more will allow us to obtain an unbiased estimate of the slope of the line *LM* or of α. The earnings-education relationship in the figure was deliberately drawn as nonlinear to illustrate that a truncated sample does not necessarily provide information on the portion of the population that is not represented in the sample. Our sample not only is truncated but also has a much higher proportion of people with a college degree than is true of the general population. This does not create problems, however, because a stratified sample (with relatively heavier weights for some portion of the population than the others) will generate unbiased estimates of population parameters, provided the sample is random and the usual conditions for unbiased estimates exist.

Suppose next that β is not zero in Eq. (4-1) and that we measure A, although its range may also be truncated. A simple

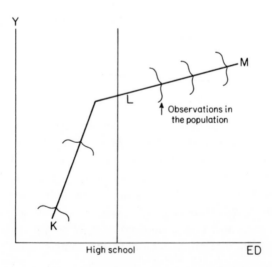

FIGURE 4-1
Hypothetical relationship between earnings and education

extension of the above discussion indicates that we can still obtain unbiased estimates of α and β from the sample, but these estimates will not necessarily apply to the portion of the sample space of A or ED not measured. In summary, the coefficients obtained from a data base in which the range of some variables is truncated, and in which some strata are sampled more heavily than others, will provide unbiased estimates of the total population parameters for the data space sample. As discussed below, only people in the top half of the IQ distribution are in the sample; thus the effects of education are specifically for people with such IQ. But since we find little evidence of an interaction of education and mental ability, the education results may well apply for the whole range of IQ.

Because this is the first study to use the sample, we will describe it in some detail: the population from which the sample was drawn; the data-collection procedure; response biases; the accuracy of results; and what information was obtained by whom.[1] Much of the technical material appears in Appendixes E, F, and G, and a summary of the important results is given at the beginning of the next chapter. Appendix E indicates how we obtain the ability measures used in the regression analysis. Since there is some ambiguity in the interpretation of the ability measures, it is recommended that these pages be examined. This chapter concludes with a brief description of the sample distribution of earnings in 1955 and 1969 by education and ability, as well as by education and occupation.

THE SAMPLE In 1969, the National Bureau of Economic Research (NBER) attempted to contact a sample of people originally surveyed by Thorndike and Hagen in the mid-1950s. The descriptions of the original sample in their report (Thorndike & Hagen, 1959) is the source of the following information. During World War II, the Army Air Corps accepted volunteers for the pilot, navigator, and bombardier training programs. The volunteers, of whom there were some 500,000, had to pass the Armed Forces Qualifying Test with a score equivalent to that of the median of high school graduates.[2] These people were then given a battery of 17

---

[1] As explained below, part of the sample was obtained and used in the mid-1950s by Thorndike and Hagen.

[2] This was about equivalent to the person's being able to complete two years of college. See Thorndike and Hagen (1959, p. 52)

tests that measured such abilities as mathematical and reasoning skills, physical coordination, reaction to stress, and spatial perception. While the tests were changed during the war, a given set of tests was used for 75,000 men in the period July to December 1943.

In 1955, Thorndike and Hagen undertook a study to determine the validity of the tests in predicting the subsequent vocational success of a random sample of 17,000 of these 75,000 individuals. Most of the 17,000 people responded to the questionnaire.[3] (The 2,000 people who were still in the military in 1955 were eliminated from our sample.)

Now let us consider the representativeness of the sample. Thorndike and Hagen (1959, p. 84) have shown that there was no significant difference in test scores between the 9,700 civilian respondents in 1955 and the 75,000 tested on the same battery. Since the test scores are also related to education, it is safe to conclude that there was no important response bias in terms of education. When compared to the United States male population aged 18 through 26 in 1943, however, the sample contains some biases. Not only was the air cadet group more educated, since all had at least a high school diploma, but the intelligence level was fairly high, since a score equivalent to the average for college sophomores was used as a preliminary screening device.[4]. Also, the tested group consisted of people willing to volunteer for the various programs. Thus, these people may be, on the average, less risk-averse than the population as a whole and thus more willing to choose self-employment and other risky operations which, on the average, pay a risk premium. However, as shown above, this will not bias out coefficients unless the degree of risk aversion, which is not measured, is

---

[3] In part, the high contact rate for people, most of whom were separated (initially) from the military for about a decade, occurred because many veterans maintained contact with the Veterans Administration through life insurance policies and disability claims. The authors were able to increase the response rate by hiring the Retail Credit Bureau to find various individuals. Some 1,500 people had died since 1943.

The questionnaire is reproduced on p. 86 of Thorndike and Hagen (1959) and in Appendix G of this volume.

[4] Some rough comparisons with the population as a whole can be found in Thorndike and Hagen (1959, pp. 110–111). The education distribution is discussed in detail below.

correlated with education. The interruption of schooling and family life by the war and the GI Bill could affect the distribution of education by ability level. But, as shown above, we can still obtain estimates of the parameters as long as we hold education and the relevant ability constant. Also, we shall argue that this interruption helps to eliminate the bias in estimating the returns from some colleges. Finally, there may be an over-representation of the successful. (See Thorndike & Hagen, 1959, p. 14; also see the discussion below on success bias.) While the differences between the sample and the United States population complicate the extrapolation of our results, a substantial benefit in comparison with the census sample is that many items that could affect income are held constant by the Thorndike-Hagen sample design.

Thorndike and Hagen's major conclusions are that, within narrow occupations there were very small differences in earnings associated with ability, but that, between occupations, there were important differences in ability and education. However, they did not present quantitative estimates of the effect of ability and education on income.[5]

In 1968, we communicated with Professor Thorndike and learned that he had retained much of the information collected for most people in the sample. Specifically, he had retained his completed questionnaires for 8,300 people; in addition, for the 9,700 civilian respondents in 1955, he had mailing addresses and a file of computer outputs. The computer output contained the test scores on each of the 17 tests, two indexes of background information whose weights were determined by the usefulness of the items in predicting success in pilot and navigational courses, respectively, monthly earnings in 1955, a three-digit job code, time on the job, number of people supervised, a job-success-evaluation code, and the army serial number. Besides some of the same items, the questionnaire included information on education *after* 1945, an occupation-earnings history, a seven-digit job code, and the social security number. After we received permission from the Air Force[6] to use the data that it had helped to collect, the NBER repunched

---

[5] See Thorndike and Hagen (1959, Ch. 3).

[6] Permission was granted by Col. John G. Dailey, Commander, Brooks Air Force Base, in a letter dated Apr. 30, 1969.

both the computer output and the educational information that Thorndike had kindly recoded from the questionnaires.

The information thus resurrected is extremely valuable because it is one of the largest samples (of people with at least a high school diploma) that contains detailed measures of income, ability, and education. The NBER decided to make this body of data even richer by conducting an additional survey of 1955 respondents to collect an occupation-earnings history through 1969, family (as opposed to individual) income in 1968, background data on the respondent, a complete post-high school education résumé (not just that of 1946–1955), health information, and other data about the individual's beliefs and activities. This questionnaire is reproduced in Appendix G. Clearly, the information on health, background, beliefs, and so on adds to the importance of the data. But from our viewpoint the reinterview was valuable because it provided information on occupations and income for up to 25 years after an individual finished his formal education.[7]

The NBER mailed a questionnaire in 1969 to the 9,700 civilian respondents of 1955. In discussing the response bias on this reinterview, it is useful to consider how many promptings were necessary to obtain a reply. The first mailing, which took place in June 1969, was made on the basis of the 1955 addresses. Approximately half the questionnaires were returned as not deliverable (although others were also not delivered and not returned). On this first mailing, about 1,400 replies were received.

Another mailing to the 1955 addresses brought the number of replies up to nearly 2,500. At this point, the NBER enlisted the aid of the Veterans Administration. Using army serial numbers, the Veterans Administration kindly provided (at no cost) nearly 4,000 new addresses. Two mailings to these addresses, in October and in November, yielded about 2,000 more replies. These 4,443 replies constitute the sample used in this study. In April 1970, however, another mailing was made to all nonrespondents. In this mailing, approximately 1,000 new addresses were obtained by examining the 1970 telephone directories of the

[7]As far as we know, the only studies that have a long span of individuals' incomes as well as measures of education and ability are those of Campbell (1965), Terman and Oden (1947), and Husén (1968). These samples are much smaller than ours and, in the case of Terman, apply to only the top 2 percent in the IQ scale.

1955 place of residence of the people for whom there had been no new address since 1955. This mailing resulted in about 650 new replies.

We had about 7,500 up-to-date addresses. The 2,200 remaining people include 300 individuals who have died since 1955 and people for whom we do not have current addresses.[8] Of the 7,500 people, about 70 percent eventually answered our questionnaire, but, as noted above, we used only 85 percent of the responding sample.[9] As will be demonstrated below, the 1969 respondents tended to be more heavily concentrated than the 1955 respondents among the more educated and mentally more able. But, given education and ability, we do not find that it is the more successful who respond. Thus, we can think of the data as a random stratified sample that will yield unbiased coefficients.

EARNINGS, EDUCATION, AND ABILITY

In Appendix E, the reader will find some technical material that examines the accuracy of the responses on education; determines the extent of response bias by education and ability level; and indicates how the ability measure was constructed and determined to be mathematical ability. At this point, it suffices to say that the education and ability measures appear to be accurate. The information in the technical sections also indicates that roughly one-fourth of the sample falls into each of the categories of high school graduate, some college, college graduate, and at least some postgraduate work. Thus, the people in our sample are better educated than both the population as a whole and other veterans of World War II. As noted earlier, the people are also brighter, since only those in the top half of the IQ distribution were allowed to take the battery of 17 tests.

Let us consider the relationship in this sample between education or ability and earnings. The average earnings levels are presented in Table 4-1 for the various education groups for 1955 and 1968.[10] Average earnings in 1955 at all higher education

---

[8] That is, for some 1,900 people, the questionnaire was returned as not deliverable, but no new address was obtained.

[9] While all the comments and results presented here apply to 4,443 people, some subsequent work has indicated there would be little difference if all 5,086 people were included.

[10] The 1968 figures are used in order to make comparisons with census data. The 1969 census data were not available when this was written. In some cases the education figures had to be corrected as described below.

TABLE 4-1 Comparison of average income by education, NBER-TH sample, and census data (in dollars)		*High school*	*Some college*	*Undergraduate degree*	*Some graduate work*
	NBER-TH				
	1955	$6,000	$6,900	$7,056	$6,964
	1968	13,944	16,920	19,044	19,506
	Census				
	1968	9,106	11,072	14,281	17,223

NOTE: These are mean incomes for those aged 45 through 54 in 1968. The average age in our sample in 1968 is 46.

levels are about 16 percent higher than those of high school graduates. In 1968, earnings of college dropouts are 20 percent greater than those of high school graduates. Earnings in 1968 are higher at the undergraduate and graduate levels. It can be seen that the sample contains people with high income by comparing the 1968 results with those for the same age group in the 1968 *Current Population Reports*. Although the data reported in our sample are for *earnings* only, they are substantially greater than the *income* estimates from the census. Since the ability level in the sample is quite high, it is not surprising that our sample is much more successful than the corresponding group of the population.

In 1968, only 1 percent of the sample received earnings below $5,500, while 10 percent received earnings less than about $9,000. On the other hand, 1 percent of the people received at least $70,000, and 10 percent had earnings above $30,000. These distributions clearly differ from those in the general population.

We now consider briefly the distribution of average earnings by mathematical ability and education.[11] In Table 4-2, earnings generally increase with ability within each educational level. It should be noted that the highest education category shown combines all Ph.D.'s, M.D.'s, and LL.B.'s. In 1955, within any ability category those with a high school degree only earn less than those with some college and those with one degree, but not necessarily less than those with some graduate work or an M.A. The highest earnings are received by those in the highest

[11] As explained in Chapter 5, mathematical ability is the only ability measure that we find to be an important determinant of income.

TABLE 4-2 *Average yearly earnings, by ability and education, 1955 and 1969 (in dollars)*

			Education			
	High school	*Some college*	*Under-graduate degree*	*Some graduate work*	*Master's*	*Ph.D., M.D., and LL.B.*
1955: Mathematical-ability fifth						
1	$5,750	$6,351	$6,450	$6,000	$5,711	$5,415
	(212)	(185)	(123)	(21)	(34)	(16)
2	5,737	6,961	6,499	6,724	5,640	7,647
	(204)	(178)	(172)	(29)	(34)	(22)
3	6,238	6,727	6,651	6,233	6,261	9,116
	(159)	(178)	(229)	(36)	(58)	(28)
4	5,989	6,935	7,262	7,902	6,078	8,548
	(136)	(200)	(256)	(40)	(72)	(52)
5	6,736	7,837	7,669	7,448	7,144	7,402
	(97)	(161)	(365)	(61)	(84)	(70)
1969: Mathematical-ability fifth						
1	$12,239	$16,886	$18,610	$14,031	$14,403	$20,461
	(219)	(202)	(124)	(26)	(46)	(26)
2	13,929	17,029	18,738	16,813	15,405	22,653
	(214)	(179)	(160)	(38)	(42)	(41)
3	14,830	16,116	20,155	20,332	14,898	23,260
	(162)	(208)	(216)	(41)	(68)	(52)
4	14,849	17,570	19,348	19,917	17,333	27,284
	(152)	(208)	(263)	(37)	(84)	(74)
5	15,961	20,295	21,429	20,011	22,233	25,888
	(92)	(162)	(352)	(71)	(112)	(102)

NOTE: Sample sizes are given in parentheses below the dollar amounts. The top fifth is ranked 5.

education categories, with incomes of those with some college and an undergraduate degree about the same. As shown in Tables 4-3 and 4-4, the earnings of M.D.'s are substantially above the incomes of others in this group. In interpreting these results, it should be kept in mind that people with greater education have had less time on the job than those with less education, and that most of those with a B.A., for example, have been working five to seven years.

TABLE 4-3 *Average yearly earnings, by occupation and education, 1955 (in dollars)*

	High school	Some college	Under-graduate degree	Some graduate work	Master's	Ph.D., LL.B., and M.D.
Managerial	$7,560	$7,860	$7,944	$8,460	$7,932	$7,776
	(245)	(357)	(378)	(48)	(40)	(15)
*Professional**	7,332	6,912	6,780	6,684	6,072	7,956
	(91)	(169)	(518)	(104)	(237)	(167)
Technical	5,796	5,892	5,016	5,880	5,340	
	(30)	(49)	(20)	(1)	(2)	†
White-collar	4,524	4,800	5,112	4,848	3,720	6,000
	(107)	(66)	(47)	(7)	(3)	(1)
Sales	6,456	7,740	7,200	6,696	7,128	6,048
	(85)	(133)	(150)	(29)	(9)	(8)
Service	4,908	4,980	5,712	5,760	7,500	7,896
	(36)	(25)	(14)	(3)	(2)	(4)
Blue-collar	5,292	5,604	5,556	5,400	4,440	4,800
	(362)	(155)	(46)	(3)	(1)	(1)
Farm	4,584	5,808	7,116	4,320	5,640	
	(30)	(22)	(23)	(2)	(2)	†
Medical		5,460	6,996	4,920	12,720	11,304
	†	(2)	(3)	(2)	(3)	(37)

* Including medical.
† No observations.
NOTE: Sample sizes are given in parentheses below the dollar amounts.

By 1969, those with more education had relatively more earnings than in 1955, compared with those at low education levels. Within any ability group, earnings increase with education except for the M.A. and some-graduate-work categories, but even in these two groups, earnings now exceed those of high school graduates—which was not true in 1955.[12] The tables also indicate that average ability rises with education. Consequently, the average earnings differences derivable from Table 4-1 will overstate the effects of education on income. Of course, the ef-

[12] The average income of Ph.D.'s (excluding M.D.'s and LL.B.'s) is about equal to that of B.A.'s in 1969. Because of the small sample sizes, this result is not reported by ability level. There are more observations in 1969 because fewer people did not report their income.

TABLE 4-4 *Average yearly earnings, by occupation and education, 1969 (in dollars)*

	High school	Some college	Under-graduate degree	Some graduate work	Master's	Ph.D., LL.B., and M.D.
Managerial	$17,937	$20,438	$22,444	$21,815	$23,221	$26,678
	(420)	(628)	(729)	(125)	(157)	(48)
*Professional**	12,598	14,112	16,862	14,329	14,364	25,270
	(17)	(60)	(297)	(88)	(234)	(276)
Technical	15,270	15,034	15,107	18,669	19,745	10,000
	(107)	(101)	(36)	(4)	(5)	(1)
White-collar	8,513	9,554	9,637	9,911	16,100	
	(30)	(26)	(14)	(3)	(1)	†
Sales	12,633	15,618	18,192	14,420	11,387	18,415
	(72)	(45)	(13)	(1)	(2)	(1)
Service	9,079	9,802	11,881	12,000		21,000
	(72)	(45)	(13)	(1)	†	(1)
Blue-collar	10,223	10,509	11,577	13,000		
	(270)	(115)	(23)	(3)	†	†
Farm	11,823	17,647	18,308	19,500	15,000	20,000
	(38)	(36)	(24)	(2)	(1)	(1)
Medical		14,875	17,333	12,975	27,667	33,139
	†	(4)	(3)	(2)	(3)	(57)

* Including medical.
† No observations.
NOTE: Sample sizes are given in parentheses below the dollar amounts.

fects of education and ability on income are not accurately reflected in Table 4-2 either, because other determinants of earnings have not been held constant, as is done in Chapter 5.

It is also of some interest to study average earnings within broad occupational groups and education classes for 1955 and 1969. In Table 4-3, 1955 earnings, education, and occupation data are given for those people who responded in 1969; in Table 4-4, 1969 data are given for the same group.[13] We have attempted to aggregate the 1955 occupation categories into broad groups corresponding to those available in 1969. The results may not be

[13] As before, the 1955 education data have been corrected to account for education prior to 1946.

completely consistent, because the 1955 job code was assigned on the basis of detailed information supplied by respondents, and the 1969 code was obtained by having the respondents report their broad occupational category. In particular, the professional-technical distinction may differ between the two years.

In both years, the rankings of occupations by average earnings are the same. At the top are the managerial, professional, technical, and sales groups, while at the lower end are the farm, blue-collar, white-collar, and service workers.[14] In 1969, at every education level except Ph.D., income in the highest-paying occupation was about twice that of the lowest-paying occupation, while in 1955 it was about $1^1/_2$ times as much.

On the other hand, within occupations there is much less earnings variability between education levels. For example, if we exclude the graduate categories, which have few entries except for the managerial and professional groups, the differences between the high school and B.A. categories average about 10 percent of the lower income. In 1969, these differences are about 20 percent. At the Ph.D. level, the differences are larger: approximately 50 percent in 1969 for managers and 75 percent for professionals, excluding medical.

From 1955 to 1969, there was a general movement from the low-paying occupations to the managerial group. This is shown most clearly for high school graduates, in that the number of managers increased by 105 even though the total number of people with just a high school education declined from 1955 to 1969. The managerial group includes all business owners, who composed about one-third of the group in 1969.

A final interesting aspect of the table is the distribution of people over occupation by education groups. In 1955, about one-half of all high school graduates were in the high-paying occupations, while about 95 percent of those with some graduate work were in these occupations. This is very similar to the distribution of people by occupation given in the Wolfle-Smith discussion. In 1969, the fractions of people in the high-paying occupations at all education levels were higher. A more detailed discussion of earnings by occupation is presented in Chapter 8.

---

[14] Since "medical" is included in "professional," we do not discuss it separately at this point.

5. The NBER-TH Sample Regression Results

In this chapter and its appendixes (Appendixes H and I), we will examine the relationship of earnings to education, ability, and several other variables, using the NBER-TH sample. An extensive discussion of how this sample was drawn, the accuracy of the data, the extent of response, and the derivation of the four major measures of ability can be found in Chapter 4. The reader may especially wish to refer to Chapter 4 for a discussion of alternative procedures and methods that could have been used in the derivation (and interpretation) of the ability measures and, to a lesser extent, elsewhere. To aid recollection, we present a very brief summary of the important information about the sample.

In 1943, some 75,000 men who had volunteered to undertake pilot, bombardier, or navigator training in the Army Air Corps, and who had scored in the top half of the Armed Forces Qualification Test, were given a battery of some 17 tests. In 1955, Thorndike and Hagen (1959) surveyed a random sample of about 17,000 men and obtained information from about 10,000 civilians and 2,000 who were still in the military. In 1969 the NBER surveyed the 10,000 civilians. About 7,500 people were contacted, and 5,200 responded. Some 800 questionnaires were received too late to be included in this study. While the 4,400 people we used in the study are brighter and more educated than the 10,000 people who responded in 1955, the respondents within each ability-education cell appear to be a random drawing from the same population.[1]

---

[1] The other people who responded in 1955 are not included in any of the analyses because of the lack of a crucial piece of education data, as explained in Chapter 4.

The major purpose of this chapter is to develop the information necessary to answer the following questions at various points in the age-income profile: What is the effect of education on income once other determinants of income are held constant? What types of ability are important determinants of income? Are there significantly different effects of education at different ability levels? What is the bias on the education coefficients from omitting ability and other variables? Are there some other unmeasured variables whose effects on earnings persist over time? In Chapter 4 we argued that a stratified sample drawn from only a portion of the population will yield results that can be generalized to a random sample of the truncated population (except for the bias problem). The results need not be capable of generalization to the whole population since the functional form may be different in the portion of the population not sampled.

SUMMARY OF RESULTS

Since this is a particularly long and, at times, technical chapter, we present first a summary of what we have found to be the major determinants of wage, salary, and unincorporated-business income. The variables that are important in some or all years in our equations for males are education, mathematical ability, being a high school or elementary school teacher, personal biography, health, marital status, father's education, and age. In addition, we find that the residual in each year consists in part of personal effects that persist over long periods of time. When we test the variables that represent coordination, verbal IQ, and spatial-perception abilities, however, there is little evidence that these variables add to earnings in this sample, which was drawn from the top half of the ability distribution.[2] Except, perhaps, for the types of abilities that were not significant, the list contains few surprises, since other investigators have often found the same types of variables (as well as a few we have not tried) to be important. There are many surprises, however, in the magnitude of the effects. We consider first the earnings differentials due to education.

---

[2]Other variables that explain income, but are not presented in the results because they are inappropriate for calculating the returns to education, include occupational dummy variables such as "business proprietor." The teaching dummy variable is included because we think it represents the nonpecuniary returns prevalent in this occupation.

The reader is once again reminded that there is some dispute about the interpretation of the factors we call mathematical ability and IQ. See Chapter 4.

The extra earnings from education are given in Table 5-1 for persons with the characteristics of the average high school graduate. In 1955, when the average age in the sample was 33, the extra earnings from education were 10 to 15 percent of those obtainable with a high school degree at all educational levels —except for the highest graduate degrees or for those whose occupation was elementary school or high school teacher. Although not shown in the table, the differentials for B.A. and B.S. holders are the same. The income differential was 70 percent for M.D.'s, 2 percent for Ph.D.'s, and 20 percent for LL.B.'s. (The Ph.D. and M.D. estimates are based on fewer than 100 and 50 people, respectively.)

In 1969, those with some college earned about 17 percent more than high school graduates, while those with an undergraduate degree, some graduate work, and a master's degree received 25 to 30 percent more.[3] Ph.D.'s, LL.B.'s, and M.D.'s earned about 25, 85, and 105 percent more, respectively, than high school graduates of the same ability level. These increases would also hold for hourly wage rates, since average hours worked are the same at all educational levels except for the combination of Ph.D., LL.B., and M.D., in which hours are 8 percent greater than those of high school graduates. In 1969, the income differentials were higher at all education levels, with the greatest percentage increase accruing to the most highly educated. Since most of the post-high school education was obtained after

---

[3] The questionnaire was somewhat vague as to whether "most recent earnings" referred to 1969 or 1968, but as explained at a later point, there is evidence that 1969 annual earnings were given.

TABLE 5-1
Increases in earnings for the average high school graduate, by education level, 1955 and 1969 (as a percentage of high school earnings)

Education	1955	1969
Some college	11	17
Undergraduate degree*	12	31
Some graduate work*	15	26
Master's*	10	32
Ph.D.	2	27
M.D.	72	106
LL.B.	19	84

*For those who do not teach.
SOURCES: Tables 5-4 and 5-8.

the tests were taken in 1943, and since evidence presented below indicates that pretest education differences had little effect on the test score, the education coefficients measure both the cognitive and affective benefits of higher education.

In 1969, we can identify the people who own their own business.[4] The earnings reported for these people probably include some return to financial investment and some compensation for extra risk. If we include a zero-one dummy variable to remove such effects, we find that the 1969 income differentials for non-business owners are 17 percent and 39 percent for those with some college and those with an undergraduate degree, respectively. A bachelor's-degree holder's performance is improved because the business owners, who have high earnings, on the average, are less heavily concentrated in the bachelor's than in the high school group.

There is one other important result in Table 5-1. In all the years studied, the returns to education display an erratic behavior in that each additional year or plateau does not add as much income as the previous one. Thus, in 1955, there is essentially no increase in income beyond the some-college level until the huge jump for M.D.'s. The increases for M.D.'s could be justified as a monopoly return, but the lack of additional income for undergraduates and those in other categories requires some explanation. This is discussed in more detail in Chapter 6, but a brief description follows.

According to Mincer (1970), people pay for general on-the-job training and higher future earnings by receiving lower wages while being trained. If, on the average, the more educated invest more in such training, differences in average starting salary by education level will be less than lifetime differences (and may even be in reverse order). The earnings profiles of those who invest more will increase faster with experience. In no more than $1/r$ years (where r is the rate of return on the on-the-job training), the returns from such investment will outweigh the costs of any current investments and people's current earnings will be above the "no investment" lifetime earnings flow. After this, the earnings profiles by education level will continue to diverge if investment continues.

Mincer's formulation also emphasizes that it is work ex-

---

[4] This category does not include self-employed professionals.

perience and not age that determines earnings. We indicated in Chapter 3 that when age is held constant, the education coefficients measure the net effect of education, that is, the increase in productivity minus the loss in work experience. The combination of these two ideas and information in Table 5-1 suggests that in 1955 those with some college and those with a bachelor's degree were near the point on their profiles where observed earnings equaled their "no investment" earnings, while high school graduates, who had more experience, were above their constant earnings level. But if those who are more educated invest more, then Mincer's model would imply that earnings of the more educated should in 1969 be even further from their constant flow than earnings of high school graduates. That is, his model implies that the 1955 results understate, and the 1969 results overstate, the effect of education on lifetime earnings.

While Mincer's theory can help explain some of our results, it is necessary to note that there exists little direct evidence on which either to accept or to refute the wage-adjustment process he predicts. Thus, it is interesting to find in this sample that, beginning in the late 1940s, the starting salary of high school graduates (in a given year) is nearly the same as that of college graduates, that graduate students receive less than college graduates, and, finally, that those with some college may earn more than those with a college degree. (These starting-salaries figures are subject to recall error since they were recorded in 1969 and are less reliable than the 1955 or 1969 contemporaneous estimates).

On the other hand, from 1955 to 1969 the growth rates in income of those with a college degree, some graduate work, and a master's degree were essentially the same. This would suggest that the difference in investment in on-the-job training was not very large at these levels. This would also reinforce the idea that the returns to education do not follow a smooth pattern as education increases.

Further evidence of the erratic nature of the returns to education is evident in the 1969 equations, in which we replace the some-college dummy variable with three separate ones for those who had one, two, and three years of college. The coefficient for completing one year of college is essentially equal to that of the some-college variable discussed above, while the coefficients for completing the second and third years of college indicate no further increase in earnings.

There is one further peculiarity to report on the returns to education. When we included a variable to represent vocational education, we obtained significant but negative coefficients. Our explanation is that those who took such courses had no intention, or chance, or perhaps lacked sufficient drive, to enter the higher-paying managerial and professional occupations.[5] Under this interpretation, the variable does not represent causation, and we exclude it from the analysis.

The returns to education given above are calculated with ability and other characteristics held constant. To derive measures of different abilities, the 1943 test scores were subjected to factor analysis, as described in detail in Chapter 4. We used the factors representing mathematical ability, coordination, verbal IQ, and spatial perception. (As explained in Chapter 4, Professor Thorndike believes that the first factor is a closer approximation to a standard IQ test than the third factor, which he contends to be more of a heterogeneous mix.) Of these four factors, only coordination is a physical skill; the others are mental. To allow for nonlinear effects of ability and changes in scores due to maturation, we divided each factor into fifths (based on the whole 1955 sample)—which for the verbal IQ factor and to a lesser degree for the mathematical factor are equivalent to tenths, since only those in the top half of the mental-ability distribution were allowed into the test program.

We find that, of these ability measures, only mathematical ability was a significant determinant of income.[6] The extra incomes above the bottom fifth are given in Table 5-2 for 1955 and 1969. The second through fourth fifths may be subject to mild diminishing returns, but the top fifth yields substantially more than the fourth.[7] The difference between the top and bottom fifth of $1,000 per year in 1955 is more important than all the education variables (except M.D.), and in 1969 the $3,350 per

---

[5] If the variable represents drive, it could be argued that those high school graduates who did not have vocational training are more like college attenders. Since the average income of high school graduates without vocational training is higher, the returns to education would be less.

[6] The second fifth was not significant, but the other three were.

[7] For 1955, a linear, continuous ability measure would be almost as appropriate as these dummy variables in the regression analysis.

TABLE 5-2
Extra income per month for those above the bottom fifth in mathematical ability, 1955 and 1969 (in dollars)

	Mathematical-ability fifth			
Year	Q_2	Q_3	Q_4	Q_5
1955	23	33	50	84
1969	69	107	143	279

NOTE: The second fifth was not significant, but the other three were. Rank Q_5 is the highest.
SOURCES: Equation 5, Tables 5-3 and 5-7.

year difference is nearly as important as an undergraduate degree. These results are of considerable interest for those interested in the relative importance of ability and education in determining the distribution of income.[8] Since our sample was drawn from only the top half of the ability distribution, it is almost certain that for those with at least a high school education, ability is a more important determinant of the range of distribution than higher education. (The range is a more interesting measure since the sample is stratified.)

An individual's score on any test at time t depends upon inherited intelligence, the quantity and quality of schooling obtained prior to t, and the individual's home environment. Evidence presented below indicates that differences in the quantity and quality of pretest education had little if any effect on scores on the particular test used. Neither environment, which presumably has several dimensions, nor school quality has been held constant in our analysis. However, since both of these variables are related to family background, which is held constant, the ability coefficients primarily reflect differences in inherited intelligence.

In the above calculations, the ability effects were constrained to be the same at all levels of education studied. Two related questions of some importance are: If this constraint is removed, do the effects of ability persist at low levels of education? What interactions exist between ability and education? We have examined these questions in some detail. For 1955, we find practically no evidence that the effect of education was different at the various ability levels, while even for high school graduates there was a return to ability. For 1969, however, we found some evidence that those who were in the fourth (and, to some ex-

---

[8] See Mincer (1970) for an excellent summary of the issues.

tent, fifth) fifth and who had graduate training received extra income. We still find that ability was an important determinant of income even for high school graduates. Finally, in our study of initial salaries, we find that ability had no effect on income except for those with graduate education. This discussion and the entries in Table 5-2 suggest that ability has little effect on earnings initially, but that over time this effect grows and perhaps grows more rapidly for those with graduate training and high ability.[9]

A basic criticism that has been made of other studies of the returns to education is that the returns obtained are biased upward because relevant abilities have not been held constant. While we have (some) measures of ability, it is possible for us to estimate the equations omitting ability and then to calculate the percentage change in the education coefficients. Because in some studies the effects of education have been estimated holding constant sociodemographic background information, it is also useful to calculate the bias on the same basis. However, as explained in more detail below, one of our important variables is a mixture of background and ability; thus we can only calculate the upper and lower bound of the bias from omitting ability. For simplicity, in this summary we use the average of these bounds.

We have calculated the bias from assuming both that each factor was the only type of ability to be measured and that all abilities should be included in our equations. In either instance we find that only the omission of mathematical ability leads to bias of any magnitude. In 1955 the bias on the education coefficients from omitting mathematical ability is about 25 percent, varying from a low of 15 percent for the some-college category to a high of 31 percent for the master's degree category.[10] In 1969 the biases are somewhat smaller, averaging about 15 percent and ranging from 10 to 19 percent. The decline in the bias over time occurs because the coefficients on ability did not grow as

---

[9] The greater importance of ability over time was also found in a study of American Telephone and Telegraph employees. See Weisbrod and Karpoff (1968).

[10] The 15 percent bias for the some-college category is higher than in other studies. This may be due to our use of mathematical ability rather than IQ.

rapidly between 1955 and 1969 as those on education.[11] In some studies, rates of return have been calculated using differences in average incomes between education groups for various age groups. In this sample, such a procedure would overstate the returns to higher education by 35 and 20 percent in 1955 and 1969, respectively. However, the biases calculated in this sample may not apply to the population, because the relationships between education and either ability or background may be different in this special sample than in the population as a whole.

We have also examined the role of various sociodemographic background factors. Several such variables are significant and important determinants of income. For example, the difference between excellent and poor health in 1969 is worth $7,000 a year, and the nearly 100 people who are single earn $2,800 a year less than others.[12] Those whose fathers' education was at least the ninth grade earn about $1,200 a year more in 1969 and $300 more in 1955 than those whose fathers did not enter high school. The other background information is contained in a biography variable that includes information on hobbies, pre-World War II family income, education prior to 1946, and mathematical ability. This measure is divided into a set of dummy variables for the fifths. We consistently found the fourth and fifth and either the second or third fifths of the biography variable to be significant and to have about the same effect as the mathematical ability.

In our analysis we also included an age variable. Since this variable only spans eight to nine years in each of our cross sections, we did not look for nonlinearities in age effects or for interactions with education and other variables.[13] We found the age variable to be quite significant and large numerically in

---

[11] The bias is also determined by δ in the equation $A = \alpha + \delta\,ED$, but because this equation would involve the sample in 1955 and 1969, and because ED changed only slightly, δ would be virtually unchanged in the two years.

[12] The health variable used was linear with 1 for "excellent" through 4 for "poor" answers. When separate dummies are used for the various categories, the coefficients confirm that the effects are linear.

[13] Some interactions can be estimated from the coefficients of the different cross sections. See Chapter 6.

1955. The difference in income between those 30 and 39 years old was about the same as the difference in income between those with a Ph.D. and those with a high school diploma. In 1969, however, the age effect was negative and insignificant. Thus, we have evidence of the familiar sharply rising age-income profile reaching a peak after the age of 40.

Our method for allowing for age effects in any cross section constrains the profiles for all educational levels to be parallel. However, the separate results for 1955 and 1969 indicate that the high school profile is less steep than the others, since the effects of education are greater in 1969. Analysis we conducted separately for each education group would indicate that there were no significant differences in age effects between the different education groups except for the graduate group in 1955, which displayed no discernible age effects.

The results discussed above were obtained from analysis of separate cross sections. It is possible to develop a combined measure of motivation, drive, personality, and whatever other characteristics persist over long periods of time by using the residuals generated in one cross section in the equations in another cross section. In principle, better results can be obtained by grouping the data. Unfortunately, because of multicollinearity, we were not able to obtain reasonable results by grouping. We used the residuals, denoted as Q, of 1955 in 1969, and vice versa. In each year, Q raised the $\bar{R}^2$ from about .1 to .33 and reduced the standard error of estimate by 15 percent.[14] However, since least-square residuals are uncorrelated with independent variables, the inclusion of Q did not alter the values of the other coefficients. The results using the Q variable are both encouraging and discouraging. It is encouraging to find that we can substantially improve the efficiency of our es-

[14] Mincer (1970) has argued that earnings data reflect not only investments in school but also investments in on-the-job training. According to his analysis, the latter investment takes the form of a reduction in earnings in the early years of working, while its payoff is in terms of a constant flow of extra earnings. Thus, those people investing more would have negative residuals in the early working years and positive residuals later. After the passage of the number of years no more than the reciprocal of the rate of return on such investment (that is, about a decade) Mincer suggests that the returns on previous investments would offset new investments. Thus, there should be no correlation between residuals calculated at this point and ones later (or earlier). Since our income differentials in 1955 are small, very little of the correlation can be attributed to Mincer's type of investment.

timates by incorporating other information on the individual. It is also encouraging that certain effects that we believe reflect personality, and so forth, persist over time.[15] The discouraging part is that the proportion of the residual that persists over time is very small. The remainder of the residual represents random events, such as luck, and/or changes in underlying characteristics.

We next turn to a detailed examination of the results. We begin with a brief discussion of the variables.

DEFINITION OF THE VARIABLES We have divided our factors into fifths as described in Chapter 4.[16] Since the individuals in our sample are within the top half of the IQ scale, these fifths approximately correspond to tenths for the population as a whole. The dummy-variable method was used to allow for nonlinearities in the effect of each ability measure.

As described earlier, the first factor, we believe, reflects a mathematical, or numerical, aptitude. The second factor represents coordinating abilities; the third factor, a verbal IQ; and the fourth factor, spatial aptitude. In the regression analysis we refer to these factors by number and by the general type of ability that they reflect.

In our analysis we have used a variable that is intended to reflect background characteristics of individuals. The variable, which was constructed by the Army Air Corps and retained by Thorndike, is obtained from the individuals' scores on navigator and pilot biography keys.[17] These keys—described in Thorndike and Hagen (1959, pp. 38–49)—were calculated from background-information items using weights that predicted success in navigator or pilot training schools.[18] In our analysis we refer to this as the biography variable. Because it reflects

---

[15] However, it may be possible to interpret our results as evidence of a Markov scheme such as estimated in Solow (1951), Cutright (1969), and elsewhere.

[16] In order to have a reasonable sample size within each ability cell, finer divisions were not attempted.

[17] We weighted the navigator scores twice as heavily as the pilot scores to form the biography variable referred to in the analysis. These weights were suggested by preliminary analysis of the data.

[18] The background-information categories were general family and personal background, major subject in college (pre-1943), school subjects studied and done well, sports participated in and done well, activities done a number of times, hobbies and free-time activities, work experience (pre-1943), and reason for choosing cadet training.

ability, education, and socioeconomic background characteristics of the individuals, it is not a pure background measure.
As we did for the ability variables, we have calculated the
sample fifths for this variable to allow for nonlinearities.

The education categories used in the regressions are high
school, some college (one to three years), undergraduate degree,
some graduate work, master's degree, and three-year graduate
degrees.[19] These are represented in the form of dummy variables, with a value of 1 if the individual is in a particular category and zero otherwise. The high school dummy variable is
omitted in the regressions. In addition, since at one time we
were not sure if there would be enough observations to study
M.D.'s and LL.B.'s separately, we included them with Ph.D. and
then created one dummy variable to represent M.D.'s—defined
as 1 if the individual is in the medical profession and zero
otherwise—and another for LL.B.'s.[20] The dummy variable for
elementary school and high school teachers (as of 1955) is
defined analogously.

Other variables included in some of the regressions are age
(in years); health (measured in 1969), with a value of 4 for those
in poor health, 3 for those in fair health, 2 for those in good
health, and 1 for those in excellent health; marital status, as a
dummy with a value of 1 for single people and zero otherwise;
and father's education, in the form of two dummies reflecting
any high school and any college education. (When there was no
answer for a variable, we either inserted the modal response, as
with age, or eliminated the observations, as with father's education.)

The dependent variable in the regressions is earnings, which
equal wage and salary income plus unincorporated-business
income. This is more appropriate than total income for measuring the returns to education.

RESULTS FOR 1955 The dummy variables for education and ability allow for all
nonlinear effects within each variable, but no interactions between ability and education. We have tested for interactions be-

---

[19] We experimented with separate variables for B.A. and for other undergraduate
degrees and for one, two, and three years of college. The results are discussed in
the text. The three-year graduate degrees are Ph.D. or equivalent, M.D., and
LL.B.

[20] Thus, both the LL.B. and M.D. coefficients must be combined with the Ph.D. coefficients to find the full effect of these educational categories.

tween education and ability by the following method. We estimated separate equations of the form

$$Y_i = a_i + \Sigma b_{ij} ED_j + \Sigma d_{ij} Z_j$$

where *ED* represents the various education variables and *Z* all
the other variables for each of the five ability levels (*i*) of factor
1.[21]

If there were no interactions between ability and education,
the estimates of b_{ij} should be the same at each of the *i* ability
levels. We can test for the equality of the b_{ij} and d_{ij} by using
analysis of covariance. The reader should note that the interactions we are testing for are second-order effects that are equivalent to $\delta^2 Y/\delta ED \delta A$.

On the basis of the analysis of covariance, we cannot
conclude that the coefficients in the various ability equations in
1955 are significantly different at the 5 percent level.[22] However,
it appeared that in 1955 the only possible significant differences
in the effect of the various abilities on income occurred in the
comparison of graduate education levels with all other levels.
We therefore decided to estimate equations using all the data
but with separate interaction terms for graduate students at
each ability level. Such equations are given as numbers 14 and
15 in Table 5-3.

All the interaction terms are insignificant with only the Q_4
interaction being positive. Thus, there is very little evidence of
an education-ability interaction in 1955. Consequently, for this
year we can omit the interaction variables while studying the
returns to education and the bias from omitting ability.

In equation 5, Table 5-3, which can be used to study the
education-earnings differentials, all the education coefficients
are significant, but their magnitudes are surprisingly small. In
Table 5-4 we summarize the effects of education on income after
holding constant ability, background factors, and age. In this
table we have calculated the percent by which average earnings
exceed (1) those of high school graduates ($6,000 per year) and
(2) the average earnings in the immediately preceding educa-

---

[21] As explained below, the first factor is the only significant one.

[22] We made both tests in pairs of the equations by ability level and a joint test for
all five ability levels. All the *F* ratios were less than 1.5.

TABLE 5-3 *Regressions for salary, 1955 (in dollars per month)*

	Constant	Some college	Under-graduate degree	Some graduate work	Master's	Ph.D. and LL.B.*	M.D.	Teacher
(1) Y_{55}	$499.6	$75.4	$ 88.0	$ 83.3	$ 28.4	$153.3		
	(5.4)	(5.9)	(7.2)	(3.9)	(1.5)	(7.1)		
(2) Y_{55}	243.9	77.1	96.8	90.3	33.7	161.2		
	(4.2)	(6.1)	(7.8)	(4.2)	(1.8)	(7.4)		
(3) Y_{55}	229.6	80.8	103.0	115.4	96.8	109.5	$292.7	$−181.1
	(3.6)	(6.2)	(8.2)	(5.2)	(4.7)	(4.7)	(6.6)	(8.0)
(4) Y_{55}	260.1	58.6	72.6	90.9	68.1	80.8	297.3	−169.1
	(4.1)	(4.5)	(5.7)	(4.1)	(3.3)	(3.5)	(6.8)	(7.6)
(5) Y_{55}	229.3	54.0	57.8	75.0	51.2	61.2	299.8	−162.4
	(3.6)	(4.1)	(4.4)	(3.4)	(2.5)	(2.6)	(6.9)	(7.3)
(6) Y_{55}	258.4	59.1	73.2	91.1	69.8	82.9	296.5	−168.2
	(4.0)	(4.5)	(5.7)	(4.1)	(3.4)	(3.6)	(6.8)	(7.5)
(7) Y_{55}	251.8	57.9	67.9	85.6	63.0	76.3	299.9	−165.7
	(3.9)	(4.4)	(5.3)	(3.9)	(3.1)	(3.3)	(6.9)	(7.4)
(8) Y_{55}	227.9	57.5	69.4	86.2	64.6	78.1	299.0	−164.0
	(3.5)	(4.4)	(5.4)	(3.9)	(3.2)	(3.4)	(6.9)	(7.4)
(9) Y_{55}	247.6	70.3	88.5	100.9	81.0	94.9	295.9	−173.3
	(3.9)	(5.4)	(7.0)	(4.6)	(4.0)	(4.1)	(6.8)	(7.7)
(10) Y_{55}	195.1	70.5	82.3	91.8	77.0	86.1	284.0	−173.4
	(3.2)	(5.7)	(6.6)	(4.3)	(3.8)	(3.7)	(6.7)	(7.9)
(11) Y_{55}	220.1	77.5	102.2	112.2	100.7	114.3	281.2	−180.1
	(3.6)	(6.2)	(8.4)	(5.2)	(5.0)	(5.0)	(6.6)	(8.2)
(12) Y_{55}	216.3	74.7	92.8	102.1	89.0	101.9	285.4	−176.3
	(6.0)	(7.6)	(4.7)	(4.4)	(4.5)	(6.7)	(8.0)	
(13) Y_{55}	188.3	73.5	94.6	104.2	92.0	105.4	283.2	−174.7
	(5.9)	(7.8)	(4.9)	(4.6)	(4.6)	(6.7)	(7.9)	
(14) Y_{55}	230.4	53.7	56.8	81.1	56.9	69.1	299.0	−162.2
	(3.6)	(4.1)	(4.4)	(3.5)	(2.6)	(2.7)	(6.9)	(7.3)
(15) Y_{55}	229.5	53.8	57.5	84.2	60.4	73.3	299.0	−160.5
	(3.6)	(4.1)	(4.4)	(3.5)	(2.5)	(2.6)	(6.9)	(7.1)

Age	Ability			
	Q_2	Q_3	Q_4	Q_5
$7.7				
(4.2)				
8.1				
(4.3)				
7.8				
(4.1)				
7.8	$ 23.4	$33.4	$50.1	$83.7
(4.1)	(1.5)	(2.2)	(3.4)	(5.7)
7.6	− 2.0	4.0	17.7	20.6
(4.2)	(0.1)	(0.3)	(1.2)	(1.4)
7.7	5.4	8.1	12.6	40.9
(4.1)	(0.4)	(0.5)	(0.9)	(2.8)
8.2	9.4	12.2	25.2	55.7
(4.3)	(0.6)	(0.8)	(1.7)	(3.8)
9.0				
(4.8)				
8.0	33.9	40.4	58.7	99.3
(4.5)	(2.3)	(2.8)	(4.1)	(6.9)
7.7	11.5	24.9	36.3	40.4
(4.3)	(0.8)	(1.8)	(2.6)	(2.9)
8.0	5.7	18.7	25.0	59.4
(4.5)	(.04)	(1.3)	(1.8)	(4.2)
8.5	18.4	23.8	38.9	76.0
(4.8)	(1.3)	(1.7)	(2.8)	(5.4)
7.8	23.3	33.1	45.8	95.9
(4.3)	(1.5)	(2.2)	(2.9)	(6.0)
7.8	25.4	33.9	46.1	96.0
(4.1)	(1.6)	(2.1)	(2.9)	(6.0)

TABLE 5-3 (continued)

| | Interactions of graduate education with: | | | | | | Father attended |
	Q_2	Q_3	Q_4	Q_5	Health	Single	high school
(1)							
(2)							
(3)							
(4)					$-34.6	$-117.5	$27.7
					(4.6)	(3.5)	(2.7)
(5)					-33.1	-121.9	26.0
					(4.4)	(3.7)	(2.5)
(6)					-33.9	-118.9	27.5
					(4.5)	(3.5)	(2.7)
(7)					-33.8	-120.4	27.4
					(4.4)	(3.6)	(2.7)
(8)					-33.0	-119.8	25.5
					(4.3)	(3.6)	(2.5)
(9)					-37.5	-126.6	36.7
					(4.9)	(3.7)	(3.6)
(10)							
(11)							
(12)							
(13)							
(14)			$15.3	-40.5	-33.7	-125.0	26.3
			(0.6)	(1.8)	(4.4)	(3.7)	(2.6)
(15)	$-12.8	$-5.2	12.4	-43.1	-33.9	-125.2	26.2
	(0.4)	(0.2)	(0.5)	(1.8)	(4.5)	(3.7)	(2.5)

* M.D.'s are also included.

NOTE: Figures in parentheses are *t* statistics.

Father attended college	Biography				Ability factor	$\bar{R}^2$/S.E.
	Q_2	Q_3	Q_4	Q_5		
						.021
						274
						.026
						273
						.058
						269
$26.3	$ 2.1	$31.9	$66.1	$90.2		.089
(2.1)	(0.1)	(2.2)	(4.5)	(6.2)		265
21.4	0.7	30.0	63.1	81.1	1	.098
(1.7)	(0.0)	(2.0)	(4.3)	(5.6)		264
25.9	0.7	30.2	64.6	86.9	2	.090
(2.0)	(0.0)	(2.0)	(4.4)	(5.9)		265
23.2	−0.7	28.5	62.6	83.0	3	.091
(1.8)	(0.0)	(1.9)	(4.3)	(5.6)		265
24.2	−0.6	28.0	61.0	81.6	4	.094
(1.9)	(0.0)	(1.9)	(4.1)	(5.6)		265
44.3						.070
(3.5)						267
					1	.066
						268
					2	.056
						269
					3	.059
						269
					4	.062
						268
21.9	1.1	30.1	63.2	81.0	1	.099
(1.7)	(0.1)	(2.0)	(4.3)	(5.5)		264
21.9	0.9	30.1	63.0	81.0	1	.099
(1.7)	(0.1)	(2.0)	(4.3)	(5.5)		264

TABLE 5-4
Percentage
increases
in earnings,
by education
level, 1955

Education level	Percentage by which earnings in each education class exceed:	
	Earnings of average high school graduate	Earnings of average member of preceding education level
Some college	11	11
Undergraduate degree (not teacher)	12	1
Some graduate work	15	3
Master's (not teacher)	10	−4
Ph.D.	2	−8
M.D.	72	
LL.B.	19	
Undergraduate degree (teacher)	−21	
Master's (teacher)	−22	

NOTE: Average age is 33.

SOURCE: Earnings of average person in each education class from equation 3, Table 5-3. Absolute increases from equation 5, Table 5-3.

tion class.[23] It should be noted that we have separate estimates for Ph.D.'s and LL.B.'s in this table but not in equation 5, Table 5-3. The equation with the separate categories yields approximately the same coefficients on the other variables as does equation 5, but to save space, it is not shown.

Table 5-4 indicates that those who continue their education (except for LL.B.'s, M.D.'s, and teachers) receive 10 to 15 percent more income at all education levels than the average high school graduate. Thus, in the second column (which compares income with the preceding educational level), there are sharply diminishing returns to education after the first three years of college, except, of course, for medical training. M.D.'s and LL.B.'s earn about 70 percent and 20 percent more than high school graduates, respectively, while teachers earn about 20 percent less.[24] However, the reader is reminded that these results are valid only for individuals around 33 years of age in 1955.

---

[23] We use equation 3 in Table 5-3 to establish the earnings level of the average high school graduate for (1) and the average person in the other education levels for (2).

[24] We consider the lower salary of teachers to be offset by a nonpecuniary reward. Thus, in our discussion we will use the salary of nonteachers.

In equation 5, Table 5-3, our ability measure is factor 1, which we interpret as a mathematical skill.[25] In the equation, the top three fifths are significant and monotonically increasing.[26] These ability effects are important since the earnings difference (per month) between the lowest and highest fifth exceeds the largest education coefficient of $75 for some graduates. We compare the results using this factor with the other ability factors later.

The biography variable is also an important determinant of income—the third through fifth fifths are again significant, with the coefficients being very similar in magnitude to those of the mathematical factor. As mentioned above, this variable reflects a mixture of mathematical ability, education, and background characteristics. Since we are holding education and ability (and some background) constant in the regression equations, the coefficients on the biography variable reflect such other background factors as parents' socioeconomic position and home environment.[27]

The other variables in equation 5, Table 5-3, are all significant except for the variable representing father's attendance at college. We consider first the age variable. Because the ages of those in the sample range from about 30 to 39 in 1955, we would expect a large impact of age on income. Thus, the highly significant coefficient, which indicates an annual earnings increase of about $95, or about $1\frac{1}{2}$ percent, is not surprising.

While testing for ability-education interactions, we automatically obtained estimates of the age effect at each education level. The coefficients of age with t values in parentheses are 12.4 (4), 6.4 (1.8), 10 (2.5), and −2 (.4) for the high school, some-college, B.A., and graduate-education categories respectively. Differences in the effect of age on income are not significant except perhaps at the graduate level.[28]

The only measure of health available is the respondents' own

---

[25] See, however, the discussion of the factors in Chapter 4.

[26] See Appendix I for a discussion of the appropriateness of the t tests given in the tables.

[27] When the variables for father's education are omitted, the coefficients on the biography variables are larger and more significant.

[28] The graduate result occurs because lawyers, who graduate sooner and who are younger on the average, receive more income. When a time-on-the-job variable is used in the graduate group, it is positive, significant, and greater than the one obtained for the whole sample.

evaluations in 1969. In view of this, the significance and magnitude of the variable in 1955 are surprising, suggesting that poor health and perhaps disability persist over time.[29] The variable for marital status, which is also taken from 1969 records, is significant, and its coefficient is larger than the effect of any of the education or ability variables. This type of variable is usually interpreted as a proxy for motivation, as well as the need for higher income for a family.[30] We have included the two father's education variables (attended high school and attended college) to represent the socioeconomic standing of the individuals' families. Since our dependent variable does not include unearned income except possibly for the earnings of the self-employed, the effect of inheritance will not be reflected in the coefficients.[31] The father's education variables will reflect, however, various types of training and motivations inculcated by parents as well as possible business contacts. The coefficients on these high school and college variables are approximately the same, although only the high school variable is significant.[32] As noted earlier, when these variables are omitted, the biography variables are more significant. We have tried including dummy variables for nine of the ten regions in which people went to high school, but none of these variables were significant. Hence, the interregional differences in the quality of high school education are not significant. Some results on the quality of college education are given in Chapter 1; more detailed analyses of high school and college quality are currently being carried out by Solmon and Wachtel.

Despite the presence of a large number of significant determinants of earnings, the fraction of explained variance in our

---

[29] Health is a much more significant determinant of income in 1969.

[30] A variable representing divorced individuals was insignificant.

[31] When the self-employed category was analyzed, as in Chapter 8, father's education was not important.

[32] Duncan, Featherman, and Duncan (1968), as well as others, have found that the socioeconomic standing of parents affects income of people with the same education. Sewell, Haller, and Portes (1969) have found that both father's education and occupation are significant determinants of occupational attainment. Subsequent work with our sample has confirmed this finding. In addition, we have found that religion and father-in-law's status likewise have a significant relationship to earnings. These new findings only change the education coefficients by a small amount and are not used, since they would necessitate recalculating all rates of return for a small refinement in the figures.

equations is only about 10 percent. While this may seem small compared with other studies of the determinants of income, there are several aspects of our sample that should be considered. First, the age variation in our study is very small, and since age increases the total variance of income without being associated with a corresponding increase in variance of the residual, samples with little age variation will have smaller $\bar{R}^2$s.[33] A comparable argument can be made because of the truncation of education and ability. Second, some studies standardize for occupations, thereby introducing more explanatory variables, a procedure that is not appropriate here.

The variables examined above explain, in some sense, part of the distribution of earnings. The distribution of the residual (the unexplained portion of earnings) is important for various aspects of human-capital and statistical theory. Appendix I contains an examination of the residuals for 1955 and 1969, as well as a study of the relative performances of equations using log earnings rather than earnings.

THE BIAS FROM OMITTING ABILITY, 1955

A primary concern of this study is the bias that occurs in the calculations of the extra income due to education when ability is omitted from the regressions. To calculate the bias from omitting ability, we compare the coefficients on the education dummies before and after including ability. To facilitate comparisons with other studies that do not have ability data, we hold constant variables that have been included in other studies. The equation without ability is called the comparison equation. The biases, calculated as the percentage differences between the corresponding coefficients in the two equations, are presented in Table 5-5.

Before examining these results, we shall explain one complication. As noted above, the biography variable contains information on mathematical ability, hobbies, and personal and family background. Since this variable remained significant after the introduction of the ability and father's education variables, it contains some information not accounted for by these two variables. If this other information is used in census studies such as Hanoch's and if we want to apply our bias corrections to

---

[33] In Hansen, Weisbrod, and Scanlon (1970), who study about the same age span, the $\bar{R}^2$s are comparable to ours.

TABLE 5-5   *Percentage biases at various education levels from omitting different types of ability, 1955*

Ability omitted	Bias at education level of:				
	Some college	Undergraduate degree	Some graduate work	Master's	Ph.D and LL.B.
A. Bias from omitting ability; age, background, and biography held constant					
1. *Factor 1*	7.8	20.4	17.5	24.8	24.3
2. *Factor 2*	−0.9	−0.8	−0.2	−2.5	−2.6
3. *Factor 3*	1.2	6.5	5.8	7.5	5.6
4. *Factor 4*	1.9	4.4	5.2	5.1	3.3
B. Bias from omitting ability; age held constant					
5. *Factor 1*	9.3	19.8	18.9	22.9	22.8
6. *Factor 2*	0.3	0.4	0.9	−0.8	−2.4
7. *Factor 3*	3.9	9.6	9.8	10.9	8.7
8. *Factor 4*	5.4	7.8	8.0	8.0	5.6
C. Bias from omitting biography and ability; age and background held constant					
9. *Factor 1*	23.2	34.7	25.7	36.8	35.5
10. *Factor 2*	15.9	17.3	9.7	36.8	12.6
11. *Factor 3*	17.6	23.3	15.2	22.2	19.6
12. *Factor 4*	18.2	15.2	14.6	20.2	17.7

SOURCE: Table 5-3. Comparison equation for section A is equation 4. Row 1 from equation 5; row 2 from equation 6; row 3 from equation 7; row 4 from equation 8. Comparison equation for section B is equation 3. Row 5 from equation 10; row 6 from equation 11; row 7 from equation 12; row 8 from equation 13. Comparison equation for section C is equation 9. Row 9 from equation 5; row 10 from equation 6; row 11 from equation 7; row 12 from equation 8.

such studies, then we should include the biography variable in the comparison equation. If we do so, the biography variable—which includes ability—will to some extent hold ability constant. Thus, the bias from omitting ability calculated from this equation will underestimate the actual bias. On the other hand, if we omit biography from the comparison equation while including it in the equation with ability, we will overstate the bias due solely to ability. Since these two alternatives bracket the desired result, we present both. Of course, if the content of the biography variable is not contained in the census data, then this latter bias calculation is the appropriate one for correcting for the effect of omitting both sets of variables.

We have calculated the bias from omitting each of the factors separately. We have also computed the bias from omitting all four factors, but since the results are quite close to those obtained from omitting just mathematical ability, they are not presented. Section A of Table 5-5 presents the bias when the age, background, and biography variables are included in the comparison equation, while section C contains the results when biography is not included. The biases from omitting mathematical ability, which appear in row 1, are substantial, ranging from 8 to 25 percent with a mean of about 20 percent. Subject to a problem discussed below, these can be considered lower bounds to the bias from omitting mathematical ability in census studies. The upper bounds, which appear in section C, average out about 50 percent greater but with a narrower range.

Table 5-5 also contains estimates of the bias from omitting different types of ability, as represented by factors 2 through 4. There appears to be no bias at all from omitting factor 2, which represents coordination. The maximum bias from omitting either of factors 3 and 4, which represent IQ and spatial perception, ranges from 15 to 23 percent with an average of somewhat less than 20 percent. In Table 5-3 only the top fifth for factors 3 and 4 is significantly different from zero in equations 6, 7, and 8. All these variables are insignificant when included in an equation with the first factor. Thus, we conclude that of the four ability measures tested, only the mathematical one is a significant determinant of income, and it is the only one whose omission results in a substantial bias.

In evaluating these bias results, the reader is reminded that one component of the bias calculation is the coefficient in the linear relationship between the omitted variable and education. But this relationship may not apply to the population as a whole because the sample is stratified, and because the war and the GI Bill may have changed the demand for college by people with various ability levels and family backgrounds.

The significance and magnitude of the mathematical-ability variable are important in terms of the calculations of the returns to education and in terms of the design of future studies. Before accepting these results, however, we must consider the possibility that the coefficient on the mathematics factor is reflecting part of the effect of education. This could occur if the scores on some of the component tests used in calculating the mathematics factor depend on differences in mathematical course work or education obtained prior to 1943 and if post-World War II education is related to mental ability. Suppose pretest education affects the test scores. Then, considering all people with graduate degrees, for example, we would expect to find higher average test scores for relatively older individuals, since it is more likely that they would have received more education prior to taking these tests. For high school graduates, of course, we would not expect to find any pattern by age, since everyone in the sample had at least a high school education when taking the tests.

In Table 5-6 we present average scores on the arithmetic-reasoning (Math B) test for various age-education cells. A quick glance at the upper education categories of some graduate work, master's, and Ph.D. indicates that there is no tendency for older people to score higher than younger people. In fact, if anything, it would appear that the reverse holds true.[34] This suggests that the Math B ability test score is not affected to any significant degree by the amount of the individual's pretest schooling. We have calculated tables similar to Table 5-6 for the mathematics (Math A) and biography scores, and again there is no evidence to suggest that schooling affects scores.

There are several other reasons for expecting that the effect of prior education on ability has little impact on the ability and education coefficients. First, the tables on initial salary (to be presented shortly) indicate that most people with such prior education had attended college only a year or two; hence the effect of differential education on the test scores should be small, especially when the data are converted to fifths. Second, the biography measure, which incorporates data on pre-1943 education, partially holds this variable constant. Third, at least half the weight in the mathematical factor is attached to tests, such as numerical operations, that are not related to college education. Finally, when we computed regressions for those with just a high school education—that is, those whose pre-1943 education was the same—the effect of ability was not statistically different from the estimates using all education groups. We conclude, therefore, that in this sample mathematical ability is a much more important variable than IQ in studying the returns to education and that the estimates of the bias from omitting this abil-

---

[34] The decrease with age may mean that recent familiarity with tests or with items stressed on tests improves scores. Because the magnitude of the age effect is the same at all education levels, however, our conclusions would be unaffected by an age adjustment. In the regressions, such a familiarity bias would be eliminated by our age variable.

TABLE 5-6 *Average scores on Mathematics B test, by age and education*

Age in 1969	High school	Some college	Under- graduate degree	Some graduate work	Master's	Ph.D. and LL.B.
43	14.0		28.3		25.7	
	(2)	*	(3)	*	(3)	*
44	18.5	23.4	31.6	31.1	32.9	33.2
	(95)	(115)	(183)	(34)	(37)	(45)
45	17.2	24.1	32.3	31.3	32.7	31.5
	(193)	(230)	(328)	(68)	(88)	(81)
46	16.9	23.4	28.5	30.9	29.0	34.2
	(195)	(263)	(286)	(49)	(102)	(73)
47	16.6	21.2	29.7	32.5	31.7	32.6
	(155)	(151)	(198)	(38)	(59)	(58)
48	16.3	21.5	30.1	31.6	29.6	28.4
	(91)	(122)	(111)	(19)	(56)	(39)
49	15.4	21.1	27.7	26.6	24.1	29.5
	(80)	(68)	(43)	(14)	(24)	(16)
50	14.7	19.4	32.7	35.9	26.1	26.6
	(81)	(55)	(35)	(7)	(21)	(8)
51	16.3	21.8	27.3	23.3	34.0	23.2
	(61)	(49)	(29)	(6)	(7)	(9)
52	15.6	17.9	27.2	26.8	32.2	19.0
	(73)	(48)	(24)	(5)	(6)	(2)
53	13.8	14.8	29.3	22.0	20.8	49.0
	(22)	(19)	(8)	(2)	(4)	(2)
Average age	47.3	46.9	46.3	46.3	46.6	46.3

*No observations.
NOTE: Sample sizes are given in parentheses.

ity are substantial. This conclusion must be qualified to the extent that Thorndike's comment that factor 1 is primarily an IQ test is correct.

COMPARISON OF RESULTS WITH THE WOLFLE-SMITH DATA Since the average age of those in the Wolfle-Smith data is approximately the same (when sampled) as the age of those in the NBER-TH data of 1955 and since the sample dates are only two years apart, it is useful to compare the results. The bias from omitting ability in the Wolfle-Smith data was about 4 percent. But this calculation was made with only IQ and age held constant, while in the above analysis we also hold background factors constant. In section B of Table 5-5 we present, for purposes of comparison, estimates of the bias from omitting each ability separately when no account is taken of background.[35] When what we call the IQ factor is omitted, the biases range from 4 to 11 percent with an average of around 9 percent, which is fairly close to the Wolfle-Smith result. When the mathematical factor is omitted, however, the bias ranges from 9 to 23 percent with an average bias of about 20 percent. (As noted in Chapter 4, there is a possibility that what we call mathematical ability is a better approximation to IQ.) Thus, the results from the two samples do not differ substantially when analyzed on a comparable basis. This suggests that mathematical ability may be more important for determining earnings than IQ. However, the Wolfle-Smith and NBER-TH tests differ in measurement as well as in concept, and we cannot be sure which is the cause of the difference in results.

The extra income from education can also be compared in the two samples. In the Wolfle-Smith study, after holding ability constant—as measured by ACE scores—we found education to be more important than in the NBER-TH data; that is, the first two years of college add 18 percent to income, an undergraduate degree adds 45 percent, and two or more degrees add 57 percent. Some of the extra returns arise because a different ability measure is used and because additional variables are included in the equation on which Table 5-4 is based. If only age and IQ are held constant, as in equation 1, Table 5-3, the income differentials of education in the NBER-TH sample are substantially greater. For example, the return to some college rises to 18 percent, which is identical to the Wolfle-Smith result, while the return to an undergraduate degree rises to about 20 percent.[36] It is not completely clear why there is such a difference between the two samples for returns to a college education. One possibility

---

[35] Age is held constant for comparability, since all people in the Wolfle-Smith sample graduated from high school in the same year.

[36] M.D. and teacher dummy variables are included in these calculations, but not in the Wolfle-Smith calculation. The discussion in this section assumes that factor 3 and not factor 1 represents IQ. If this is not the case, there is less agreement between the samples.

lies in the nature of the samples. The NBER-TH sample is drawn from a group more homogeneous with respect to such unmeasured variables as personality and drive than the Wolfle-Smith sample, because the population of the latter was composed of all high school graduates from Minnesota.[37] Second, the Wolfe-Smith sample may be more affected by response bias (see Chapters 3 and 4).

The above discussion exhausts the implications of the data for 1955 when treated as a single or isolated cross section. Later, we study the implications of using information from other years.

EARNINGS DIFFERENTIALS IN 1969

When comparing the 1955 and 1969 results, it is important to keep in mind the slight differences in definition for the income and education variables. Since nearly 10 percent of our sample completed their education after 1955, for 1969 we use education as reported in 1969, but as pointed out earlier, about 10 percent of the questionnaires contain inconsistent replies on education in the two years. The 1969 earnings variable differs from that of 1955 because in 1969 respondents were asked to report earnings from their main job only, and in 1955 they were asked to report total earnings.[38] About 10 percent of the sample indicated that they held more than one position in 1969, a fact that we ignore in our analysis.[39]

The first question to consider is whether there are any important interactions between education and ability.[40] Once again,

---

[37] In addition, if the returns to education interact significantly with experience and are very concave with respect to age, then the average return from the sample with variable age will be less than that from the sample with a fixed age, but this should only explain a small portion of the difference.

[38] We omit from the analysis the 50 people not reporting income in 1969.

[39] We have calculated the income change from 1968 to 1969 for those with more than one job in 1969. Assuming that they also had two jobs in 1968, we would expect them to have a relatively smaller growth in income than others. This is the case at all education levels. We can adjust their 1969 earnings to have the same average growth as single-job holders in the same education groups. When this is done, average incomes rise by 0.5 to 1.5 percent in the various education levels. Since such small differences would not affect our results significantly, we have not corrected the 1969 data. Note that these results strongly imply that the "current" earnings figures are for 1969 rather than 1968.

[40] As was the case with the 1955 data, preliminary analysis indicated that factor 1 was the only important ability factor. Factor 3—an IQ measure—was occasionally significant and negative.

the F statistics used in the analysis of covariance are less than 1.5; hence, we cannot reject the hypothesis that all the coefficients in the individual education regressions are equal to the corresponding coefficients in the overall regression. There is, however, some tendency for the graduate education coefficients to be higher at the high ability levels. Thus, we also computed some equations with interaction between graduate education and the high ability fifths. In equations 14 and 15 in Table 5-7 we present the equations with interactions. For each ability fifth, the effect of ability is greater for graduate students than for other students; however, only in the case of Q_4 is the difference significant, although Q_5 has a t value greater than 1.0.[41] For graduate students the effect of ability can be determined by adding together the ability coefficients such as Q_2, with the coefficient on the interaction term involving Q_2. Thus, at the graduate level, compared to the bottom fifth, the effect of ability is about $150, $210, $350, and $415 per month for the second to fifth fifths, respectively. Although the effect in the top fifth is larger than that in the fourth fifth, the interaction coefficient is not significant because the top fifth has a much bigger impact than the fourth fifth—$204 versus $94—at the other education levels. Since the interactions here are fairly weak, we conduct our analysis of the returns to education and the bias from omitting ability using equations without interactions.

We consider now equation 5 in Table 5-7, which contains the mathematical-ability, biography, and background variables. All the education coefficients, the top three fifths of the mathematical factor, the second, fourth, and fifth fifths of the biography variable, the background variables, and the M.D. and teacher dummies are significant.[42] Most of these variables, as well as

---

[41] Because there are 20 possible education-ability cells, 5 percent of the time, or once, we would find one of the interaction terms to have a significant t value even if its true value were zero. However, we would not expect to find all four coefficients positive.

[42] The M.D. and teacher variables are not quite correct, since they are measured as those who were M.D.'s and teachers in 1955. When we added a separate variable for lawyers, both the Ph.D. and lawyer coefficients were significant, while the other coefficients were unaffected. In a weighted regression that attempts to correct for heteroscedasticity, the coefficients on the some-graduate-work and master's variables change by about 15 percent, while the ability variables increase by about $60. There were some noticeable changes in a few of the other variables.

TABLE 5-7 *Regressions for salary, 1969 (in dollars per month)*

	Constant	Some college	Under-graduate degree	Some graduate work	Master's	Ph.D. and LL.B.*	M.D.	Teacher	Age
(1) Y_{69}	$1,164.7	$276.4	$499.4	$376.2	$318.0	$926.6			
	(37.2)	(6.4)	(11.9)	(5.3)	(5.4)	(14.8)			
(2) Y_{69}	1,360.2	274.8	493.2	370.8	313.9	920.6			$-5.9
	(6.5)	(6.4)	(11.6)	(5.2)	(5.9)	(14.6)			(1.0)
(3) Y_{69}	1,321.9	276.9	498.3	421.6	527.6	857.7	$508.9	$-522.5	-4.7
	(6.4)	(6.5)	(11.8)	(5.9)	(7.9)	(12.9)	(4.0)	(6.9)	(0.8)
(4) Y_{69}	1,454.2	206.4	388.9	336.4	412.1	728.3	486.1	-524.9	-1.9
	(4.7)	(4.6)	(8.6)	(4.6)	(6.0)	(10.5)	(3.7)	(6.4)	(0.3)
(5) Y_{69}	1,355.7	192.9	340.8	287.1	351.0	670.0	493.7	-496.2	-1.7
	(4.4)	(4.3)	(7.5)	(3.9)	(5.1)	(9.6)	(3.8)	(6.1)	(0.3)
(6) Y_{69}	1,461.9	208.0	391.2	337.5	410.9	734.3	474.5	-516.5	-2.3
	(4.8)	(4.6)	(8.7)	(4.6)	(6.0)	(10.6)	(3.6)	(6.3)	(0.4)
(7) Y_{69}	1,425.8	204.9	382.9	330.6	403.1	723.7	485.5	-517.9	-1.8
	(4.6)	(4.5)	(8.4)	(4.5)	(5.8)	(10.5)	(3.7)	(6.2)	(0.3)
(8) Y_{69}	1,367.5	205.1	383.5	331.1	339.8	723.4	488.1	-511.2	-0.9
	(4.4)	(4.5)	(8.5)	(4.5)	(4.9)	(10.5)	(3.7)	(6.3)	(0.1)
(9) Y_{69}	1,416.5	234.5	425.0	371.3	440.9	757.1	495.6	-522.5	1.0
	(4.6)	(5.2)	(9.6)	(5.1)	(6.4)	(11.0)	(3.8)	(6.4)	(0.2)
(10) Y_{69}	1,215.7	252.9	430.2	353.1	443.6	776.7	514.9	-515.8	-4.8
	(5.9)	(5.9)	(10.0)	(4.9)	(6.6)	(11.5)	(4.1)	(6.4)	(0.8)
(11) Y_{69}	1,300.7	278.0	498.3	424.4	526.6	864.1	499.6	-543.8	-5.5
	(6.2)	(6.5)	(11.8)	(6.0)	(7.9)	(13.0)	(3.9)	(6.8)	(0.9)
(12) Y_{69}	1,294.0	270.1	478.8	403.6	504.1	838.6	510.2	-540.0	-4.8
	(6.1)	(6.2)	(11.2)	(5.6)	(7.5)	(12.5)	(4.0)	(6.7)	(0.8)
(13) Y_{69}	1,211.7	267.1	477.9	404.2	500.2	840.3	509.6	-531.3	-3.5
	(5.8)	(6.2)	(11.3)	(5.7)	(7.5)	(12.6)	(4.0)	(6.6)	(0.6)
(14) Y_{69}	1,358.8	195.3	346.9	229.9	282.5	602.2	490.7	-485.4	-1.7
	(4.4)	(4.3)	(7.5)	(2.8)	(3.5)	(7.6)	(3.7)	(5.9)	(0.3)
(15) Y_{69}	1,373.6	196.1	348.7	150.3	204.8	521.4	489.0	-487.4	-1.8
	(4.5)	(4.3)	(7.6)	(1.3)	(1.8)	(4.4)	(3.7)	(6.0)	(0.3)

TABLE 5-7 *(continued)*

	Ability				Interaction of graduate education with:				Health	Single
	Q_2	Q_3	Q_4	Q_5	Q_2	Q_3	Q_4	Q_5		
(1)										
(2)										
(3)										
(4)									$-208.6	$-225.5
									(-7.9)	(2.1)
(5)	$ 68.8	$ 107.1	$143.7	$ 278.9					-205.6	-236.8
	(1.3)	(2.1)	(2.9)	(5.5)					(7.8)	(2.2)
(6)	-16.7	-38.5	72.7	-8.1					-208.1	-230.2
	(0.3)	(0.8)	(1.5)	(0.2)					(7.9)	(2.1)
(7)	14.9	41.9	26.7	57.5					-208.0	-225.1
	(0.3)	(0.8)	(0.5)	(1.1)					(7.9)	(2.0)
(8)	33.0	32.0	36.0	117.4					-205.7	-225.2
	(0.7)	(0.6)	(0.7)	(2.4)					(7.8)	(2.0)
(9)									-215.5	-250.1
									(8.2)	(2.3)
(10)	81.5	121.5	176.2	318.2						
	(1.6)	(2.5)	(3.6)	(6.5)						
(11)	35.1	8.7	121.5	57.5						
	(0.7)	(0.2)	(2.6)	(1.2)						
(12)	-9.0	53.6	54.0	102.2						
	(0.2)	(1.1)	(1.1)	(2.1)						
(13)	53.1	73.7	73.7	192.2						
	(1.1)	(1.5)	(1.5)	(4.0)						
(14)	70.3	110.7	106.0	261.3			$179.8	$ 87.2	-204.7	-242.4
	(1.4)	(2.2)	(2.0)	(4.7)			(1.9)	(1.0)	(7.8)	(2.2)
(15)	55.2	89.5	93.6	248.8	$96.1	$121.5	260.6	168.0	-204.5	-241.8
	(1.0)	(1.6)	(1.7)	(4.4)	(0.7)	(0.9)	(2.0)	(1.4)	(7.8)	(2.2)

*M.D.'s are also included.

NOTE: Figures in parentheses are *t* statistics.

Father attended high school	Father attended college	Biography				Ability factor	$\bar{R}^2$/S.E.
		Q_2	Q_3	Q_4	Q_5		
							.062
							954
							.062
							954
							.077
							947
$115.0	$112.4	$125.4	$101.1	$178.3	$236.5		.100
(3.3)	(2.6)	(2.5)	(2.0)	(3.6)	(4.8)		938
107.9	96.8	119.2	91.8	167.0	205.9	1	.112
(3.1)	(2.2)	(2.4)	(1.8)	(3.4)	(4.2)		934
113.7	112.7	126.6	103.1	178.9	236.9	2	.105
(3.2)	(2.6)	(2.6)	(2.0)	(3.6)	(4.7)		938
114.4	108.6	122.0	97.1	173.4	228.2	3	.104
(3.3)	(2.5)	(2.5)	(1.9)	(3.5)	(4.6)		938
110.9	108.8	120.3	92.4	168.3	219.8	4	.105
(3.1)	(2.5)	(2.4)	(1.8)	(3.4)	(4.4)		938
137.3	152.9						.095
(3.9)	(3.6)						941
						1	.087
							942
						2	.078
							947
						3	.078
							946
						4	.080
							946
107.8	96.4	120.1	92.4	167.7	205.8	1	.113
(3.1)	(2.2)	(2.4)	(1.8)	(3.4)	(4.1)		934
107.8	97.3	120.7	92.9	167.9	204.5	1	.113
(3.1)	(2.2)	(2.4)	(1.9)	(3.4)	(4.1)		934

age, were significant in 1955. The age result for 1969 is discussed in more detail below.

The percentage increases in earnings due to increases in education implied by this equation are presented in Table 5-8, for a person with the ability and background of (1) the average high school graduate and (2) the average member of the preceding education level. As compared to just going to high school, earnings increased by 17 percent for some college attendance, 25 to 30 percent for obtaining an undergraduate through a Ph.D. degree; 84 percent for obtaining a law degree, and 160 percent for completing a medical degree. Each of these numbers is larger than the corresponding entry for 1955 (Table 5-4). The greater importance of education with the passage of 14 more years can be explained either by the proposition that the age-income profile is steeper for the more educated in this range or by the proposition that because of shifts in supply and demand, the relative wage rate of the more educated was greater in 1969

TABLE 5-8 *Percentage* *increases in* *earnings, by* *education level,* *1969*	*Percentage by which earnings in each* *education class exceed:*	
	Earnings of average *high school graduate*	*Earnings of average* *member of preceding* *education level*
Some college	17	17
Undergraduate degree *(not teacher)*	31	11
Some graduate work	26	−3
Master's (not teacher)	32	4
Ph.D.	27	−8
M.D	106	
LL.B.	84	
Undergraduate degree *(teacher)*	−14	
Master's (teacher)	−13	

NOTE: Average age is 47.

SOURCE: Earnings of average person in each education class from equation 5, Table 5-7. Absolute increases from equation 3, Table 5-7.

than in 1955. We discuss this question in more detail in Chapter 6.

Several comments about the pattern of results in Table 5-8 are in order. First, in an equation not shown, we have replaced the some-college dummy variable with separate variables for one, two, and three years of college. We find that the absolute increase in earnings (over high school) for the first year is the same as for the some-college variable and that neither of the next two years adds anything to income.[43] Second, as shown in the second column of Table 5-8, an undergraduate degree causes another jump in income, although the increase is smaller than that for the first year of college. The erratic nature of the returns to education is made more evident by the decrease in earnings from an undergraduate degree to some graduate education and the large increase for three-year-graduate-degree holders. Third, when a dummy variable for business owners is included, the constant term and all the various education coefficients fall, but the decreases in the high school and some-college categories are larger. If calculated for non-business owners, the income differentials in Table 5-8 would be 17 and 39 percent for some college and a bachelor's degree, respectively.

We next examine the effects of ability and background. As noted earlier, only factor 1, the mathematical-ability factor, has significant coefficients and displays the expected monotonic patterns. From equation 5, Table 5-7, it is clear that the impact of this mathematical skill is important, with those in the top fifth receiving about $3,300 a year more income than those in the bottom fifth—an increase midway between that of the some-college and the undergraduate-degree variables. The biography variable has significant coefficients, which (except for a small insignificant drop in the third fifth) increase monotonically. Although the magnitudes are not quite as large as those of mathematical ability, the effect of the top fifth in biography is as important as that of some college education.

We now examine the effect of age on earnings. Before discussing this subject in detail, we remind the reader that the age variation in this sample is only eight to nine years. Because of this small range, no attempt was made to find nonlinear age ef-

---

[43] The information currently available from the 1955 questionnaire does not allow us to break down the some-college category to investigate this question.

fects or to discover interactions with education in 1969.[44] Hence, our results should not be extrapolated to other ages.[45] Whenever age is included in an equation, its coefficient ranges from −2 to −6, but it is always insignificant. (In 1955 it was about +7 and significant.) A common finding in studies of age-income profiles is that the peak earnings occur in the late forties or early fifties of a person's lifetime.[46] Since the average age of people in this sample was 47 years in 1969, a negative coefficient is not surprising, and the insignificance could arise because the peak is near the mean of 47.[47] There is, however, one other result to report. A good argument could be made that time on the job (after education is completed) is more important than age, and that such work experience is not completely collinear with age and education because of delays in entering or finishing education. We attempted to measure such a concept by a variable defined as 1969 minus the year of first job after completing school. (This year was determined from the job-income history.)[48] When this time-on-the job variable is used, we always find a significant coefficient of about +10, even if age is added to the equation. Since the education coefficients are not much affected by this variable, however, we shall not pursue these results any further at this time.

As was the case in 1955, the background and individual characteristics are important. The health and single coefficients are both significant, negative, and in excess of $200. Each of the two father's education coefficients are about $100 and significant. Thus, the health and single effects are as great as that of the

---

[44] We tested for age-education interactions by running separate regressions for the various education categories. The age variable was never significant.

[45] It is possible to study these questions by combining the 1955 and 1969 cross sections.

[46] See, for example, Becker (1964), Miller (1960), and Mincer (1970). Some recent work at the NBER by Fuchs suggests that when earnings are converted to wage rates per hour, this peak is not discernible.

[47] Moreover, in the next chapter we will present evidence that from 1968 to 1969 average income (after adjustment for secular changes in wage rates) declined in this sample.

[48] We should note that for some people the "first job" entry appears to refer to the date they began in their current job.

some-college variable, while the influence of father's education is equal to that of the third fifth of ability. As was the case in 1955, the quality of high school education, as measured by a set of dummy variables, did not determine earnings. The $\bar{R}^2$ values in 1969 of about .11 are slightly greater than those in 1955.

THE BIAS FROM OMITTING ABILITY, 1969 We turn now to the question of the bias from omitting ability. The information obtained on this question is very important, since this is the only large sample with information on income, ability, and education for people in their late forties and early fifties. In Table 5-9, we present the bias from omitting separately each of the ability factors, using a variety of assumptions

TABLE 5-9 *Percentage biases at various educational levels from omitting various types of ability, 1969*

		Bias at education level of:			
Ability omitted	Some college	Under-graduate degree	Some graduate work	Master's	Ph.D. and LL.B.
A. Bias from omitting ability; age, background, and biography held constant					
1. *Factor 1*	6.5	12.4	14.6	14.8	8.0
2. *Factor 2*	−0.8	−0.6	0.3	0.3	−0.8
3. *Factor 3*	0.7	1.5	1.7	2.2	0.6
4. *Factor 4*	0.6	1.4	1.6	3.0	0.7
B. Bias from omitting ability; age held constant					
5. *Factor 1*	8.7	13.7	16.2	15.9	9.4
6. *Factor 2*	−0.4	0.0	−0.7	0.2	−0.7
7. *Factor 3*	2.5	3.9	4.3	4.5	2.2
8. *Factor 4*	3.5	4.1	4.1	5.2	2.0
C. Bias from omitting biography and ability; age and background held constant					
9. *Factor 1*	17.8	19.7	22.8	20.6	11.5
10. *Factor 2*	11.4	7.8	9.3	7.0	3.0
11. *Factor 3*	12.7	9.8	11.1	8.8	4.4
12. *Factor 4*	12.6	9.6	11.0	9.5	4.4

SOURCE: Table 5-7. Comparison equation for section A is equation 4. Row 1 from equation 5; row 2 from equation 6; row 3 from equation 7; row 4 from equation 8. Comparison equation for section B is equation 3. Row 5 from equation 10; row 6 from equation 11; row 7 from equation 12; row 8 from equation 13. Comparison equation for section C is equation 9. Row 9 from equation 5; row 10 from equation 6; row 11 from equation 7; row 12 from equation 8.

about the other included variables. Sections A and C yield lower and upper bounds to the percentage bias when background factors are held constant. When mathematical ability is omitted (section A), the biases at the various education levels range from 7 to 15 percent, with an average of about 10 percent. In section C, the upper bounds of such biases range from 18 to 23 percent, with an average of about 20 percent. Both the lower and upper bounds of the bias are substantially less than the corresponding estimates for 1955, because the coefficients on education grew more rapidly than those on the ability, biography, or background variables.

Mathematical ability is only one of the many types of ability that could affect income and whose omission could bias the education coefficients. In Table 5-9 we also present the biases from omitting physical coordination, IQ, and spatial-perception measures. The biases from omitting any of these average about 2 percent or less in section A and 10 percent in section C. Both these upper and lower bounds are much smaller than when mathematical ability is the omitted variable. (The biases using an equation in which all the ability variables are included were nearly the same as in the mathematical-ability rows.) Since the upper bound on the bias from omitting these three abilities does not exceed 10 percent, we conclude that in 1969, as well as in 1955, the returns to education are not greatly affected by the omission of coordination, IQ, and spatial-perception abilities. It would still be possible, however, for any of these abilities to be significant determinants of income. But in equations 6, 7, and 8 in Table 5-7, the only significant coefficient for the ability dummies is the top fifth of factor 4. When factors 2, 3, and 4 are added to equation 5, no additional coefficients are significant.

We have also made some calculations of the bias when only age is held constant. The results are given in section B of Table 5-9. Once again, omitting mathematical ability yields a large bias—about 12 percent—while omitting the other abilities implies biases of 4 percent. In 1955 the comparable biases were twice as large.

INDIVIDUAL EFFECTS PERSISTING OVER TIME In the preceding analysis we have treated the two cross sections separately. It is possible to make use of the continuous-cross-section nature of the data to obtain more efficient estimates of the coefficients and to allow for unmeasured personal character-istics that persist over time.[49]

It can be demonstrated that if we were to regress $Y_{69} - Y_{55}$ on our independent variables (and include a new one for the change in education), the estimates would equal the difference between the coefficients estimated in 1969 and 1955. There is, however, an advantage in using the individual's residual in one time period in the regression for the other. That is, the residual consists of $\delta_t P_i + u_i$, where P_i represents the *i*th person's various unmeasured characteristics, such as personality, that persist over time; u_i is a random element; and δ_t is the effect on income in period t of the P_i. Let $q_{it} = \delta_t P_i + u_i$. If we include q_{i55} in our 1969 regressions, or vice versa, then we incorporate an imperfectly measured estimate of P in our analysis. Measurement error will generally lead to biased estimates of the coefficient on q and all variables with which q is correlated. But since q_t is constructed to be orthogonal to all the independent variables in the equation in year t and since these variables are unchanged from 1955 to 1969 (except for a few changes in education), each q is approximately orthogonal to the other variables. Hence, the other coefficients are practically unchanged when q is included.

We do not present the entire equation, but concentrate in-stead on the coefficient of q and the change in the explained variance. When we use the 1955 residual in 1969, the coefficient of q is 1.7 with a t value of 35. The $\bar{R}^2$ rises from .11 to .34, and the standard error of the equation declines from \$934 to \$785. When the 1969 residual is used in the 1955 equation, the coeffi-cient is .15 with a t value of 35. The $\bar{R}^2$ rises from .10 to .33 and the standard error declines from \$264 to \$227.[50]

---

[49] In principle, it is possible to obtain, with certain grouping techniques, unbi-ased estimates of the coefficients of the measured and unmeasured variables even when they and income are correlated with the unmeasured personal char-acteristics. However, this procedure proved to be infeasible because of mul-ticollinearity.

[50] The comparisons are with equation 5, Table 5-7, and equation 5, Table 5-3. Since the coefficients of the q variables should equal the ratio of the coefficients of the unmeasured characteristic in the two years, it might be expected that their product would be 1. However, because in both cases personality and so on are measured with error, the q coefficients are biased downward, and their product is less than 1.

The residual in any year can be partitioned into p and u.[51] It is interesting to calculate the extent to which the variance of the residual is due to the variables represented by p. Since p and u are assumed to be uncorrelated, var p + var u = var q. An estimate of var q is the (squared) standard error of the regression equation when q is included, while an estimate of var u is the corresponding statistic when q is not included. Using this information, we calculate var p expressed as a fraction of var p + var u to be 30 percent for 1969 and 26 percent for 1955.

Thus, based on observations 14 years apart, we estimate that about 30 percent of the original unexplained variance (after eliminating the influences of the measured variables) is due to variables whose effects persist over time. The other 70 percent of the variance is due to random events such as luck and changes in unmeasured variables.[52] This conclusion is discouraging in two regards. First, there apparently are some systematic but unmeasured determinants of income that are more important than all the education, ability, and background variables that we have studied. Second, random events (and changes in the unmeasured but systematic variables) are the most important determinants of income within a given age cohort. Finally, as demonstrated earlier, very little of the correlation between the residuals should be attributable to investments in on-the-job experience as formulated by Mincer (1970), since 1955 should be close to what he calls the overtaking point, where a person's current and discounted lifetime earnings are equal.

EARNINGS ON INITIAL JOB The last earnings to be examined are those obtained on the person's first job after completing his education. There are several difficulties in using this information. First, there is the possibility of error because of the long time between event and recall in 1969. As demonstrated in Appendix H, we judge this memory lapse to be important for estimates of 1958 earnings, and the initial job occurred earlier than 1958 for nearly all the people in our sample. A possible offset to this greater-time-lapse aspect is

---

[51] Earlier we used δ, but since δ is just a scaling vector, it can be ignored.

[52] However, since both our education and ability measures cover limited ranges, the importance of ability and education relative to the unmeasured variables is understated compared with the population as a whole.

that the first position is a much more important event to the individual than other ones.[53]

Another problem with the initial-job data is that there is a correlation between education and the starting date. Because of inflation and technical change, wages increase over time; hence the average initial salaries of the more educated would tend to be overstated relative to those of high school graduates.[54] The adjustment for inflation and technical change given in footnote 53 assumes that the coefficients on the education variables change proportionately with the passage of time, but for reasons explained in Chapter 2, the relative wages at different education levels (at given age or experience levels) can shift over time. While such a structural change would hardly be expected to be important over the space of five or maybe even ten normal years, we do not have the luxury of five or ten normal years, because the period before 1943 is far removed from that of the late 1940s and early 1950s.

For these reasons, we resorted to simpler methods in analyzing the data. In Table 5-10, we present (for those instances in

---

[53] There is some partial evidence on the reliability of the earnings-on-initial-job estimates. Thorndike and Hagen asked the same question in 1955. If there are memory lapses, it seems likely that the longer the recall period, the greater the errors should be. Unfortunately, Thorndike and Hagen had not transcribed the initial-earnings data to the IBM sheets, and the NBER has not yet coded these data from the original questionnaires. However, Dr. E. Mantell, who has used the NBER-TH sample to write a dissertation on engineers, has collected the data for some 300 people for whom the year of initial job was the same in the 1955 and 1969 responses. He finds that the mean income reported in 1955 was $3,905 with a standard error of $2,039, while that reported in 1969 was $4,094 with a standard error of $1,473. This difference, which is only one-seventh of a standard error, is not significant at the 5 percent level. It might be noted that if people do not recognize the amount of inflation since the 1940s, they may tend to overstate their initial-job earnings in 1969. In a regression of the two responses, Mantell obtains

$$Y_{I,69} = 1,378 + .070 Y_{I,55} \qquad \bar{R}^2 = .25$$
$$\phantom{Y_{I,69} = 1,}(4.9) \quad (10.3)$$

Thus while the mean estimates of two estimates are reasonably close, the individual estimates are not strongly correlated. Hence, the differences in the two responses do not solely represent an equally poor recall or inflation.

[54] This difficulty can be overcome through such devices as deflating starting salaries by a wage index and by including a time trend. Once the equation is estimated, it is easy to convert back to money wages at various education levels for each year.

			Ability fifths			
Year	*1*	*2*	*3*	*4*	*5*	*Total*
High school						
1939	$1,878	$2,096	$1,769	$ 900	$1,359	$1,671
	(10)	(14)	(10)	(6)	(14)	(54)
1940	1,781	1,857	1,103	1,985	1,228	1,659
	(14)	(24)	(9)	(14)	(14)	(75)
1941	2,734	1,642	1,785	2,335	1,233	1,975
	(22)	(30)	(28)	(19)	(11)	(110)
1942	2,325	2,024	2,443	1,889	1,850	2,190
	(18)	(14)	(14)	(11)	(1)	(58)
1945	2,822	3,767	4,989	4.077	2,401	3,818
	(13)	(23)	(13)	(12)	(3)	(64)
1946	3,528	3,431	3,240	3,259	3,376	3,392
	(44)	(31)	(22)	(27)	(13)	(137)
1947	3,233	3,736	3,392	2,760	3,500	3,328
	(12)	(11)	(13)	(8)	(2)	(46)
Some college						
1940	2,708	1,815	1,594	1,323	1,422	1,624
	(4)	(8)	(14)	(8)	(15)	(49)
1941	2,104	2,392	2,519	1,727	1,554	2,012
	(11)	(6)	(10)	(10)	(12)	(49)
1945	4,229	4,432	3,713	4,027	4,711	4,180
	(18)	(10)	(12)	(17)	(9)	(66)
1946	3,560	3,517	3,267	3,321	3,246	3,361
	(24)	(24)	(32)	(41)	(33)	(154)
1947	4,172	3,572	4,112	4,896	3,544	4,089
	(22)	(22)	(24)	(24)	(19)	(111)
1948	5,326	3,998	4,194	4,181	4,206	4,377
	(22)	(23)	(21)	(26)	(19)	(111)
1949	4,668	3,293	4,211	3,951	3,743	3,894
	(10)	(18)	(11)	(12)	(7)	(58)

TABLE 5-10 Initial annual salaries for selected years, by mathematical ability and education (mean income in dollars)

NOTE: Dollar entries are mean income. Sample sizes are given in parentheses below dollar amounts. Rank 1 is the lowest ability fifth.

TABLE 5-10
(continued)

	Ability fifths					
	1	*2*	*3*	*4*	*5*	*Total*
Undergraduate degree						
1946	3,370	3,375	3,444	3,233	3,543	3,443
	(5)	(8)	(16)	(11)	(32)	(72)
1947	4,050	3,408	3,917	3,427	3,230	3,464
	(6)	(13)	(20)	(23)	(48)	(110)
1948	3,654	3,615	3,399	3,845	3,936	3,755
	(20)	(30)	(32)	(47)	(74)	(203)
1949	3,783	3,649	3,320	3,402	3,590	3,518
	(24)	(38)	(44)	(59)	(59)	(224)
1950	4,788	4,100	3,120	3,576	3,976	3,808
	(17)	(25)	(32)	(41)	(43)	(158)
1951	4,118	4,329	3,920	4,222	4,600	4,297
	(11)	(17)	(14)	(24)	(28)	(94)
Graduate study						
1946	3,408	2,841	2,600	4,188	2,671	3,081
	(6)	(8)	(8)	(9)	(15)	(46)
1947	2,240	3,075	3,070	2,411	4,111	3,460
	(2)	(8)	(15)	(9)	(32)	(66)
1948	2,987	3,147	3,053	3,244	3,482	3,242
	(14)	(17)	(20)	(31)	(37)	(119)
1949	2,824	2,988	3,066	3,615	3,492	3,298
	(16)	(24)	(16)	(26)	(54)	(136)
1950	3,107	3,515	3,467	4,208	3,290	3,579
	(15)	(13)	(18)	(36)	(44)	(126)
1951	3,583	3,781	3,490	4,306	5,207	4,223
	(12)	(13)	(20)	(18)	(27)	(90)
1952	3,028	4,650	4,581	5,211	5,462	4,738
	(8)	(10)	(14)	(11)	(16)	(59)
1953	4,137	5,198	4,711	3,560	5,454	4,715
	(4)	(12)	(13)	(10)	(11)	(50)

which we have reasonable sample sizes) average starting salaries by mathematical-ability fifths, education, and year of starting salary.[55]

Consider first the high school graduates. Although it is not shown, about one-half had earned a living before 1943, but of the rest a majority started work in 1946.[56] In 1946 there is no evidence of a positive effect of ability on salary, and indeed there could even be a negative effect. None of the other years has enough observations to analyze the separate fifths.[57]

About one-third of those with some college had their first job before 1946. Fairly large groups of people began to work in each of the years between 1946 and 1948. It is encouraging to note that their starting salaries increased from 1946 to 1949 and that the salaries in 1946 were about double those before the war. In the years 1946 to 1948, we can compare the average income of the bottom two fifths with that of the top two fifths. We find the former to be larger by $250 in 1946, smaller by $420 in 1947, and larger by $550 in 1948. Using all five fifths of those averages, there is no evidence of incomes increasing with ability.

Very few people had finished their undergraduate studies and started to work before 1946.[58] From 1946 through 1951, there are large numbers of people with undergraduate degrees starting to work. The average starting salary rises in each year except for 1949.[59] In comparing the average starting income in the top two fifths with the income in the bottom two fifths, we find that

[55] Because we suspected that many people were reporting salaries other than their first, we constructed a comparable set of tables in which individuals were included only if the date of their starting salaries minus the date they terminated schooling was less than three years. In those instances in which we had large samples, for example, undergraduates around 1950 and high school graduates in 1946, the two sets of estimates were close; hence we decided to ignore the restriction and use the larger sample (1,000 more observations).

[56] The relatively large numbers in 1947, 1948, and 1949 presumably reflect later discharge dates from the military.

[57] Although education in these tables is defined from the data in 1969, when the corrected 1955 education is used, essentially the same results are achieved. The 1969 education is used because the question in 1969 asked for first salary after completion of education as reported in 1969.

[58] Including those with graduate education, there were only 4 percent. However, some graduates who began working in the late 1940s and early 1950s had completed their undergraduate work earlier.

[59] In 1949, the starting salary of those with some college as well as various national figures such as wage income declined.

in half the years the bottom fifths have more earnings, and in the other half the top fifths have more. Thus, the effect of ability on earnings still is not evident.

It is useful at this point to compare the starting salaries at the various educational levels. Since we have found that ability does not affect starting salaries, we can use the average in each year. In 1946 average incomes are $3,392, $3,361, and $3,443 for those with a high school degree, some college, and an undergraduate degree, respectively. The differences in income are not significant.

It is interesting to speculate on why people coming on the market in 1946 with different amounts of education and ability received the same starting salary. One possibility is that, though ability and education add to skills, employers had no way of knowing who was better qualified and, on the average, offered the same wage to all these education and ability levels.[60] If this is correct, then as the workers' performances are monitored over time, we should find the effects of ability and education becoming more important, which is indeed what we have found to be the case. This is the opposite of the role of ability hypothesized by Lydall (1969). It also seems to run counter to the human-capital theory, since those with more training do not earn more when coming on the market. There is, however, a way to reconcile these results with the human-capital theory. As explained in detail in Mincer (1970) and Becker (1964), those with more education could be undertaking more on-the-job training and "paying" for the investment with lower current wages. In addition, those with some college education could have been tempted by very good job offers while the others finished their degrees.

The average starting salaries in 1947 and 1948 give some credence to these ideas. In these two years, those with some college received between $500 and $1,000 more in starting salary than those with undergraduate degrees. Also during these two years, high school graduates received slightly smaller starting salaries than undergraduate-degree holders. Finally, it might be

---

[60] Weisbrod and Karpoff (1968) have presented some evidence that when professional and mangerial employees are separated by quality of school and performance in school, starting salaries are the same, but salaries after 15 years differ significantly.

noted that in 1949 and 1950, when the some-college samples are smaller, it is still true that the starting salary of the college dropouts exceeds that of those with an undergraduate degree.

In order to obtain a large enough sample to permit analysis at the graduate level, we combined the three categories of graduate training. Since the average salaries of the three groups were quite close in each year, there is little danger of aggregation bias. The majority of these students finished their education between 1947 and 1951, although about 25 percent—many of whom were Ph.D.'s—began to work after 1951. In this graduate education category, we do find some evidence of the effect of ability on income. The bottom two fifths fall short of the top two in every year from 1946 to 1952. That ability is significant here and not at other education levels can be explained by the proposition that only at this education level is academic performance—which is related to ability—considered an indicator of employee quality, thus influencing starting salaries.

Consider next the difference in average starting salary of graduate students and college graduates. In each year from 1946 through 1954 (except 1953) college graduates earned as much on their first job as graduate students or earned more.[61] While the large percentage of pre-college teachers in the graduate group presumably holds down the average, the starting salaries for Ph.D.'s and LL.B.'s were about the same as the average for all graduates. Thus, once more we find that starting salaries do not rise, and may even fall, with education.

---

[61] The samples in both education groups are small in 1953.

6. Age-Earnings Profiles

In the previous chapter we examined the data for 1955 and 1969 extensively and the data for the initial year, 1958, and 1968 more briefly. There the discussion was centered on the importance of education and other variables in each separate year. In this chapter we make use of such information to construct age-earnings profiles from 1946 to the present.[1] The time-series profiles can be used to examine several questions that generally have been studied only with the use of cross-section data.

First, numerous studies have documented that earnings rise with age at least until middle age. Some economists have theorized that this age-earnings relationship occurs because people invest in on-the-job training that is general and not firm-specific. If such investment increases with education, an age-income profile could initially lie below the profile of those in the next highest education level, but rise more steeply. Moreover, the earnings profile of an "investor" will intersect the profile of the noninvestor, alike in all other capacities, after no more than $1/r$ years, where r is the rate of return on investments in on-the-job training.[2]

An alternative explanation of the rising age-earnings profile is that, because of difficulties in measuring potential productivity and a general uncertainty about the abilities possessed by individuals, firms (as well as governments and universities) are

[1] These are ex post profiles because they are based on incomes actually received by individuals in the same sample. The profiles are only approximate because some interpolation is needed within the sample period and, more seriously, because our sample results apply only to people aged 22 through 47 and must be extrapolated through age 65.

[2] See the excellent summary in Mincer (1970).

engaged in a continual sorting and monitoring process based on performance on the job. If firms initially have little knowledge about potential productivity and if most training on the job is not firm-specific, then starting salaries need not differ by education or ability level. However, if successful performance is dependent upon or correlated with education and ability, then, over time, individuals with more education and ability will be promoted more quickly and will obtain relatively higher incomes. We later present some evidence that is consistent with this explanation.

Second, we can examine the importance of holding ability and other variables constant in constructing age-income profiles. Because omitting ability biases the estimates of the extra earnings from education, differences *between* profiles will be overstated when ability is omitted. Moreover, as the (same) people age, even *within* an education level where, say, average ability is constant, the growth in average income will partially reflect the changed importance of ability.[3] Thus, in the NBER-TH sample, age-income profiles at various education levels are steeper (relative to the high school profile) after standardizing for ability and family background.

SHAPE OF PROFILES There are several reasons for supposing that the impacts of education on earnings could change over time. First, changes in supply and demand for the differently educated groups will change relative wages. Second, inflation will increase earnings and the values of the education coefficients (although not necessarily the ratio of one to another). Third, there may be a distributed-lag effect of education on earnings due to institutional factors associated with promotion policies and sorting methods or due to the possibility that skills of the highly educated benefit relatively more from aging. Finally, the effect of experience on earnings may vary with education, for there may be more investment in training at different education levels. It should be noted that the last two reasons apply to profiles based on cross-section or time-series data and that the first two reasons apply only to time-series data.

---

[3] In profiles based on cross-section data, ability need not be constant over different cohorts with the same education. See Appendix J.

We can use the tables for initial-year salary and our estimates of the education coefficients for the years 1955, 1968, and 1969 from Chapter 5 to calculate points on the age-income profiles at the various education levels. For the reader's convenience, we present in Table 6-1 these basic data. In Appendix J, we indicate how to interpolate between these years and extrapolate beyond 1969 to obtain the complete profile.[4] Table 6-2 contains the ratios of earnings at various education levels to the earnings of the average high school graduate for each year. The numbers not in parentheses are based on earnings calculated for people with the same characteristics as the average high school graduate.[5]

[4]The data in Table 6-1 have been estimated from regression equations for individual years. The same results would have been obtained by regressing differences in income between years on the determinants of income.

[5]The numbers in parentheses are obtained when only age is held constant.

TABLE 6-1 Income at various education levels, 1955, 1968, and 1969 (in dollars)	Education level	1955	1968	1969
	A. Age, background, ability, and biography constant			
	High school	$ 6,000	$13,968	$13,212
	Some college	6,600	15,852	15,423
	Undergraduate degree	6,720	17 232	17,280
	Some graduate work	6,900	16,908	16,635
	Master's	6,612	17,906	17,402
	Ph.D.	6,140	16,715	16,774
	M.D.	10,332	26,693	27,154
	LL.B.	7,150	24,189	24,274
	B. Age constant			
	High school	6,000	13,968	13,212
	Some college	6,970	16,970	16,620
	Undergraduate degree	7,320	19,070	19,140
	Some graduate work	7,385	18,700	18,430
	Master's	7,080	20,000	19,540
	Ph.D.	6,489	19,996	20,040
	M.D.	10,840	29,920	29,330
	LL.B.	7,560	26,617	26,676

TABLE 6-2
Percentages by
which earnings of
those with higher
levels of
educational
attainment
exceed those of
the average high
school graduate,
selected years

	1946	1955		1958	1968	1969	
Some college	0	11	(16)	10	14	17	(26)
Undergraduate degree	2	12	(22)	7	23	31	(45)
Some graduate work		15	(23)	13	21	26	(40)
Master's		10	(18)	4	28	32	(48)
Ph.D.		2	(8)	12	43	27	(52)
M.D.		72	(81)	85	91	106	(122)
LL.B.		19	(26)	31	89	84	(102)

The high school profile rises less rapidly than all the others: in every case the entries are larger in 1969 than in 1955. To compare the steepness of the non-high school profiles, we calculate for each education level the percentage change in the Table 6-2 entries; the larger this change, the steeper the profile. These percentage changes, as given in Table 6-3, indicate that the Ph.D. and LL.B. profiles are the steepest, with the some-college and M.D. categories the flattest for the period 1955–1969.[6] Thus, an M.D. earns a large income immediately after graduation, but over time his income grows less rapidly than that of any other group. A lawyer initially earns considerably less than an M.D. but more than a Ph.D. In spite of the faster earnings growth of Ph.D.'s than lawyers, and lawyers than M.D.'s, the income rankings of these three groups are the same around the age of 50 as they are in early years.

A proposition that has been widely accepted in human-capital literature is that the higher the education level, the steeper the age-income profiles. This is not entirely borne out by our results. Although it is true for the high school, some-college and undergraduate-degree comparisons, there appears to be no significant difference between the undergraduate-degree, M.A., and some-graduate-work groups, while the undergraduate-degree growth rate exceeds that of the some graduate work. These conclusions are based on profiles calculated in each instance for a person with the ability and background characteristics of the average high school graduate, whereas most

[6]It should be noted that even if the 1955 entry for Ph.D.'s in Table 6-2 were three times as large, the Ph.D. profile would still be the steeper.

	Background, ability, biography, and age held constant, 1955–1969	Age held constant
Some college	55	60
Undergraduate degree	158	104
Some graduate work	72	72
Master's	220	166
Ph.D.	1,250	550
M.D.	47	51
LL.B.	342	292

TABLE 6-3 Percentage growth in earnings at various education levels relative to growth in the earnings of high school graduates, 1955 to 1969

previous studies of profiles have been based on mean earnings by age and education level. For comparison, the numbers on the right in Table 6-3 represent the growth in earnings at each education level holding only age constant. As noted in the previous chapter, the percentage biases from omitting ability and biography are smaller in 1969 than in 1955; hence the ratios of the unadjusted to the adjusted means are greater in 1969, and the profiles based on mean income indicate much less relative growth for those with undergraduate degrees, master's degrees, LL.B.'s, and Ph.D.'s. (The rankings are the same.) This finding and the material on bias adjustment by cohort given in Appendix J suggest that profiles estimated from census data in which ability is not held constant should be viewed cautiously.

Since the initial salaries of those with high school, some college, and an undergraduate degree were about the same and since incomes of the latter two groups were about 10 percent above high school incomes in 1955, the profiles of these two groups were equally steep in terms of experience. (In terms of age, the more educated have a steeper profile.) However, initial earnings in 1947–1949 for those with some college exceeded the initial earnings of B.A. holders, suggesting that the undergraduate-degree experience-earnings profile may be steeper.

These points on the age-earnings profiles describe the effect of education on the distribution of income at different points of time, and in light of some recent literature (Lydall, 1969) it is interesting to consider the relative importance of the effects of education and ability over time.[7] In Table 6-4 we present estimates of the extent to which earnings at the five ability levels differ from the earnings of the average high school graduate. In 1955, those in the top fifth earned about 9 percent more and those in the bottom fifth 8 percent less than the average, and in 1969 the corresponding figures are 15 and −10 percent. Thus, over time the earnings of those at the low end of the ability scale grew less quickly; for the middle fifths, the growth rate was about the same as that of the average high school graduate.

These data can also be used to determine the relative importance of the effects of education and mental ability on earnings. In 1955, the difference between the top and bottom ability fifths of 17 percent is greater than the differential at all education levels except for M.D. and LL.B. (see Table 6-2). In 1969, the 25 percent differential is greater than that of the some-college coefficient and is quite close to all other education coefficients except those for LL.B. and M.D. Since our sample was drawn only from those in the top half of the Armed Forces Qualifying Test distribution, it is almost certain that for those who are at least high school graduates, ability is a more important determinant of the range of the earnings distribution than is education.

The differential growth rates in ability coefficients also suggest to us that the data are more in conformity with a sorting or filtration process than with Mincer's postschooling-investment model. Because of the correlation between steepness and ability, Mincer's model would require that investment be

[7]In this discussion we are assuming that the inclusion of any other variables in the equation would change the ability and education coefficients proportionately. However, because college quality may be correlated with ability but not education, its inclusion could reduce ability coefficients more.

TABLE 6-4 **Percentages by which earnings of high school graduates of a given ability exceed those of the average high school graduate, 1955 and 1969**		

Ability fifth	1955	1969
1	−7.6	−10.0
2	−3.0	−3.9
3	−1.0	−0.4
4	2.4	2.9
5	9.2	15.0

NOTE: Rank 5 is highest.

greater for the more able. But since ability does not interact with nongraduate education and since the effects of ability grow less quickly than the effects of education, it would also be necessary to have smaller investments by ability at the higher education level. Furthermore, the effects of family and personal background, health, and so on, also grew at varying rates between 1955 and 1969; thus differential investments would be needed for each of these categories. In short, our results have to undergo much ad hoc reasoning to be made consistent with the postschooling-investment model, whereas in the filtration theory, different variables can have different effects over time on performance and on promotions.

The above analysis has been based on average income for people with a given set of characteristics. However, within each education level there is a substantial amount of variation in income even after eliminating the effects of the other measured variables. Table 6-5 contains the regression standard error for each education level for 1955 and 1969. During this period, the range of increase of the standard error (of the residual) was between 214 percent for some college and 286 percent for graduate study. Since the growth in the standard error is greater than the corresponding increase in earnings at each education level (after standardization for the various factors), the distribution about the profiles fans out with age; but, contrary to the findings in Mincer, the increase is not monotonically related to education.[8] Moreover, the differences in the percentage increase between high school and college graduates are quite small, and

---

[8]This difference in results might disappear if the effects of ability and the other variables were not eliminated.

TABLE 6-5 Standard errors of annual earnings after removal of the effects of measured variables, by education level, 1955 and 1969 (in dollars)	1955	1969	Percentage change, 1955–1969	Percentage growth in average earnings
High school	$2,700	$ 9,600	255	120
Some college	3,750	11,800	214	133
Undergraduate degree	3,200	12,000	275	157
Some graduate work	2,950	11,400	286	172

the increase in the standard error relative to the mean earnings is greatest in the high school category.

The preceding discussion of age-income profiles was based on age levels included in our sample, but in order to calculate rates of return, it is necessary to construct the complete profiles. A detailed description of the procedures used is given in Appendix J, and only a brief account will be presented here. From 1955 through 1968, we interpolated incomes of each education group on the basis of mean incomes for the nationwide age-education group corresponding to our sample. Prior to 1955, we used the median income of white males together with our initial-year-income estimates. The complete profiles through 1969 are presented in Appendix J, Table J-4, and some are graphed in Figure 6-1. This graph is in line with the previous discussion and, in addition, indicates the intersection points of different profiles. Because the latter occur in interpolated areas, however, the particular dates and, hence, ages may not be accurate.

Our age-income profiles can be compared with the standard finding in cross-section studies that all age-income profiles reach a peak and then decline at some age above 40. This result is less likely to occur using time-series profiles because of increases in money wage rates over time, attributable to inflation and productivity increases. We removed these effects by deflating by a series on median earnings for white males, and the results, which are not presented, indicate that, at every education level except high school, the peak in the deflated-earnings series occurs in 1968, when the average age was 46.[9] For high school graduates, the peak occurs one year later, although earnings in this year are barely above those of the preceding year. Since 1965 through 1969 were years of high employment, it is not likely that business-cycle influences are a cause of these peaks. All the profiles are concave, with earnings growing faster in early years than in years close to the peak earning period. In general, then, these ex post profiles, after removing inflation and productivity effects, are qualitatively very similar to those found in cross-section studies.

---

[9]As explained in Chapter 5, the current-salary question referred to main job only. But adjusting the 1969 data for those with more than one job by the 1968–1969 income growth of those with one job would raise the average 1969 earnings by less than 2 percent at each education level and would not alter the above conclusion.

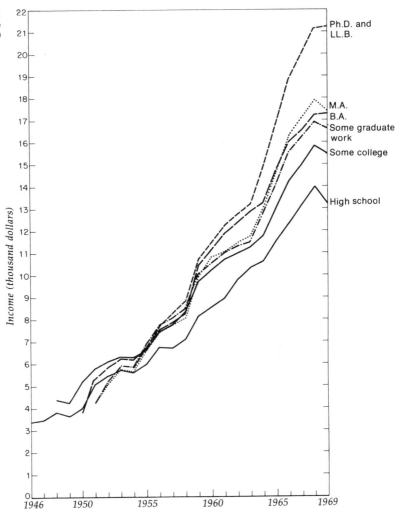

FIGURE 6-1
*Ex post age-income
profiles, 1946–1969*

**CROSS-SECTION
PROFILES** The information in our sample can also be used in conjunction with cross-section data sets from the late 1940s to construct ex ante profiles.[10] We adjust the data by using our estimates of the bias on the returns to education due to omitting ability and background factors. The interesting uses of these profiles are the comparison of the ex ante and ex post rates of return and the comparison of rates before and after adjusting for the bias.

[10]These data appear in Miller (1960) and for 1949 are similar to those in Becker (1964).

7. Rates of Returns to Education Based on the NBER-TH Data

In previous chapters we estimated the effect of education on earnings at several points in time. The extra income resulting from education is not constant from year to year. There are several possible explanations for this variation. For example, while education may better equip a person to handle very difficult jobs, he may only be responsible for these jobs after gradual promotions. Hence, more highly educated people will gradually display the extra marginal product gained from education, and earnings differences will grow over time.[1] Alternatively, skill levels may change over time because of maturation or, later in life, because of mental and physical deterioration. These changes need not be constant for people with different education levels. Finally, educational earnings differences may vary by age because people "invest" in on-the-job training as defined by Mincer (1970).

Thus, to determine if the extra earnings from education are enough to justify the investment in schooling, it is customary to compute the internal rate of return or the present discounted value of the incremental income stream arising from education.[2] With I_t representing the costs of an incremental investment in education, PDV the present discounted value of the additional net income stream obtained from the investment, r the internal rate of return on the education increment under discussion, i the interest rate, and X_t the extra income earned in year t at-

---

[1] Earnings and promotions can also reflect the benefits from on-the-job training.

[2] If Mincer (1970) is correct, this is the combined rate of return to education and general on-the-job training.

tributable to education, the two concepts can be expressed as

$$0 = \sum_{t=1}^{n} \frac{X_t - I_t}{(1 + r)^t} \tag{7-1}$$

$$PDV = \sum_{t=0}^{n} \frac{X_t - I_t}{(1 + i)^t} \tag{7-2}$$

While a substantial body of literature exists on the relationship between the two formulas, for our purposes the rate of return as defined in Eq. (7-1) is sufficient.[3] This rate of return clearly depends upon the cost of investment I_t and the profile of the extra income due to education X_t.

COST OF THE INVESTMENT The relevant costs of an investment in education are not the same for an individual as for society. For an individual, the costs consist of earnings forgone while attending school, tuition, fees, and other school-related expenses.[4] Since the latter expenses are quite small and since data on tuition and fees are readily available, the only difficulty in estimating costs is in measuring forgone earnings. We estimate forgone earnings at each ability level from the data on earnings on initial job by education level but reduce it by an estimate of student's summer and part-time earnings.

From society's viewpoint, direct costs are all the resources used in educating individuals. In general, it is not appropriate to use the average expenditure per pupil at higher education institutions as the resource cost if average and marginal costs are not the same. Because of lack of information, however, we will follow other investigators and will use the average rather than the marginal cost. In addition, we do not distinguish between graduate and undergraduate costs, although we do follow Becker and others in attributing a fraction of total educational costs to research.[5]

[3] For a discussion of the relationship between the concepts, see the articles in Soloman (1959).

[4] The arguments summarized in Bowman (1966) that alternative costs are irrelevant when there are compulsory-school-attendance laws are not appropriate at this level of education.

[5] A discussion of cost calculations appears in Appendix K.

It is necessary at this point to distinguish between an ex post and an ex ante rate of return to education. We define an ex post return as the rate that an individual actually receives from his investment in education; that is, we use the *actual* differences in income that occur in each year during the working lifetime of two individuals alike in all respects but education. We define the ex ante return as the rate that an individual expects to make at the time he undertakes the investment;[6] that is, we use earnings that the individual anticipates will occur in future years of his working life.

Ex post returns should be calculated by using earnings of a group of individuals throughout their working lifetimes. Although no such (longitudinal) study has ever been completed, the NBER-TH sample, which spans at least 25 years of working lifetime, can be used to approximate a life-span.[7] If the economy is on a balanced growth path, this ex post rate of return will also be received by individuals in other cohorts. Of course, the economy may not be on a balanced growth path. Given the rapid increase in educational attainment after World War II, we would not be surprised if the rate of return realized by individuals educated in the late 1940s were greater than the return that will be realized by individuals currently going to college.

The expected, or ex ante, rates of return can be estimated in as many ways as expectations can be formed. The method that has been most often used in economics and that we will follow involves converting cross-section earnings data of cohorts to an expected time profile. The conversion process assumes, among other things, that the economy is on a balanced growth path. Because this method has often been used in the literature, we shall not discuss it here in detail (see Miller, 1960; Becker, 1964; and Hanoch, 1967). Basically, the method assumes that one can estimate what an average person with a given amount of education and other measured characteristics will be earning n years later on the basis of the average income currently being earned

---

[6] For simplicity, we shall assume that an individual decides at the end of high school the number of additional years of schooling he will obtain. This assumption allows us to avoid the "option" benefit of education discussed in Weisbrod (1964).

[7] Rogers (1967) has used sample data to approximate an ex post return. In addition, Project Talent (1964) plans to follow a group of students from elementary and high school through their lifetimes, but the study began only in 1960.

by people with the same characteristics, but in a cohort n years older. When this assumption is applied to all other cohorts, it is possible to estimate age-income profiles at any education level. These age-income profiles must then be adjusted for mortality rates and technological-change rates.[8]

In Appendix J, we present our estimates of the age-earnings profiles by education level for people with a given set of personal characteristics. We use these profiles, together with the cost estimates presented in Appendix K, to estimate the rate of return to various levels of education.

We calculate these returns for individuals in our sample under the following assumptions. First, to obtain rate-of-return estimates applicable to the population as a whole, we do not include GI education benefits as offsets to forgone earnings. Second, we assume that, as in our sample, the average age of people about to undertake higher education in 1946 was 24. We also calculated a rate of return for people identical to those in the sample, but who were 18 in 1946. Since these rates of return

[8] As shown in Becker (1964), the mortality adjustment does not have a large impact on rates of return, and it will be omitted here.

TABLE 7-1 *Ex post rates of return to higher education*		Private			
		Not deflated		Deflated	
Educational categories		*After tax*	*Before tax*	*After tax*	*Before tax*
High school to:					
Some college		15.0	14.8	11.7	11.5
B.A. (not teacher)		9.7	10.7	7.3	8.2
Some graduate (not teacher)		7.0	8.0	4.7	5.6
M.A. (not teacher)		7.7	8.5	5.4	6.2
Ph.D		3.6	4.4	1.4	2.2
LL.B.		11.3	11.8	9.0	9.4
Some college to B.A.			7.4		5.2
B.A. to LL.B.			13.1		11.0

NOTE: In these calculations we have assumed that the differences in income (in current prices) for the various education categories will remain at 1969 levels for the next 18 years.

are very similar, we restrict discussion to rates of return to 24-year-olds.

In Table 7-1, we present four types of rates of return: deflated, not deflated, private, and what we and others call social.[9] The social return, however, does not include the value of any externalities. The costs used in calculating the social rates of return are forgone earnings set at three-quarters of the earnings of high school graduates (until a B.A. is obtained) plus the resource cost per student in higher education. The private costs are forgone earnings plus expenses for tuition and college-related items. In neither case do we allocate any of the costs for current consumption or future nonmonetary benefits from education. While some of the future benefits may be negative—for example, alienation—the sum of these benefits is probably positive. Thus, we probably underestimate the total return to education. The undeflated returns indicate what individuals actually received, while the deflated returns eliminate the effects of inflation on the level of earnings differentials and yield a real rate of return.

[9] In extrapolating to age 65 we have assumed that current-dollar income differences between education groups remain at the 1969 level. This assumption is supported by evidence in Miller (1960) and Becker (1964). However, we do test the sensitivity of our results to this assumption.

	Social				
	Not deflated			Deflated	
Biased	Whole sample	High ability		Whole sample	High ability
15.9	13.7			10.5	
12.2	10.0			7.6	
9.4	7.4	8.4		5.1	6.1
9.9	8.0	8.9		5.7	6.6
7.3	3.8	4.9		1.7	2.7
12.5	11.1	11.7		8.7	9.4
	7.0			4.9	
	12.3			10.1	

The undeflated social rate of return from completion of high school to a bachelor's degree is 10 percent. (There is no difference between a B.S. and a B.A.) This estimate is admittedly based on a number of assumptions that may be inappropriate. Perhaps the assumption based on the least amount of information is that current-dollar differences in income will remain at their 1969 level for 18 more years. However, even if we let this difference grow at the rate of 3 percent a year, so that the difference is 70 percent larger by the end of 18 years, our estimate of the rate of return rises only from 10 to 10.4 percent. If this difference declines at the rate of 3 percent a year, the rate of return falls from 10 to 9.4 percent. Another possible source of error is that our estimates of the average resource cost of educating a student may not be accurate. If we decrease these costs by 10 percent, the rate of return increases trivially from 10 to 10.1 percent. A halving of these costs raises the rate of return to 10.7 percent. Another possible source of error is in our estimates of forgone earnings, which happen to be equal to about four times the resource costs. Since forgone earnings enter the rate-of-return calculation in the same way as resource costs, changes in the rate of return of the same magnitude as given above (0.1 and 0.7 percentage points) would require errors of only 2.5 and 12 percent in the forgone-earnings estimates. While a 2.5 percent error in our initial-earning series is quite possible, a 12 percent error is not as likely, and even this error would not greatly affect our calculations. Thus, we conclude that the rate-of-return estimates are not sensitive to these assumptions or estimates.

If we deflate all incomes by the Consumer Price Index (CPI), which we assume increases beyond 1969 at the rate of 2 percent per year, the social rate of return falls sharply from 10 to 7.6 percent. It is often thought that the CPI is biased upward because of its inadequate treatment of quality changes. If we were to allow for a bias of 1 percent per year in the CPI, the deflated social rate of return would be about 8.7 percent. In either case, the inflation since 1946 has had a fairly large effect on the rate of return.

The calculations given in Table 7-1 are for a person with the ability and background characteristics of the average high school graduate in our sample. Except for graduate education, these estimates also apply at other levels of ability because (1) forgone earnings are the same at all ability levels, (2) for subsequent earnings the effect of ability is the same at all education levels, and (3) we assume that tuition payments do not vary with ability. This does not mean that standardization for ability and background is unimportant. In the *Biased* column of Table 7-1 we present social undeflated rates of return when ability, background, and biography are not held constant. In this instance, the social rate of return is about 12.2 percent rather than 10 percent.

Finally, we consider the private rate of return to a B.A. degree. On a before-tax basis, the estimate is 10.7 percent (and 8.2 percent when deflated). Private returns, however, should be calculated on an after-tax basis. Although we have not had the time and resources to adjust our profiles using progressive tax rates, we have made the following rough adjustment. We use an average tax rate of 12.5 percent for those with at least a B.A. and 10 percent for everyone else, and we assume that part-time earnings of students are not taxed. Considering that no one in our sample earned much more than $100,000 in 1969, these assumptions probably overstate the average tax burden. Using these tax rates, the private rate of return declines from 10.7 to 9.7 percent.

RATE OF RETURN TO COLLEGE DROPOUTS Next we consider the rate of return for those who attended but did not graduate from college. As shown in Table 7-1, the social rate of return is 13.7 percent (16 percent with no ability and background standardization) but falls to 10.5 percent when the effects of inflation are eliminated. That the rate of return to some college is substantially more than for college graduation (13.7 versus 10 percent) is surprising in that previous studies have generally concluded the opposite (see Becker, 1964; and Morgan & David, 1963). Part of the explanation may be the greater concentration of business owners in our sample in the some-college group. (In 1969 about 30 percent of the some-college group were business owners.) The "earnings" figures reported by the self-employed may include a return to financial investment in their businesses. A rough adjustment for such returns can be made by holding constant self-employment via a dummy variable. The results of such equations for 1969 were reported in Chapter 5. But even if the same 25 percent adjustment found for business owners in 1969 is made for each year, the rate of return to some college is unchanged, and is still slightly greater than the rate for an undergraduate degree.

Our primary explanation for this better performance of the people with some college is the following. By the end of World War II, the men in our sample ranged in age from 22 to 30, with an average age of 24. Many of these men were married and had children before, during, or right after the war. Despite the availability of the GI Bill, many married men probably could not afford to wait to start providing for their families. Thus, in an equation explaining years of schooling, those married before 1949 obtained about two-thirds of a year less schooling after controlling for ability, family background, and age. It seems likely that those who dropped out for family reasons are much more like the college graduate with respect to personality, other unmeasured aspects of ability, and so on. Thus, our estimates may be better than those obtained from census data. Incidentally, a similar conclusion also applies to the high school–bachelor's degree rate-of-return estimate.

The private before-tax and after-tax rates of return are both about 15 percent.[10] This rate of return indicates that many more high school graduates could have profited from attending college for some time. In the above calculations we assumed that the average stay in college was two years. In analyzing the 1969 earnings data, however, we found that all the increase in income from some college occurred in the first year. If this finding is extrapolated to all points on the age-income profile, the rate of return to the first year of college is above 20 percent. On the other hand, as shown in Table 7-1, completing the last two years of college yields rates of return about one-half as large as those for the first two years.

RATE OF RETURN TO GRADUATE EDUCATION
The social and private rates of return from high school to some graduate work and an M.A. are about 7 to 8 percent, while the return to a Ph.D. is about 4 percent.[11] In these calculations, we have eliminated the nonpecuniary return to elementary and

---

[10] It is possible for the after-tax rate to exceed the before-tax rate. Although taxes reduce the return to education, they also reduce the opportunity cost more than proportionately, since we assume summer earnings of students to be tax-free.

[11] There are only about 50 Ph.D.'s in our sample.

high school teachers but not to college teachers.[12] Therefore, these low rates are indicative of diminishing returns to education. Indeed, the return from B.A. to Ph.D. is negative, although this presumably reflects some nonpecuniary factors.[13] Some types of graduate training, on the other hand, yield larger returns. Thus, the social rate of return from high school to an LL.B. is 11.1 percent, and that from a B.A. to an LL.B. is 12.3 percent. Although we have not calculated the return to M.D.'s because there are so few in the sample, it is clear from the discussion of their age-income profiles that their rate of return is higher than that of LL.B.'s.

In 1969, the effect of graduate education in the top two mathematical-ability fifths was about 10 percent greater than the effect in the bottom three fifths. We have estimated the rates of return in the graduate categories for those in the top two ability fifths.[14] These estimates, which are presented for the social rate in Table 7-1, are generally about one percentage point above the average rates. In the bottom fifths, the corresponding rates are about one percentage point below the average. Even for people with the highest ability, returns to a general graduate education appear low.

**EX ANTE RETURNS
TO EDUCATION**

The ex post rates of return indicate what was earned, on the average, by those in our sample who invested in higher education in 1946. An estimate of the rate of return that could have been expected in 1946 can also be calculated.

It is useful to determine if ex ante returns calculated with various assumptions are good approximations to ex post rates —then we would have more faith in ex ante estimates of the rate of return from the 1968 *Current Population Reports* or the 1970

---

[12] In Chapter 8 we find that in the managerial and owner categories those with a B.A. and M.A. have about the same income. There should be no differences within these occupations in nonpecuniary returns at the B.A. and M.A. levels. This suggests that our rates of return to an M.A. are not being affected by other nonpecuniary factors. However, Ph.D.'s within these occupations earn about 20 percent more than B.A.'s. If this is indicative of the extra monetary and nonmonetary income attributable to a Ph.D., the rate of return from a B.A. to a Ph.D. would still be less than the rate of return from high school to B.A.

[13] These results are similar to Hunt's ex ante rates (1963).

[14] This was accomplished by increasing the existing graduate profiles by 5 percent in 1969 and by interpolating the difference between zero and 5 percent from 1955 to 1969.

census. Second, the bias in our sample from omitting ability and sociodemographic information is larger than that generally allowed for in other studies, so that it is difficult to compare our ex post returns to ex ante estimates of others.

Expectations can be formed in many ways. For simplicity we make the types of assumptions that other economists have made and ignore the shifts in wages implied by known changes in education levels between cohorts. Using data in Miller (1960) and the correction procedures given in Appendix J, it is possible to estimate ex ante returns in 1946 and in 1949 for 24-year-old high school graduates contemplating one to three years or four or more years of college.[15] In Table 7-2 we present estimates of the various ex ante rates of return from high school to some college, and from high school to four or more years of college.

Consider first the returns to attending college for two years. In 1946, the social rates of return are about 11 and 12 percent, with technical-change rates of 1 and 2 percent, respectively.[16] One assumption that is crucial for this analysis concerns the bias correction for ability and other omitted variables. The rates of return just noted are based on the assumption that the bias correction derived from our sample is applicable to each cohort in the census. This assumption could be wrong either because the bias shifts from one cohort to another or because the sample bias results are not applicable even to the corresponding cohort in the census. Using the method described in Appendix J, we can allow the bias to shift by cohort. Such shifts, which raise the income differences in the oldest cohorts of 1946 and 1949, increase the rate of return by about one-half a percentage point.

Next, suppose the bias in the NBER-TH sample is not the same as the (unknown) bias in the census. We can still estimate the rate of return for the people in our sample by developing estimates of the age-income profiles to apply to the income of our sample cohort in 1946. We assume the census bias to be the same in each cohort. Therefore, the census age-income growth

[15]In making these calculations, we adjust the data for technical change but not for mortality. As demonstrated in Becker (1964, p. 131), the effects of mortality on rates of return are less than one-half of one percentage point; hence, we ignore the adjustment in all our calculations. We allow for technical change by assuming both 1 and 2 percent per year growth rates.

[16]These estimates are about as sensitive as the ex post returns to the various assumptions made on costs.

TABLE 7-2
Ex ante rates of return to higher education, 1946 and 1949

Type of return	1946 from high school to:		1949 from high school to:	
	Some college	At least a B.A.	Some college	At least a B.A.
Social rates of return				
1 percent technical change	11.1	8.3	6.7	9.1
2 percent technical change	12.2	9.4	7.8	10.2
Allowing δ to change and 1 percent technical change	11.6	8.7	7.3	9.7
No bias correction (1 percent technical change)	15.2	11.4	8.9	12.1
All incomes adjusted to NBER-TH sample level and 1 percent technical change	12.8	9.3	7.1	9.5
Private rates of return, before tax				
1 percent technical change	13.3	9.6	7.5	10.1
2 percent technical change	14.4	10.7	8.6	11.2
Allowing δ to change and 1 percent technical change	13.5	9.9	8.0	10.7
No bias correction (1 percent technical change)	17.8	12.9	9.8	13.4
All incomes adjusted to NBER-TH sample level and 1 percent technical change	14.2	10.1	7.7	10.3

NOTE: Shifts in δ are explained in Appendix J.

rates can be used to generate income profiles at each education level in our sample. In 1946, this procedure requires us to double all the income levels presented in Miller (1960). With the resource costs unchanged, this adjustment increases the social rate of return by nearly two percentage points, for example, from 11 to 12.8 percent. It is interesting to observe that if we had not made a correction for bias, the rate of return (with 1 percent technical change) would have been 15 percent rather than 11 percent.

Table 7-2 also contains estimates of private before-tax rates of return. These estimates are about two percentage points higher than the social rates, while the after-tax private rates, although not presented, are about one percentage point higher than the social rates.

Consider next the 1949 ex ante rates. The 1949 sample differs from the 1946 sample in several ways. The 1949 figures are based on a larger sample, represent the entire rather than just the nonfarm population, measure income rather than earnings, and are from a period in which reconversion from wartime was mostly finished. Finally, the period from 1946 to 1949 witnessed a substantial inflation.

The rates of return for some college in 1949 are about four percentage points lower than in 1946, but as discussed below, the returns to at least a B.A. are about the same in the two years. Although the differences between the 1946 and 1949 samples cited above may explain the difference in the return to some college, it is not clear which of these is operative or which of the two years is the more appropriate for comparison with our ex post rates.

We turn now to consider ex ante rates of return to those who graduate from college. For these individuals, the average length of college schooling is about five years (Becker, 1964).[17] As shown in Table 7-2, the expected social rate of return in 1946 for college graduates over high school was about 9 percent. These estimates are raised by one percentage point when calculated from our sample by using the census profiles (fifth row). Also, when we allow the bias correction to change with cohorts, the rate is raised one-half a percentage point. The private rates of return are about one percentage point higher than the social rates.

These rates of return are three to five percentage points below the rate for college dropouts. Of course, those with more than four years of college include many receiving nonmonetary returns. But, while all the master's degree and Ph.D. holders who taught undoubtedly received low monetary incomes in 1946, a large proportion of those with graduate training were lawyers and medical doctors who received (although not necessarily reported) large incomes.

In 1949, the rates of return to at least a B.A. are only slightly

---

[17] We have analyzed these data assuming that for the fifth year students would earn one-fourth of the starting salary of a B.A., which is essentially that of a high school graduate with five years on the job, and that the resource and tuition costs are the same as for undergraduates. This probably understates costs and overstates rates of return, because it costs more to educate M.D.'s and Ph.D.'s and because law and medical students receive few scholarships.

higher than those in 1946. However, these now exceed the returns to some college by two or three percentage points. It might be noted that our estimates for 1949 involving no bias correction are quite close to those of Becker (1964), although there are some slight differences in treatment of the data.[18]

It is interesting to compare our ex post and ex ante estimates of the rate of return. Since the cross-section data are in constant prices, the comparison will be made using the deflated ex post returns. The 1946 ex ante and ex post returns to some college are the same, while the ex ante return to four or more years appears to be slightly above the weighted average of the corresponding ex post returns.[19] These results suggest that ex ante rates are good approximations to ex post rates.[20] There are, however, some other factors to consider. First, if the Consumer Price Index is biased upward, then we are understating the deflated ex post rates. Second, our ex post profiles are interpolated on the basis of a national series in which high school graduates suffer relatively more in recessions. Although it is proper to include the effect of fluctuations in ex post rates, we have not included them in our ex ante calculations and have therefore overstated the ex post rates relative to the ex ante rates. Third, the ex ante returns are calculated assuming that the bias corrections from our sample apply to the whole population. An adjustment for these factors probably would not alter our basic finding of approximate equality between the ex ante and ex post results.

Finally, we consider the question of whether investments in education, ignoring consumption aspects and externalities, are worthwhile. From a social point of view, this involves comparing our rates of return to education with alternative returns available to society. Assuming a fixed amount of saving and investment in society, the appropriate alternative rate is that obtainable on physical investment, which is usually thought to be

[18]For example, Becker's social rate for at least a B.A. for an 18-year-old is 12.5 percent, while ours for a 24-year-old is 12.1 percent.

[19]Although the ex ante estimates in the table are lower than those found elsewhere in the literature, our estimates are close to those of others when we do not standardize for ability and background factors.

[20]M.D.'s and teachers (not college) are included in the ex ante but not in the ex post calculations. This difference probably reduces the ex ante rate slightly.

about 12 to 15 percent in constant prices. Comparing this with our estimates of the deflated social rates, we conclude that, except perhaps for the some-college category, there is overinvestment in education from society's viewpoint.[21] This conclusion, of course, assumes that there are no consumption, nonmonetary, or external benefits from education. Moreover, the higher rate of return to some college may be due to the inclusion of returns to financial capital of business owners, who are concentrated more in the high school and some-college categories than in the college-graduate groups. We suspect that this concentration reflects the availability of capital through Veterans Administration loans and that the some-college results may not be applicable to the population as a whole. If we adjust the income differentials by including a dummy variable for business owners, the some-college rate of return is unchanged, while the return from a bachelor's degree is raised to $12^1/_2$ percent, which is competitive with the return from physical assets.

From a private viewpoint, however, the appropriate alternative return is best represented by an after-tax ex post rate of return on common stocks. A reasonable estimate of this rate is perhaps about 10 percent in nominal terms. Since the private after-tax rates differ by less than one percentage point from the before-tax rates, we conclude that, in addition to obtaining some college education, obtaining a B.A. or an LL.B. degree is a profitable investment, although it appears to be advantageous to drop out after two years of college.

There are several reasons why the private return to education is close to the rate earned on common stocks, though the social rate is less than that earned on physical capital. First, tuition does not cover the full cost of the education. Second, the rate of return on common stocks from 1929 to 1960 was probably held down by the increases in corporate tax rates. Third, the income-tax laws do not treat forgone earnings as taxable income; hence, individuals in effect are allowed to "expense" this investment cost rather than depreciate it (although, of course, this is partially offset by not allowing depreciation of tuition).

---

[21] However, for those with a B.A., obtaining an LL.B. may be worthwhile. These conclusions do not necessarily apply to M.D.'s, as we have not included them in our analysis.

8. Within-Occupation Regressions

All but the most primitive economies are characterized by a division of labor into various occupations that differ in terms of such characteristics as the tasks performed, status, and average wage levels. In this sample, as in others, the more highly educated tend to be concentrated in the higher-paying occupations. A question that naturally arises is whether this concentration is due to the affective and cognitive skills produced by, or associated with, education or whether it is due to the use of education as an entry card. In Chapter 9 we attempt to answer this question using information from earnings functions within various occupational groups that are estimated here.

Such occupational earnings equations are of interest in themselves. They indicate both the extent to which success in different occupations depends on ability and education, once entry into an occupation has been achieved, and the extent to which education, ability, and prior work experience impart specific skills. The equations can also be used to examine several other important problems involving, for example, age-income profiles by education level in various occupations, or the degree of riskiness in education-occupation groups. These within-occupation regressions, however, are not appropriate for determining the returns to education. Such equations do not take into account the increases in earnings attributable to entering higher-paying occupations.

SUMMARY   Using the NBER-TH data, we have analyzed separately three broad occupational categories: professional, technical, and sales; managerial and business owner; and white-collar, blue-

137

collar, and service.[1] We make use of the estimated equations, which are presented and discussed in detail later, in several different ways. First, we calculate the average earnings and their variance after standardizing for differences in such characteristics as mental ability, family background, and age. Second, we indicate which variables determine earnings within an occupation.

In Table 8-1, we present mean earnings for 1955 and 1969 and the percentage change in earnings over this period by education and occupation level for people with the same measured characteristics.[2] In 1955, this "standard" high school graduate would have earned a low of $400 per month as a white-collar employee and a high of $628 in managerial work. His professional and sales salaries would be close to his managerial salary, and his technical, blue-collar, and service earnings would be intermediate. In 1969, the rankings over occupations of the high school graduate's earnings are about the same, except that owners and managers do substantially better than professionals and salesmen. As might be expected, the growth rate in earnings is lowest in the service and blue- and white-collar occupations, and is highest for technicians, owners, and managers.[3]

In 1955, incomes earned in the various occupations were about the same at all education levels, but by 1969 incomes were higher for those with more education. Thus, the percentage growth in income is substantially greater at the undergraduate-degree and Ph.D. levels than at the high school or some-college levels for professional, technical, sales, and owner-manager groups. When calculated for people in the top ability fifth, the profiles are steeper.

---

[1] These categories were chosen in order to obtain a sufficient number of observations while maintaining homogeneity with respect to average income levels. (See the tables in Chapter 4.) Moreover, as will be shown below, the variance of the unexplained residual is approximately constant for the suboccupations in a group, but the variances differ between the occupations.

[2] A separate profile can be constructed for each ability and background characteristic. The discussion that follows is for a person of the average age, in the third fifth in ability and biography, whose father attended high school but not college, who is married, and who is in excellent health.

[3] Miller (1960) finds a similar pattern.

TABLE 8-1 *Average monthly earnings, by occupation and education, 1955 and 1969 (in dollars)**

	High school	Some college	Under-graduate degree	Some graduate work	Master's	Ph.D.
Professional						
1955	$ 606	$ 628	$ 599	$ 607	$ 601	$ 589
1969	1,238	1,324	1,483	1,315	1,366	1,684
Percentage change	(104)	(111)	(148)	(117)	(127)	(186)
Technical						
1955	497	519	490	498	†	†
1969	1,320	1,406	1,565	1,397	†	†
Percentage change	(166)	(171)	(219)	(181)		
Sales						
1955	623	645	616	624	†	†
1969	1,309	1,395	1,554	1,386	†	†
Percentage change	(110)	(116)	(152)	(122)		
Blue-collar						
1955	463	485	496	488	†	†
1969	897	929	992	1,056	†	†
Percentage change	(95)	(92)	(100)	(116)		
Service						
1955	454	475	486	478	†	†
1969	851	883	946	1,010	†	†
Percentage change	(87)	(86)	(95)	(111)		
White-collar						
1955	400	422	433	415	†	†
1969	794	826	843	907	†	†
Percentage change	(99)	(96)	(95)	(119)		
Owner-manager						
1955	628	644	638	697	618	643
1969	1,613	1,708	1,816	1,793	1,873	1,961
Percentage change	(157)	(165)	(184)	(157)	(203)	(205)

*Calculated for people of average age, Q_3 in ability and biography, father attended high school, married, in excellent health, not an M.D. or a teacher.

†No observations.

SOURCE: Derived from Table 8-3.

It is often of interest to know the riskiness attached to earnings within education and occupation groups.[4] Since some of the variability arises from measurable characteristics in each education group, we have calculated a conditional variance defined as $\sigma^2 = [1/(N-k)] \Sigma(Y_i - Z_ib_i)^2$. Z_i represents independent variables, and $N-k$ and b_i are the degrees of freedom and the coefficient estimates, respectively, from regressions described in this chapter.[5] It should be noted that

[4] The variance is a complete measure of riskiness only if the distribution of errors is normal or if the utility function is quadratic.

[5] These regressions include the personality variable q and hence differ from those in Table 8-3.

TABLE 8-2
"Conditional" standard errors in monthly earnings, by occupation and education, 1969 and 1955 (in dollars)

	1969					
	High school	*Some college*	*Undergraduate degree*	*Some graduate work*	*Master's*	*Three-year graduate degree*
Professional	$274	$500	$674	$ 461	$302	$ 293
	(11)	(49)	(257)	(75)	(195)	(197)
Technical	577	579	458	*	*	*
	(85)	(82)	(29)	(3)	(4)	(1)
Sales	548	614	865	*	*	*
	(56)	(80)	(90)	(6)	(3)	(2)
Blue-collar	165	182	244	*	*	*
	(211)	(87)	(18)	(1)	(0)	(0)
Service	177	228	244	*	*	*
	(50)	(32)	(11)	(1)	(0)	(1)
White-collar	127	194	212	*	*	*
	(24)	(21)	(11)	(3)	(0)	(0)
Owner-manager	907	884	911	1,158	960	1,261
	(299)	(501)	(610)	(112)	(136)	(36)

*Too few observations to calculate the standard error.

NOTE: The number of observations is given in parentheses beneath the standard error. For the factors that were held constant, see first footnote to Table 8-1.

these variances overstate the riskiness of the various occupations, because some of the residual reflects individual characteristics that we have not measured.

In Table 8-2, we present estimates of the corresponding standard errors (σ) for various education and occupation groups in which we have at least 10 people. Since we would expect individuals to have sorted themselves out by 1969, the results for that year are more interesting. We consider first the ranking of occupations by variability. For this purpose we exclude the graduate levels of education for which we have estimates of the variance in only two occupations. Using 1 for the lowest σ and 7 for the highest, the average ranks over the three educational levels are white-collar, $1^1/_3$; blue-collar, 2; service,

			1955			
High school	*Some college*	*Undergraduate degree*	*Some graduate work*	*Master's*	*Three-year graduate degree*
$203	$172	$171	$180	$145	$ 28
(77)	(156)	(488)	(98)	(220)	(16)
114	134	124	*	*	*
(24)	(45)	(20)	(1)	(2)	(0)
191	434	219	249	*	*
(72)	(124)	(139)	(28)	(9)	(7)
102	146	113	*	*	*
(293)	(135)	(44)	(3)	(1)	(1)
103	167	118	*	*	*
(28)	(18)	(14)	(2)	(2)	(4)
83	74	85	*	*	*
(91)	(61)	(45)	(7)	(3)	(1)
282	279	280	320	197	178
(195)	(334)	(362)	(45)	(27)	(14)

$2\,^2/_3$; professional, $4\,^1/_3$; technical, 5; sales, $5\,^2/_3$; and owner-manager, 7. Except for the switch in position between service and blue-collar, these rankings correspond to those of average earnings in 1969; that is, occupations paying lowest (highest) also have the lowest (highest) variability in earnings. Examination of the variability by education within each occupation indicates that in 1969, but not in 1955, σ increases with education, although in 1969 the managerial and technical occupations are exceptions to this rule.[6] Finally, we note that there are much greater differences in the variances between occupations (given education) than between education levels (given occupation).

Since average earnings in 1955 do not differ much by education (after standardization) in any occupation, it is not surprising that very few education coefficients are significant in the 1955 equations. On the other hand, the larger educational earnings differences in 1969 (Table 8-1) result in more of the 1969 education coefficients being significant. These coefficients differ by occupations, with service and white- and blue-collar groups displaying smaller effects of education. Both the average level of earnings and the coefficients suggest that around the age of 47, education has imparted skills that are more important in occupations that require leadership and judgment.[7] The ability-measure coefficients tend to corroborate this conclusion. Only the mathematical measure is significant, but it is not important in the service, white-collar, and blue-collar occupations.

A more detailed summary of these findings by occupation may be of some interest to the reader. For the professional group in 1955, we find the top two mathematical-ability fifths and the top three biography fifths significant but all the education coefficients except M.D. insignificant and small. In 1969, the B.A., M.D., and LL.B variables are significant, as are the top two ability fifths and the highest biography fifth. For managers and business owners, all the education coefficients are small and insignificant in 1955. In 1969, the B.A., M.A., and LL.B. coefficients, the top ability fifth, and the top two biography fifths

---

[6]The increase of σ with education and the higher concentration of the more educated in the higher-variance occupations help to explain the heteroscedasticity discussed in Appendix I.

[7]However, the differences could be explainable by differences in investment in on-the-job training or by small sample sizes in some cells.

are significant. When owners and managers are analyzed separately for 1969, we find that for managers the B.A., M.A., and LL.B. coefficients as well as the top ability and biography variables are significant; for owners, only the B.A. and LL.B. variables are significant. This result for managers is consistent with the results of our study of top corporate managers, presented in Appendix L. For the white-collar, blue-collar, and service group, we find the B.A., some-college, and top biography coefficients significant in 1955, while in 1969 only the B.A. variable is significant.[8]

Thus in 1955 mathematical ability, the information contained in the biography variables, and to a minor extent education affect income within occupations. The result for education is not surprising, since for the sample as a whole its effects are not large, and education coefficients are nearly always smaller within occupations.[9] In 1969, on the other hand, the effects of education are more pronounced, while the ability factors are still important.

Tables 4-3 and 4-4 (pages 66, 67) indicate that many people switched occupations between 1955 and 1969. We can use the 1955 occupation as an indicator of the time spent in a particular occupation or, alternatively, of the type of training received in the past within each occupation. We find that those in the service, white-collar, and blue-collar group in 1955 earn substantially less in 1969 (regardless of occupation in 1969) than those who were in other occupations in 1955. In both the managerial and professional categories, 1969 income is highest for those who were in the same occupation as they were in 1955. Those who switched from professional to managerial, or vice versa, received about $2,000 a year less in 1969 than those who remained in their 1955 occupation. This strongly suggests that there is some specific training in the managerial and professional categories. However, the fact that those with training in

[8] We excluded M.A.'s and Ph.D.'s because there was only one person in each category.

[9] These results on ability and education are similar to those found in the Wolfle-Smith data. In Thorndike and Hagen's study, however, there were only very few more finely defined occupations in which ability was significant. Thus, some of the importance of mathematical ability may be due to differences in ability requirements among suboccupations. In addition, the ability requirements for suboccupations in the professional category may be correlated with nonpecuniary returns.

law do exceptionally well as owners or managers suggests that some skills produced by education are fairly general.

Although the results are not presented here, we have estimated the 1969 equations after including the 1955 residual, with the latter calculated from the individual's 1955 occupation. This variable is highly significant in all occupations with a coefficient of about 1.5 and a t value in excess of 15, and its inclusion increases the $\bar{R}^2$ values by about .2. In these equations this "residual" variable is not orthogonal to the other independent variables because of changes in occupations between 1955 and 1969. Nevertheless, it is clear that it explains more of the variance in earnings than the education or ability variables, even within occupations. The above results are based on a detailed regression analysis of earnings by occupation, to which we now turn.

TABLE 8-3 *Occupational regressions, 1955 and 1969 (in dollars per month)*

	Constant	Some college	Undergraduate degree	Some graduate work	Master's	Ph.D.	LL.B.*	M.D.*	Teacher
(1) Y_{55}	$ 276.3	$21.9	$ -7.1	$ 1.1	$ -5.5	$ -17.5	$ 40.8	$321.9	$ -159.9
	(2.8)	(1.0)	(.3)	(.0)	(.2)	(.5)	(1.1)	(7.5)	(4.0)
(2) Y_{69}	876.8	86.4	244.9	77.1	127.6	445.8	583.7	903.7	-197.8
	(2.0)	(1.1)	(3.0)	(.7)	(1.3)	(4.0)	(5.8)	(7.8)	(2.4)
(3) Y_{55}	397.2	16.4	9.9	69.5	-9.5	15.3			
	(3.0)	(.5)	(.3)	(1.2)	(1.2)	(.2)			
(4) Y_{69}	1,781.1	94.7	202.9	179.8	259.3	347.4	666.6		
	(3.6)	(1.2)	(2.6)	(1.5)	(2.3)	(1.6)	(2.0)		
(5) Y_{55}	268.5	21.2	32.5	24.8					
	(4.5)	(2.1)	(2.4)	(.7)					
(6) Y_{69}	865.7	31.8	94.0	158.2					
	(4.6)	(1.5)	(2.6)	(1.8)					

*Those with LL.B.'s and M.D.'s are also included in the Ph.D. category.

NOTE: Figures in parentheses are t statistics. Rank 5 is highest. N is sample size.

PROFESSIONAL, TECHNICAL, AND SALES

Consider first the 1,686 individuals in the professional, technical, and sales group in 1955. In equation 1, Table 8-3, we have included the following as determinants of earnings: age; the mathematical factor; the biography variable; the five education variables; background variables; doctor, teacher, and lawyer dummies; and dummies for the sales and technical suboccupations.[10] The most noticeable difference between this equation and the corresponding one using all the data (that is, all occupations combined) is that none of the five basic education variables is significantly different from zero, and all their coefficients are extremely small. On the other hand, the top two

[10] As before, the people who are lawyers and M.D.'s are also included in the Ph.D. category; hence the significance test given in the table is for the difference from the Ph.D. effect and not the difference from high school.

We also examined the effects of the three other ability factors. Since none of these were significant, the results are not presented.

Age	*Ability*				*Technical*	*Sales*	*Service*	*White-collar*	*Health*
	Q_2	Q_3	Q_4	Q_5					
$ 7.6	$ 27.3	$ 38.3	$ 43.2	$ 80.0	$-109.4	$17.0			$-19.8
(2.7)	(1.3)	(1.9)	(2.1)	(4.0)	(4.0)	(1.1)			(2.0)
5.8	103.2	110.0	130.5	291.5	81.7	70.6			-157.4
(.6)	(1.5)	(1.6)	(1.9)	(4.4)	(1.1)	(1.1)			(4.6)
8.2	20.5	15.5	48.0	74.8					-45.0
(2.2)	(.5)	(.4)	(1.3)	(2.1)					(2.4)
-1.7	29.8	22.8	90.4	224.7					-256.7
(.2)	(.3)	(.3)	(1.0)	(2.6)					(5.6)
5.8	2.9	- 3.5	5.4	24.1			$-9.9	$-63.0	-25.0
(3.3)	(.3)	(.3)	(.4)	(1.6)			(.6)	(6.4)	(3.7)
-.3	19.3	5.1	55.5	30.0			-46.0	-103.3	-22.8
(.1)	(.7)	(.2)	(2.0)	(.9)			(1.9)	(3.4)	(1.5)

TABLE 8-3 *(continued)*

Single	Father attended high school	Father attended college	Q₂	Q₃	Q₄	Q₅	Occupation	R̄²/N
$-108.9	$16.1	$ 6.2	$ 20.8	$ 44.7	$ 55.6	$ 66.7	Professional, technical, and sales	.12
(2.7)	(1.2)	(.4)	(1.1)	(2.3)	(2.9)	(3.4)		238
−259.2	87.6	−83.5	105.4	48.4	39.7	145.0		.21
(2.1)	(1.9)	(1.5)	(1.6)	(.7)	(.6)	(2.2)		728
−144.0	47.2	15.8	− 92.3	−57.7	15.2	16.5	Managers and owners	.03
(1.4)	(1.9)	(.5)	(2.4)	(1.5)	(.4)	(.5)		336
117.6	91.7	157.4	90.6	54.4	203.8	199.7		.05
(.5)	(1.6)	(2.2)	(1.1)	(.6)	(2.4)	(2.3)		1,085
− 74.2	5.6	17.5	8.0	26.5	34.7	43.3	Blue-collar, white-collar, and service	.11
(2.6)	(.6)	(1.2)	(.7)	(2.1)	(2.6)	(3.0)		115
− 98.5	20.5	− 1.8	− 5.8	43.1	30.6	3.0		.04
(1.5)	(.9)	(.1)	(.2)	(1.4)	(1.0)	(.1)		208

mathematical-ability fifths and the top three biography fifths are significant, and their magnitudes do not differ much from those obtained when using all the data. The M.D. and teacher dummies are significant, and their magnitudes are substantial, while the dummy for lawyers is not significantly different from that of Ph.D.'s or high school graduates. This is in line with our earlier profile discussion in which we found that the M.D. profile starts high and is fairly flat, whereas the lawyer profile starts low and climbs faster. These findings suggest that educational differences (including M.D.) have no effect on incomes within the professional occupation, but that differences in mental ability have a substantial effect. (There are enough people at all the education levels to ensure that the result cannot be attributed to small sizes in any of the categories.)

Incomes of technical workers are about $1,200, or 15 percent below incomes of those in the professional or sales occupations. Finally, as far as the background factors are concerned, the single (marital-status) and health variables are significant, while the father's education variables are not. The magnitude of the single variable is about the same as for the entire sample, but the coefficient of the health variable is only about half as large.

Since census results generally indicate a positive influence of education on earnings within occupations, we must ask whether our results are due to standardizations for ability and background factors, some of which cannot be done with census data. In an equation (not shown) containing only the age, education, and suboccupation dummies as independent variables, none of the five basic education dummies is significant. One possible explanation for the difference between this and census results is that only those in the top half of the IQ scale are considered here, and dummies are included here for M.D.'s and teachers. In addition, census equations usually span a wider age interval.

Equation 2 in Table 8-3 is the corresponding 1969 equation for the professional, technical, and sales occupation, but because of switches in occupation there are now 1,324 people in this group.[11] There are some important qualitative as well as quantitative differences between the 1955 and 1969 results. Perhaps of most interest is the fact that the B.A. and Ph.D. coefficients are highly significant and their magnitudes fairly substantial in 1969. For example, after standardizing for ability and background factors, B.A. holders receive incomes 20 percent above those of the average high school graduate in this occupation, and Ph.D. holders receive earnings about 40 percent higher. In addition, incomes of M.D.'s are well over double, and incomes of LL.B.'s are about double, those of the average high school graduate. The other education coefficients are all positive, but their magnitudes are less than that of B.A. The top two mathematical-ability fifths are again significant, with magnitudes about the same as when all the data are used, but only the top biography fifth is significant. This general pattern of results corresponds to that for the sample as a whole in that educational effects become much more important than ability effects over time. Once again, the sales suboccupation dummy is insignificant, but now the technical suboccupation is also, indicating

---

[11] We also exclude people with zero income, and this number differs in the two years.

that although technical workers start more slowly their incomes are equal to those of professionals by the age of 47.[12]

Data are available on whether the individual is a self-employed professional in 1969. When a dummy variable for the self-employed is added to equation 2, its coefficient is $630 and it is highly significant, suggesting that the self-employed, other than lawyers and doctors, do substantially better than the non-self-employed.[13] The self-employed lawyers and M.D.'s, in turn, earn higher incomes than other self-employed individuals.[14]

Since data are available on an individual's occupation in 1955, it is possible to test the proposition that individuals who were in the same occupation in 1955 and 1969 earned higher incomes than those who switched into the professional group after 1955. In an equation (not presented here) that includes dummy variables representing the 1955 occupation of the individual, those who were in the professional and technical, sales, and managerial categories in 1955 received over $4,000, $2,000, and $1,500 a year more, respectively, than those in the white-collar, blue-collar, and service group. Hence, experience gained in other occupations is not as useful as in the professional occupation, although sales experience is more valuable than managerial, which in turn is more valuable than "other" occupational background. (The greater impact of sales may be because the group studied in 1969 is professional, technical, and sales.) While the above results are useful for studying the relative importance of specific and general experience, the equations cannot be used directly to examine the effects of education in 1969 (within the occupation), because occupation in 1955 is partially determined by education. Thus, with the introduction of the 1955 occupations, the coefficients on Ph.D. and B.A. are substantially smaller.

MANAGERS AND BUSINESS OWNERS The results for the 1,000 managers and business owners in the sample in 1955 are presented in equations 3 and 4 in Table 8-3.

[12]As mentioned in Chapter 4, the 1955 and 1969 definitions of the technical occupation may differ, in which case no significance should be placed on the difference between the 1955 and 1969 results.

[13]Since most M.D.'s and some lawyers are self-employed, the M.D. coefficient drops from $904 to $487, the LL.B. coefficient from $584 to $286, and the Ph.D. coefficient from $445 to $428.

[14]As is the case with owners, the earnings of self-employed professionals may include a return on financial capital.

In equation 3, the only significant variables are age, the top fifth of mathematical ability, health, and the second fifth of biography. Again, education coefficients are insignificant and income levels do not differ much from those of high school graduates.[15] In the 1969 regressions (involving 1,700 people), both the B.A. and M.A. coefficients are significant, but earnings at these levels exceed a high school graduate's earnings by about 15 percent only. Since in this occupation we would not expect differential nonpecuniary rewards to those with master's and undergraduate degrees and since the income in these two education groups is nearly the same, we can conclude that the low rate of return to a master's degree (discussed in Chapter 6) is not attributable to nonpecuniary returns. The other education coefficients are positive, with *t* values greater than 1, and the overall education pattern is monotonic. The LL.B. dummy is large and significant, indicating that the average income for managers trained as lawyers is about 66 percent higher than that of the average high school graduate in the group, and 50 percent greater than that of those with a B.A. or M.A. The top ability fifth and the top two biography fifths are significant, and each adds to income about the same amount as does possession of a B.A. degree. The father's college variable is significant, and its coefficient is substantially larger than it is in the sample as a whole, a result that may stem from the relative importance of business connections in this occupation.

When dummy variables are included to reflect the 1955 occupations, the magnitudes of the education coefficients are reduced. Those in 1955 occupations other than white-collar, blue-collar, and service do much better in 1969, with the professional group receiving about $4,500, managers $6,500, and sales personnel $5,500 more than those in the blue-collar, white-collar, and service occupations in 1955. Thus, once again, there appears to be more specific training within the occupation, but with people in sales having training that is more readily transferable than that of other outsiders.

Data are available in 1969 to run the regressions separately for owners and managers. For the managerial group, the significant variables are B.A., M.A., Ph.D., LL.B. (as compared with high school), the top ability and biography variables, health, and the

[15]Although the equation is not presented, this result holds also when only the education variables are included.

father's high school and father's college variables. Within the managerial group, education and high ability, along with some type of social connection, are important determinants of earnings.[16]

We present in Appendix L a separate study based on data made available by Lewellen (1968) of earnings of top corporate executives from 1940 to 1963. We find that those with an undergraduate degree earn slightly more than those with graduate training, with both groups earning about 40 to 50 percent more than high school graduates. Since ability is not held constant in these regressions, we reestimated the NBER-TH sample equations without including ability and found that incomes of undergraduate-degree holders and those with graduate work were 30 and 45 percent, respectively, above incomes of high school graduates.[17]

On the other hand, for owners in 1969, only the B.A. and marital-status variables are significant. This is a particularly surprising result, since one would expect skills depending on both education and mental ability to play a major role in determining the success of those who attempt to earn a living on their own.[18] The difference in results between the managerial and owner groups is also surprising, in that one of the roles of an owner is to manage. However, the owner results may be obscured because the income data are "profits," which consist of earnings and return to financial investment, and because one would generally expect capital to be more rapidly available to the more educated, if only because of family wealth. However, our study includes the father's education and biography variables that are intended to reflect this effect, and as noted earlier, people in our sample had access to Veterans Administration loans.

[16]Indeed, those with an M.A. earn about $1,600 a year more than those with a B.A.

[17]These results are surprisingly close in view of the following differences in the data. First, since the Lewellen sample consists only of successful managers, we would expect the effects of education to be underestimated. Second, in Appendix L income is defined as the present discounted value of after-tax compensation, whereas in the NBER-TH sample it is defined as before-tax earnings. From information in Lewellen, it appears that earnings in this occupation understate the return to education for the most successful. Finally, both the time period and average age in the two samples differ, and the results in the Lewellen sample change over time.

[18]Clearly, other types of abilities may be important in determining income, although the other ability factors we tried were not significant.

WHITE-COLLAR, BLUE-COLLAR, AND SERVICE We have combined the blue-collar, white-collar, and service occupations and have included intercept dummies for the latter two.[19] The Ph.D. and M.A. education dummies are excluded, since only one Ph.D. holder and one M.A. holder are in this broad occupational group. The results for 1955, presented in equation 5, Table 8-3, indicate that the significant ability and education coefficients are the B.A., some-college, and top biography variables, with the magnitude of the education coefficients indicating incomes about 10 percent above the income of the average high school graduate. White-collar workers earn about 25 percent less than blue-collar workers; those in the service trades earn about the same amount. Once again, the health and single variables are significant.

By 1969, there was a substantial drop in the number of people in this broad occupation—from 756 to 497.[20] In the equation for 1969, when all the ability and background factors are included, only the B.A. variable is significant, with a coefficient about 10 percent greater than high school earnings. This coefficient is about one-third as large as it is when all the data are analyzed, indicating that much of the income difference attributable to educational attainment arises from entering other occupations. Neither the mathematical-ability nor biography variables follow the expected monotonic pattern, with the only significant variable being the fourth fifth of the mathematical factor. In general, it appears that mental ability plays no role within this occupational group, and the effect of education is not very large. Further, the variables reflecting the other abilities are not significant determinants of earnings in this group.

In 1969, both the white-collar and service occupations pay significantly less than the blue-collar occupations, with average earnings being about 12 and 5 percent lower, respectively, than that of the average blue-collar worker. We have included dummy variables representing the individual's 1955 occupation. The results, not recorded in Table 8-3, indicate that the 1955 professional occupational experience contributes the most to white-collar earnings in 1969. Those who were professionals in 1955 receive about $800 more per year than those who were

---

[19]Farm workers were excluded from our study.

[20]However, since the 1969 occupation was that reported by the individual, the response may be affected by status considerations. In 1955 these occupations were assigned on the basis of job descriptions.

white-collar employees. This result differs from the other case studies in that being in a different occupation in 1955 adds more to 1969 income than being in the same one.

It is interesting to compare the 1955 results with those obtained using the Wolfle-Smith data, because the two samples are very similar in terms of age and calendar time. In the Wolfle-Smith study, the same occupational groups were used, except that the professional, technical, and sales group was combined with the managerial category. Within this broad occupation, there was no noticeable effect of education on income, but mental ability played an important role. This result is remarkably similar to the one we obtain for our professional, technical, and sales group, in which no education variable is significant but the top two mathematical fifths and the top three biography fifths are significant. Again, in our 1955 managerial equation, no education variables are significant, but in this case only the top mathematical-ability fifth is significant. In the other broad occupation group in the Wolfle-Smith study, neither the education nor the ability variables are related to income.

In summary, the results for the two sets of data are very similar qualitatively, thus lending support to our earlier conclusions. It is important to recall, however, that these results are valid only for individuals about 33 years of age. Analysis of NBER-TH data suggests that even within occupations the effects of education are much more important for individuals aged 45 to 50.

9. Education as a Screening Device

In Chapter 1, we hypothesized that a possible role of education is as a credential, license, or screen. By this we mean that entry into some high-paying occupations is not free to all, but generally requires that a person of a *given* skill level also possess a *minimum* level of educational attainment. In this chapter we consider reasons why firms might use education as a screening device, and we develop and implement a test for the existence of screening. If screening based on education occurs, then a person with more education earns more income partly because he is allowed to hold a high-paying job. Concomitantly, some people with low educational attainment who also want and could manage the high-paying jobs are excluded from them. Thus, part of the income differential attributed to education arises from an income redistribution due to restricted entry and not to an increase in skills. This implies that the returns to society from educational programs may be overestimated by conventional measures.[1]

REASONS FOR USING EDUCATION AS A SCREEN   A general assumption made in most research in the human-capital area is that each person is paid a (real) wage rate equal to his marginal product (less any costs for general training). Although this conclusion is valid in a perfectly competitive world, some deviations from competition, such as the existence of costs of obtaining information, may invalidate it. A firm may have knowledge about the marginal productivity of some factors of production; for example, a manager can determine that all models of a particular machine will produce 100 units of out-

---

[1]However, if education is not available for screening, other sorting devices have to be used, but should they be less expensive than education, the social rate of return will be overestimated.

put per hour. People, however, cannot generally be classified into types that produce specific numbers of units of output, because a person's productivity level depends upon a complex set of inherited and acquired skills. Further, not only are individual skills difficult to identify and measure, but various skills also are more useful in some occupations than others. These last two points are illustrated by the occupational regressions using both the Wolfle-Smith and NBER-TH samples. For example, the coefficients on mental ability and education are greater in the managerial and professional occupations than in the white-collar or blue-collar occupations. Moreover, as reported in Chapter 8, these variables, plus measures of family and personal characteristics, explain less than 30 percent of the earnings variance in any of our occupations. Thus, either luck or some other unmeasured variables are very important determinants of earnings in the occupations.

Even though an employer might find it impossible to predict in advance the marginal productivity of any worker in all possible positions in his firm, the competitive outcome could result if a trial-and-error procedure were followed. That is, the firm could pay a piece rate for each position and could allow individuals to fill the positions they desired. There are such jobs as fruit picker and some sales positions that are based on a piecework system, but most occupations are not. Instead, most positions pay a person a fixed amount each hour, day, week, month, or year, and indeed there may be good economic reasons for paying these fixed sums per period. If the output is produced by an assembly line or other team of workers or if there is no directly observable physical output, it may be extremely difficult or costly to measure the output of each worker.[2] But, in any event, firms agree to hire people for at least a limited time and pay them these fixed sums regardless of how well or how poorly they perform. Firms therefore have some incentive to try to hire people whose marginal product will be at least equal to the wage payment. Of course, workers also have an incentive to perform, since firms will try to fire those whose marginal product can be judged to be less than the wage (after training periods are over). Moreover, because of union rules or the expenses associated with hiring and firing, there is often an

---

[2] What, for example, is the marginal product of a bureaucrat?

explicit or implicit agreement by the firm to retain a worker for relatively long periods —subject to his not being grossly incompetent or insubordinate and to cyclical conditions. Finally, when there is a division of labor, it may be very costly to allow a trial-and-error system in which an individual demonstrates how good he is, since an error at one point might cripple a whole production line. Thus, when the labor market is one in which people are paid a fixed period wage and hired for a relatively long time, firms have an incentive to try to sort people by types and levels of skills to find the right person for the right job.

There are many ways in which firms can perform such sorting and matching. One way is to administer tests to measure skill levels, and another is to observe performance on a simpler job. Firms can also use such characteristics as neatness, sex, age, and so forth, as indicators of a person's productivity.[3] Another possible signal is education, upon which this chapter will focus.

Before proceeding with the discussion of education as a signaling or screening device, several comments are in order. Many people have long maintained that the United States has been, and is increasingly becoming, a country concerned with credentials, with education being one of the major credentials (Miller & Reissman, 1969). While economists are predisposed to find a rational explanation for business behavior, as for example in the preceding discussion, the use of education may be dictated partially by snobbery, ignorance, or irrational prejudices. Distinguishing between rational and irrational behavior is important, but since our test for the existence of screening is not based on the assumption of rational firm behavior, we have no way of knowing whether such behavior prevails.

Second, it should be recognized that our screening model does not imply that education is a license absolutely required for a position. If firms, while sorting and matching people, do not get enough applicants with the preferred education to fill positions, some people with less education will be accepted. Moreover, the number of such people accepted as, say, managers will depend on the business demand for managers and the

---

[3]For a lucid discussion of the economics of signaling see Spence (1972). Arrow (1972) has applied this theory to the education market. Both these papers, which appeared after we finished this work, go further than we do by arguing that people decide rationally whether to obtain the signal, that is, to go to college.

supply of college graduates to this occupation, both of which are likely to fluctuate over time. While it is possible in some time period for no one to be accepted whose education is too low, our test for screening requires some people with less than the normal amount of education to be working in the occupations in which education is used as a screening device.

Let us suppose that firms have a number of sorting devices available to match persons and positions. Each sorting method entails direct costs such as salaries of personnel interviewers and indirect costs such as mistakes made on the job. In a more formal sense, the firm should consider as the indirect costs the expected difference between the wage payments and the marginal product of all people who will be hired for a position by a given sorting method.[4] For any particular job, the firm should adopt the sorting method that is cheapest to use, but of course the method may differ for different jobs. Suppose that successful performance in, say, the managerial occupation depends upon the individual's possessing a complex set of talents and skills, including intelligence, leadership, and judgment. Firms might attempt to develop and use tests for these skills in recruiting people for the particular occupation. But the development of tests and the examination of recruits can be expensive and may not be very useful if the appropriate skills are not easily measured and mistakes on the job are expensive.

Suppose, however, that firms either know (from past experience) or believe that educational attainment is correlated with the necessary complex of skills.[5] This does not mean that all college graduates and no high school graduates have the necessary skills, but that a significantly larger percentage of college graduates are so endowed. Thus, to save on hiring costs, firms may decide to use information on educational attainment available at a near-zero cost as a preliminary screening device.[6] Other criteria may also be used in hiring a person, and retention and especially promotion may well depend on performance on the job.

[4]If the firm is risk-averse, it might also consider the variance in the mistakes.

[5]It is likely that in past decades high school was the screening level for high-paying jobs, as indeed it may be now for some types of lower-paying jobs.

[6]See Arrow's recent paper (1972) for a rigorous theoretical treatment of some of the problems involved in hypothesizing that education is used as a filtering device.

The case for screening based on education can be thought of as one of market failure arising from the cost of obtaining knowledge. Some people with whom we have discussed this argument believe that the expenses associated with hiring people (based on, say, a formula predicting who could finish college) would be small enough—given the proportion of earnings differentials we attribute below to screening, and the small return to a college degree—to make it profitable for some rational firms that rely heavily on the high-paying occupations to hire many (or only) high school graduates. Since these firms would have lower costs and higher profits, they would expand, other firms would stop paying a premium to college graduates, and the screen would be eroded.

There are several responses to this argument. First, even if the screening function were to vanish in the long run, its consequences would be observable before then.[7] Second, even when there is a profit to be made by discovering and exploiting available information, the actual discovery may not occur for many years.[8] Thus, the use of education as a screening device is certainly not a proposition which should be rejected out of hand.

As a corroborative bit of evidence, we note that in the last few years so-called diploma mills have become a matter of concern to the educational community. For a fee, these schools grant diplomas by mail without requiring attendance or much, if any, work. Consequently, it is difficult to see how these schools

[7]Analogously, in the long run, with perfect competition, there are no excess profits or rates of return on capital. But in the short run, while capital is being expanded, excess profits could exist and be measured.

[8]As an example, we offer the first part of this study. Two large and rich samples for investigating the rate of return to higher education net of the effect of ability and family background are the Wolfle-Smith and NBER-TH samples, both of which were available in the 1950s. The only prior analysis of the Wolfle-Smith data consists of the original few cross tabulations for males in the Wolfle-Smith report in 1956, with some slight extensions in Denison (1964). (Data were also collected for females but were used for the first time in Chapter 3 of this volume.) We have learned that the data for people of Minnesota were intact and accessible until 1966 at the University of Minnesota, but were permanently or temporarily lost when some operations were moved. The Thorndike-Hagen sample was sitting unused in a basement at Columbia Teachers College for over a decade despite the fact that it is mentioned in Hunt (1963) and was known at least to Lee Hansen. Both samples would have provided data for a series of very useful and important articles in a highly competitive profession. Why did it take up to 15 years for these data sources to be resurrected?

could be adding much to a person's level of skills. Yet the fact that people are willing to pay the fees suggests that the diploma is useful to them, and clearly one possibility is that it is useful in passing an educational screen. It is also worth noting that the uproar over the diploma mills has not come from businesses that feel cheated, but from the more respectable members of the academic community. In addition, casual evidence—such as newspaper advertisements that list a college diploma as a prerequisite—suggests the existence of screening. However, this is far from conclusive, since many jobs may, in fact, require specialized knowledge attainable only in college.[9]

Because these suggestions are not in any way conclusive, it is necessary to construct a more formal test for the existence of screening. Before doing this, we shall define more precisely the concept of screening itself. *Screening based on educational attainment occurs when, because of lack of educational attainment, a person is excluded from an occupation in which he would have a higher marginal product or higher (discounted) earnings.* This definition introduces the idea of different occupations or jobs—a necessary concept because if a person's marginal product and wage rate do not differ across occupations, then he cannot be excluded on the basis of his education from all occupations in which his marginal product would be highest.

The test for screening thus involves comparing the actual and expected fractions of people in different occupations at various education levels. If the actual fraction of people in the high-paying occupations is less than the expected fraction at low levels of education, but not at high ones, and if the occupations are ones in which we might a priori expect some screening, this suggests that screening is, in fact, present.

The initial step in determining the expected distribution is to estimate the potential income that any individual could earn in various occupations. If we then assume that the individual chooses the occupation that yields the highest income, we can estimate the distribution of individuals over occupations that would prevail with free entry. If we assume further that the po-

---

[9]In addition, firms may hire people at low hierarchical positions to sort people for high-level positions. Individuals with low education may be able to master the low-level job but not the high-level one; hence, firms would not be willing to hire them at all.

tential earnings in an occupation are equal to a person's marginal product in that occupation, we can estimate the portion of observed educational earnings differences due to skills produced by education and the portion due to screening.

Assume that there are n occupations and that for each individual, earnings in occupation i (y_i) are determined by a set of characteristics (X) as follows:

$$y_i = X\beta_i + u_i \qquad\qquad i = 1,n \quad (9\text{-}1)$$

where u_i is a random disturbance and β_i is a vector of coefficients for occupation i.[10] If all the variables (X) that influence income in a systematic way are observable, we can estimate the potential earnings of any individual in the ith occupation by substituting his X values in Eq. (9-1). As long as we can ignore the random-disturbance term, our model predicts that all individuals with identical X characteristics will choose the same occupation if occupational choice is based on maximum earnings.[11]

Is it proper to ignore the error term? If the disturbance is interpreted as a chance or luck factor about which the individual has no knowledge when he is making his decision, then we are justified in ignoring it when comparing potential income and occupational choice unless there is differential risk and people are not neutral toward risk. Also, if the disturbance term is the same in all occupations for an individual, then even if he is aware of the disturbance, the rankings of occupations by earnings will not change. In either of these cases, the expected distribution of individuals over occupations can be readily determined simply by evaluating Eq. (9-1) for each occupation for the known X's and selecting the maximum income. In this case,

---

[10]Of course, any individual has only one occupation, but we can estimate a separate equation for each occupation based on the people in that occupation. The problems involved in this method are discussed below.

[11]This result holds only because we assume that occupational choice depends solely on income. If the choice also depends on nonpecuniary factors valued differently by various individuals, then all individuals need not choose the same occupation. This problem is ignored in the following discussion, since it does not present any difficulties as far as our test for screening is concerned. See, however, the section below on risk aversion.

as just noted, all individuals with a given set of characteristics will be in one occupation.[12]

The problem is more complicated if one does not want to ignore the random-disturbance terms or interpret them in this way. If the jth individual is aware of his disturbance terms and if they differ by occupation, the incomes that must be compared are $X_j \beta_i + u_{ij}$ and not just $X_j \beta_i$. Since we do not know the u_{ij}, we cannot determine which occupation a particular person will choose, but by making various assumptions about the distribution of the error terms, we can estimate the probability that a person with a given set of X's will choose a particular occupation. An important question concerning the error terms is whether they are correlated for the jth individual over the various occupations. In some instances, a person will know that his particular job is paying him more than he could expect if working for another firm in the same or a different occupation. For example, a person would know if he married the boss's daughter, or if he had stumbled into a good job offer. Indeed, the theory of information costs in job search would lead to the occupational distribution described by Eq. (9-2).[13] When the errors arise for these types of reasons, we can assume that the disturbances are not correlated over occupations. A much more important explanation for the errors, however, is that there are some X's we have not been able to measure or hold constant. If these X's are important income determinants in different occupations, then the regression errors will be correlated across such occupations. We discuss below the importance of a nonzero covariance of errors across occupations.

Assume for the moment that errors are not correlated over occupations and that the errors in each occupation are normally distributed. Then the *probability* that an individual chooses the mth occupation is given by[14]

$$P_m = \int_0^\infty f_m(z) \prod_{i \neq m} F_i(z) dz \qquad (9\text{-}2)$$

---

[12]All people with a given education level need not be in the same occupation. Other variables in X, in addition to education, can affect occupational choice.

[13]For an analysis of the effects of job-search costs on employment choice, see Holt (1970).

[14]Eq. (9-2) also holds for nonnormal distributions.

where $F_i(z)$ is the cumulative normal density and $f_m(z)$ is the normal density function with mean $\bar{Y}_m$ and variance σ_m^2.[15] Basically, P_m is the sum of all products representing the probability that potential income in the mth occupation takes on a certain value, times the probability that all other potential incomes, given by $\underset{i \neq m}{\Pi} F_i(z)$, are less than this value. Unfortunately, P_m cannot be expressed in a simpler form even if the means and variances of all the incomes are known. However, an approximation to P_m can be obtained by numerical integration. Since an equation analogous to Eq. (9-2) holds for every occupation, we can obtain estimates of the distribution of individuals by occupation.

When there are only two occupations, the problem can be expressed in an alternative form that provides some additional insight. Let the two occupations be 1 and 2, with mean incomes $\bar{Y}_1$ and $\bar{Y}_2$ such that $\bar{Y}_1 < \bar{Y}_2$. We are interested in determining the fraction of people in the population for whom Y_1 will be greater than Y_2. If earnings in both occupations are normally distributed, then $Y_3 = Y_1 - Y_2$ will also be distributed normally. To find the probability that Y_3 is nonnegative, we need to integrate from zero to infinity the normal curve with mean $\bar{Y}_1 - \bar{Y}_2$ and variance $\sigma_1^2 + \sigma_2^2 - 2\sigma_{12}$. In the normal distribution, half the people are found to the right, and half to the left, of the mean. Thus, if the mean of $\bar{Y}_3$ were zero, that is, if $\bar{Y}_1$ equaled $\bar{Y}_2$, then half the people would choose each occupation, but if $\bar{Y}_1$ were less than $\bar{Y}_2$, fewer than half the people would choose 1. For a given variance of Y_3 and mean income in occupation 2, the proportion that will choose occupation 1 will decrease as $\bar{Y}_1$ falls. Also, for a given $\bar{Y}_1 - \bar{Y}_2$, the proportion that will choose 1 will decrease as the variance of Y_3 decreases.

This formulation also is useful in assessing the importance of the assumption of a zero correlation of the errors over occupations. Assuming that the errors in each occupation are indepen-

---

[15] As an estimate of this variance for the mth occupation (σ_m^2), we use the conditional variance based on $\hat{Y}_m - \bar{Y}_m$. The assumption that this variance is the same for people not in m as for those in m when estimating what those not in m would earn in m seems reasonable, since individuals are supposed to be identical on the average after standardizing for all the characteristics used in the regression analysis. We shall later discuss circumstances in which this assumption is not reasonable.

In the calculations, ∞ was replaced by the mean plus three standard deviations.

dent is the same as assuming that σ_{12} is zero. If, however, some variable X_1, whose coefficient is of the same sign in both occupations, is omitted, then σ_{12} will be positive and we shall overestimate the variance of Y_3 and the fraction of people in occupation 1, which has the lower mean earnings. Thus, if we improperly ignore positive values for σ_{12}, we will bias the tests against acceptance of the hypothesis of screening. On the other hand, if σ_{12} is negative because the coefficient of an omitted X is positive in one occupation and negative in another, then the test we use will be biased in favor of accepting screening. Such a bias might arise if, for example, initiative and independence were rewarded in the managerial category while their opposites were rewarded in white-collar or blue-collar jobs. We judge the positive correlation to be more likely. Now let us drop the assumption of only two occupations. When there are many occupations, the problem becomes intractable computationally if we assume that the distributions are not independent. That is, suppose that there is a positive correlation between the u's for an individual across occupations. In this case, the expression for the probability that an individual will choose a given occupation cannot be written in a simplified form such as Eq. (9-2), but must be expressed as a multiple integral, the evaluation of which, although possible numerically, would be very tedious. However, this is not a serious problem, since the independence assumption does not seem unreasonable, and as shown above, it biases the results in the direction of rejecting the screening hypothesis.

Before we present the results of our calculations, two points should be considered. First, if some occupation-education cells are empty, we cannot estimate $\hat{Y}$ in these cells. For example, in the NBER-TH sample there are no individuals with Ph.D.'s in the blue-collar, white-collar, or service occupations. Thus, the calculations given below are based on the assumption that all occupations are open to those at the high school, some-college, and B.A. education levels, but that at the graduate levels—which will not be studied—some occupations are irrelevant. Second, we are assuming that the individual's occupational choice depends only on the monetary income he can expect to earn. If occupational choice depends also on such factors as nonmonetary returns and fringe benefits not included in money income and if these vary across occupations, then our expected distributions will be inaccurate. This problem is discussed in more detail below.

We consider first the results for 1969 for the seven broad occupational groups discussed in Chapter 8. The occupational regressions used for this purpose are those discussed in the preceding chapter, except that they include as an additional independent variable the residual from 1955.[16]

Table 9-1 contains the expected and actual occupational distributions for the high school, some-college, and B.A. education categories, together with the means and standard deviations of the corresponding earnings levels.[17] The entries in column 4 are the differences between the expected and the actual percentage of people in each occupation at each of three educational levels. The most striking result is that for the high school group, the actual fractions of people in the three lowest-paying occupations are considerably greater than the expected fractions. In the some-college group, the same pattern is found, though less pronounced numerically, and for the undergraduate-degree holders, the actual and expected distributions are essentially the same in the lowest-paying occupations.

In general, then, under the assumptions of free entry and income maximization, very few people at any education level included in our sample would choose the blue-collar, white-collar, or service occupations. In practice, however, a substantial fraction (39 percent) of high school graduates, a smaller fraction (17 percent) of the some-college group, and only 4 percent of the B.A. holders enter these occupations. Since the discrepancy between the expected and actual distributions is directly related to education, we conclude tentatively that education itself is being used as a screening device to prevent those with low educational attainment from entering the high-paying occupations.

We find a pattern of differences between expected and actual

---

[16]The reason for including this residual is that it represents "individual effects" (that persist over time) which, if omitted, would invalidate the assumption that errors are independent across occupations.

[17]These means differ slightly from those in Table 4-2, since in these we exclude individuals who in 1969 did not report the educational achievement of their fathers. The standard deviations are calculated *after* removing the effects of all variables included in our equations.

TABLE 9-1 *Expected and actual distributions of individuals, by education and occupation, 1969*

	Number of people (1)	Actual per- centage (2)	Expected percent- age (3)	Col. (3) − col. (2) (4)	Mean income per month (5)	σ income (6)
High school						
Professional	11	1.5	9.5	8.0	$ 960	$ 274
Technical	85	11.5	21.0	9.5	1,220	577
Sales	56	7.6	22.0	14.4	1,120	548
Blue-collar	211	28.6	1.3	−26.3	844	165
Service	50	6.8	1.4	−5.4	824	177
White-collar	24	3.3	.5	−2.8	754	127
Managerial	299	40.6	42.4	1.8	1,485	907
Some college						
Professional	49	5.8	14.8	9.0	1,260	501
Technical	82	9.6	19.1	9.5	1,285	579
Sales	80	9.4	21.8	12.4	1,300	614
Blue-collar	87	10.2	.8	−9.4	882	182
Service	32	3.8	1.2	−2.6	840	228
White-collar	21	2.5	.6	−1.9	785	194
Managerial	501	58.8	39.8	−19.0	1,680	884
B.A.						
Professional	257	25.0	17.8	−7.2	1,412	674
Technical	29	2.8	14.1	11.3	1,370	458
Sales	90	8.8	25.5	16.7	1,490	865
Blue-collar	18	1.8	.9	−.9	950	244
Service	11	1.1	.9	−.2	920	244
White-collar	11	1.1	.4	−.7	840	212
Managerial	610	59.4	38.3	−21.1	1,850	911

fractions within the high-paying occupations that is not as readily explainable. The expected always exceeds the actual percentage by about 10 to 15 percent in the technical and sales occupations, while in the professional occupation the expected percentage is too high in all but the B.A. group. In the managerial occupation the expected percentage falls short of the actual by a substantial amount except at the high school level, where the two percentages are approximately equal. These consistent differences at all education levels might be explained by a combination of risk- and status-related nonmonetary rewards.

A risk-averse individual may select his occupation on the basis of the variance of income as well as the mean. Column 6 of Table 9-1 presents the (conditional) standard error of earnings for each occupation and education level, which we interpret as a measure of risk.[18] Since the standard errors in column 6 are positively correlated with mean earnings in column 5, our estimates of the expected fractions for the low-paying occupations may be too small for any particular education level. But unless high school graduates are more averse to risk, this does not explain the differences between actual and expected fractions that prevail *across* education levels, since occupational standard errors do not differ much by education. If there are differences in risk preference, then our previous estimates of the rate of return to education would be biased upward, because an income-determining characteristic correlated with education would not have been held constant.[19]

The differences in column 4 could also arise because of non-pecuniary rewards that vary by occupation. We would expect status, one form of nonmonetary return, to be highest for the managerial group, in which case our method will underestimate the fraction of people expected in the managerial category. Since the actual does exceed the expected percentage by about 20 percentage points at the some-college and bachelor's-degree levels, the extremely small difference at the high school level can be interpreted as limitations imposed by screening. Further, a much higher percentage (43 percent) of the people in the owner-manager group were owners at the high school level than at other education levels. Owners cannot be screened out of working for themselves if they can raise financial capital, which was available to those in our sample through the Veterans Administration.

The status and risk arguments may help to explain some of the actual occupational choices, but they do not necessarily weaken the evidence supporting the screening hypothesis.

---

[18]The standard error is not the only possible measure of risk. For a discussion see Tobin (1958).

[19]This assumes that education does not make people more willing to bear risk.

There are, however, some other possible objections to the test for screening that must be considered.

First, for the conclusion on screening to be meaningful, those with little education must be capable of working in the high-paying occupations. Clearly, some people with just a high school education are so capable, since over 60 percent of the high school group are employed in the managerial, technical, sales, or professional groups (although very few are in the last named).[20]

Second, the differences between expected and actual distributions reflect any existing entry restrictions or immobilities and any deviations from the principle of income maximization in addition to the type of screening mentioned above. But unless there are reasons to suppose that such factors are correlated with education, they cannot explain or justify the findings in Table 9-1.

Third, the earnings data used in the calculations are for individuals whose average age is 47 years. To the extent that lifetime earnings follow widely diverse patterns in different occupations at different education levels, the use of income from only one year may be an inappropriate indicator of lifetime earnings. However, the relative positions of occupations in terms of mean income and variance are fairly constant from 1955 to 1969, and as shown below, we also find evidence of screening in 1955. Furthermore, screening is hypothesized to take place when individuals first enter the job market, whereas the expected distributions calculated above refer to individuals at the average age of 47. Now, it might be argued that even if there were no initial job screening, many people might enter the white-collar, blue-collar, and service occupations at first simply because they involve well-defined, straightforward jobs and then move into other occupations such as sales and managerial in later years. However, it is hard to believe that such voluntary occupational switches into preferred jobs do not occur by the age of 47.

Fourth, suppose that the blue-collar, white-collar, and service occupations were substantially overrepresented in our sample

[20]Of course, the high school graduates employed in the lower-paying occupations may actually have less ability, but our calculations adjust income for the effects of ability.

at the high school level. Then the actual distributions in the population in these occupations could approximate our estimates even if no screening were practiced. There are two reasons for believing that nonrepresentativeness is not a serious problem. First, if the actual sample distribution differs from that of the population because the sample consists of more able (or otherwise better-endowed) people, then the expected sample distribution will differ in a corresponding manner from the expected population distribution. Second, there is no reason to suspect that the low-paying occupations are oversampled at the high school level, a condition that is required to be consistent with our observed results.

Fifth, there may be nonmonetary rewards other than status that differ by occupation. Suppose, for example, that those in the blue-collar, white-collar, and service occupations prefer (attach a value to) working in these jobs as compared with any others and choose their occupation on the basis of the monetary and nonmonetary returns. Because we have ignored the nonmonetary aspects in the calculations given above,[21] these expected distributions will underestimate the number of people in the blue-collar, white-collar, and service occupations. It would appear, then, that by assigning the appropriate monetary value to the privilege of working in the blue-collar, white-collar, and service occupations, we can explain the discrepancies between the actual and expected distributions in these occupations without relying at all on the screening hypothesis.

There are, however, a number of problems with this explanation. If we assign to all education levels the same nonpecuniary reward that allows us to explain the actual distribution of people at the high school level, we will overestimate the expected number of people in the low-paying occupations at the some-college and B.A. levels. Second, this argument ignores the possibility that those in the high-paying occupations may themselves be receiving a nonmonetary reward due to better working conditions or status differences.

Moreover, it should be recognized that if nonmonetary returns differ by occupation, it must also be argued that the monetary returns to education used in calculating rates of return overstate the total rate of return to education because the

[21]Except for pre-college teachers.

high school category contains the largest proportion of people in the low-paying occupations.

The final, and most important, qualification to the test for screening is that the calculations are based on the assumption that there are no unmeasured occupation-specific skills. Since we can only observe an individual in one occupation, we calculate his expected earnings in other occupations from the mean and variance of people with the same set of measured characteristics, for example, education, ability, and age. Unfortunately, these measured characteristics explain only a small portion of the variance in earnings in the various occupations. Some of the unexplained variance undoubtedly occurs because of luck or other temporary factors, but the rest occurs because some types of skills, talents, and abilities have not been measured. For simplicity, if all these *unmeasured* skills are represented by a single variable X, then in the implementation of the test for screening we are assuming that the mean and variance of X are the same in each occupation.

If X is more important for performance in one occupation than in others, we would expect both the effect of X on earnings to be higher in this occupation and more people with high X values to choose employment in this occupation. But unless X is correlated with education, we will underestimate or overestimate the potential earnings in the various occupations equally at each education level and will obtain an equal "misallocation" of people at all education levels. (We would not call such a misallocation evidence of screening.) Suppose, however, that both X and education are highly rewarded in a particular occupation; then the average error that arises from using the mean earnings of people in an occupation to estimate the potential earnings there of people in other occupations will be correlated with education. For example, suppose that high school graduates who are managers have compensated for their lack of education by being innately more able (in a broad sense not measured here) than other high school graduates and college graduates who are managers. Then, as long as this ability is an important and recompensed characteristic of a manager, we would assign in our calculations too high an earnings figure to high school graduates who were not managers and would improperly conclude that screening existed.

We have no way of determining the importance of the omitted variables, nor do we know of any studies that would be informative. Nevertheless, if the calculations had been performed with census data, mental ability would have been an obvious candidate for the omitted (occupation-specific) variable. Indeed, in our equations we do find that mathematical ability has a bigger effect on earnings than do other variables in the higher-paying occupations. The omitted-variable argument would lead us to expect the fraction of people at each education level in the managerial occupation to be larger the higher the ability level, and to expect high school graduates who were managers to be more able on the average than other high school graduates. Analysis of our sample indicates that both these expectations are borne out, but that the effects are not pronounced. For example, the mean ability level of managers is .47 and .62 for high school and college graduates, respectively, while the corresponding means for all high school and college graduates are .43 and .60.[22] Consequently, to the extent that the omission of other occupation-specific skills follows the same pattern as that of mental ability, the problems caused by their omission may not be serious.

We consider very briefly now the results for 1955. Table 9-2 contains the expected and actual distributions for 1955, calculated in the same manner as were those for 1969.[23] Subject to the same qualifications, these results tend to support the screening hypothesis. The differences between the actual and expected percentages in the blue-collar, white-collar, and service occupations combined are about 40 percent, 12 percent, and 0 percent for the high school, some-college, and B.A. categories, respectively. Thus, as in 1969, people are apparently being screened

---

[22]Those in the top fifth receive a score of .9, and each successive fifth declines by .2.

[23]Two general points should be made concerning the comparability of the two years. First, as mentioned in Chapter 8, the occupational classifications may differ slightly because the 1955 categories were determined by aggregating each individual's description of his job into broad groups, whereas in 1969 each individual selected the broad occupation that included his job. In particular, the distinction between the technical and professional groups may differ considerably between samples. Second, the number of individuals in a particular educational group will differ in 1955 and 1969, since about 7 percent of the sample attained more education in this period, and since there was a 10 percent response variation on education.

TABLE 9-2 *Expected and actual distributions of individuals, by education and occupation, 1955*

	Number of people (1)	Actual percentage (2)	Expected percentage (3)	Col. (3) − col. (2) (4)	Mean income per month (5)	σ income (6)
High school						
Professional	77	9.9	5.1	−4.8	$580	$203
Technical	24	3.1	3.2	.1	469	114
Sales	72	9.2	8.9	−.3	576	191
Blue-collar	293	37.6	5.1	−32.5	439	102
Service	28	3.6	5.0	1.4	418	103
White-collar	91	11.7	1.8	−9.9	382	83
Managerial	195	25.0	67.5	42.5	625	282
Some college						
Professional	156	17.9	3.2	−14.7	603	172
Technical	45	5.2	3.5	−1.7	491	134
Sales	124	14.2	19.6	5.4	629	434
Blue-collar	135	15.5	5.1	−10.4	467	146
Service	18	2.1	5.6	3.5	457	167
White-collar	61	7.0	1.3	−5.7	398	74
Managerial	334	38.3	58.4	20.1	654	279
B.A.						
Professional	488	43.9	3.8	−40.1	576	171
Technical	20	1.8	3.7	1.9	438	124
Sales	139	12.5	10.5	−2.0	597	219
Blue-collar	44	4.0	4.3	−.3	479	113
Service	14	1.3	4.3	3.0	479	118
White-collar	45	4.0	1.4	−2.6	412	85
Managerial	362	33.0	69.6	36.6	664	280

out of the high-paying occupations at the low education levels, but not at the high ones.

The major difference between the two years is that in 1955 the expected number of owner-managers substantially exceeds the actual number at all three education levels; in 1969 the reverse is true except at the high school level (where the expected equals the actual). One possible explanation for the 1955 results is that many managerial positions are eventually filled by individuals who in their early years are in the professional, technical, and sales occupations.

EARNINGS DIFFERENCES DUE TO SCREENING We can use these estimates of expected distributions to determine what income differentials attributable to education would have been in the absence of screening. Such returns are of interest because they represent the extent to which those presented earlier reflect increases in productivity, rather than "discrimination" in the job market. To calculate returns to education, we weight the earnings differences due to education in various occupations by the expected distribution of people across occupations. These returns are upper bounds to those that would actually occur because they do not allow for income levels to adjust as the occupational distributions change.[24]

In Table 9-3 we present the percentages by which earnings in the some-college and B.A. categories exceed high school earnings for the actual and expected distributions for 1955 and 1969. In 1955, the earnings differentials due to education under the assumption of no entry barriers are only about one-half to one-third as large as the actual ones. In 1969, the expected differentials are about one-half as large as the actual ones. This suggests that screening accounts for a substantial portion of educational earnings differentials. The implications of this for rates of return to education are discussed below.

[24]These are unadjusted estimates in that they do not allow for differences in ability, background, age, and so on. Because they are compared with estimates obtained by weighting the same earnings figures by the actual distributions, however, the percentage differences between these two sets of estimates will probably be reasonable approximations to the adjusted income differentials.

TABLE 9-3 *Earnings differentials attributable to education, for actual and expected occupational distributions, 1955 and 1969 (as a percentage of high school income)*

	Actual distribution		Expected distribution	
	1955	*1969*	*1955*	*1969*
Some college	15.2	24.3	5.0	12.5
B.A.	17.4	42.3	7.4	24.3

The private rate of return to education is higher when screening exists than it would be under conditions of free entry into all jobs. This follows directly from the finding just given that expected income differentials are about one-half to one-third as large as the actual ones, and from the fact that the private costs of education are not likely to change much as a result of screening.[25] Moreover, if firms respond to increases in the supply of educated people by raising the screening level, wages in the high-paying occupations need not adjust. This might explain why the private rate of return to college did not change much from 1939 through 1969.

The social rate of return to education, on the other hand, may or may not be higher when there is screening. The reason for this is that, although educational income differentials are again higher under screening, education also serves to provide firms with information that allows them to reduce sorting costs. Hence, if educational screening were not practiced, additional costs would have to be incurred by firms and by society in order to replace this sorting function of education. Calculation of a social return to education when screening is practiced thus requires that we subtract from costs an amount equal to the cost of the best alternative sorting technique. Hence, the social return may be high even if education does not substantially increase individual productivities. Since we have no evidence on the cost of alternative sorting techniques, we do not present estimates of the social rate of return that would prevail in the absence of screening. We conjecture, however, that this rate is substantially lower than the estimates given earlier in this book, in which no attempt was made to account for screening.

While the purpose of this study is to determine the effect of education on income and to examine the cause of this effect, we feel that it is important to explore briefly the implications of screening for educational policy.

We assume that screening has two major effects—it saves

[25]The existence of screening will affect opportunity costs because it will increase the number of individuals in the low-paying occupations, thus depressing average earnings of those at low education levels. Hence, when there are only two levels of education, screening will reduce the average earnings of those with low education, but when different levels of education are used as a screen for different jobs, it is not clear whether wages of high school graduates will increase or decrease as a result of screening.

businesses and society some of the costs of sorting people, and it redistributes income. If society is not in favor of such a redistribution, it can use its tax and transfer schemes to undo the effect of screening on the income distribution. Under this scheme, the private individual return to education would be reduced until it equaled the return that would exist if there were no screening. To the extent that individual demand and social supply of education are based on the rate of return, this would reduce the number of people obtaining higher education.

Since determining the exact taxes and transfers to use would be difficult, other approaches should be considered. The problem of redistribution arises when some qualified individuals are not allowed into occupations because of their education level, a practice that is followed because firms save on costs by using the free information on schooling to sort people. This suggests two possibilities: eliminate the informational content of the screen or charge businesses for the information.

The informational content could be eliminated either by not giving firms access to a person's education level or by giving everyone the same education. The problem with the former is that it is unrealistic. There are several objections to the latter. First, if the education were to be similar in nature and quality to that currently given, it would be a very expensive use of resources to achieve the stated purpose. Second, if everyone had the same education, firms either would base their screening on the quality of the education or would have to spend other resources in obtaining information. In either case the resources spent on education would only garner the skill benefits. Finally, it is likely that not everyone would want the same level of education or have the capacity to achieve it.

Alternatively, businesses could be taxed annually for employing educated people. They would then have to weigh these costs against the extra sorting costs in finding the appropriate people among the less educated. We would expect some additional hirings among the less educated as well as a partial sharing of this tax (through a reduction in income) by the educated. Both these shifts would tend to reduce the return on education toward the one implied by perfect competition.

As noted above, one effect of screening is to reduce sorting costs for individual firms. However, society as a whole pays for these costs by devoting resources to higher education, whereas if there were no screening, alternative sorting policies would have to be developed by firms. Presumably, employers, looking for specific employee characteristics in different occupations, would develop tests to provide information on these characteristics. Alternatively, the testing would not necessarily have to be developed and administered by individual firms, but could be done by one or a few centralized agencies or even by the government itself. This type of sorting procedure would probably be cheaper in terms of resource cost than using the educational system.

Finally, society could consider the redistributive return as equivalent to a monopoly return on a product that it supplied. Under this interpretation, the government could capture the excess return by substantially raising the tuition components of the investment cost. Such a scheme could be accompanied by an educational-loan plan, so that educational opportunity would be made available to all, and those who achieved an education would not receive an excess return due to entry restrictions into certain occupations.

Appendix A: Problems in Measuring Education

In this appendix, we shall compare various possible measures of the quantity and quality of education. Since we are interested only in higher education, we shall restrict our discussion to this area, although much of the material is relevant for the lower grades. Suppose we begin by assuming that the quality of education is known, and that the problem is one of measuring quantity. The quantity of post-high school education could be measured in terms of years, courses taken or passed, number of days, or number of class hours. The ideal measure for our analysis is, of course, the one that exactly determines earnings. That is, if one more day of classes attended adds to income, we should measure education in days (Denison, 1964).

It is useful at this point to consider briefly the possible ways in which education may add to skills, since this may provide guidance in selecting a measure of quantity. Education can develop cognitive and affective skills.[1] Cognitive skills include reasoning and problem-solving ability and knowledge of particular abstract and applied subjects; affective skills include discipline, tolerance, and social poise. Consider the former aspect. Abundant evidence exists that schooling can teach some individuals facts and methods of thinking—two components of knowledge. While some attendance in class is probably necessary for gaining knowledge, much of the learning can be gained through homework and conversations with fellow students. Moreover, except perhaps for vocationally oriented knowledge, there need not be a close connection between knowledge gained and the length of the school year or number of courses,

---

[1] For an interesting discussion of these topics along with some partial tests for the relative importance of the two types of skills, see Gintis (1971).

because the difficulty of courses may be adjusted to the size of the average course load. This suggests that no quantitative measure of schooling is a very accurate gauge of the amount of knowledge gained through schooling. While such studies as Project Talent may eventually develop measures of both pre- and postcollege knowledge, there are no existing bodies of data that include this information as well as income. Consequently, years of schooling does not seem inferior to any of the other measures that have been suggested to represent the increase in cognitive skills.

Next consider the affective impact of education. Education can impart patterns of behavior that are useful in earning a living.[2] While one approach to teaching discipline (broadly defined) is through the carrot-and-stick method, it is not clear how many applications of the carrot-and-stick are necessary to accomplish the desired goal. Further, for attributes such as social polish and tolerance, it would seem that exposure to the college atmosphere is as important as the number of courses attended. Thus, in the absence of more direct measures of the affective output of education, years of schooling would seem to be a not unreasonable proxy.

As far as we know, there have been no empirical tests of the comparative performance of different ways of measuring education, such as those mentioned above. The measure we generally employ is the number of years of college completed; in order to measure the nonlinear effects of education on income, however, we use a zero-one dummy variable for each discrete possibility.[3]

Measuring the quality of education is also difficult. Differences in quality presumably should be interpreted as differences in educational output (received by an individual) for a given quantity of input. In order to implement this definition, educational output must be defined. Most investigators have defined this output in terms of knowledge gained from schooling as measured, for example, by aptitude tests (Bowles, 1970; Astin, 1968). Others have suggested that the major output

---

[2] In addition to creating these patterns, education may sort out people who do not have certain minimum acceptable levels of behavior. For example, those people who are "troublemakers" may be dropped from school.

[3] In some of our samples, vocational schools are included as a separate category.

of education takes the form of better behavior and work habits (Gintis, 1971). Since it is not possible to find direct measures of output in samples with income data, it is common to use inputs as a proxy for outputs. The distinction between cognitive and affective outputs noted above may be important because different types of inputs may be required to produce them. That is, it is possible to find studies that rank colleges and even departments within colleges on the basis of the reputation of the teachers, teacher-student ratios, and facilities per pupil. Such measures may be appropriate for cognitive, but not for affective, output.

The problem is made more complicated because education can be specific or general. An education is specific if it is useful in only a small set of occupations. To the extent that only specific education adds to income, then the quality of this education only should be considered in our analysis. Much specific education is given in graduate schools; hence, for graduate students the quality of the undergraduate school may be irrelevant, while that of the graduate school is important.

A few studies have tried to adjust for the quality of schooling. For example, Weisbrod and Karpoff (1968) found that income earned after 15 years out of college by professionals and managers at American Telephone and Telegraph was related to the quality of their colleges.

Appendix B: Tables to Chapter 3

Definitions of symbols used in the following tables:

Education

H   High school education only

M   Armed Forces and company schools

V   Correspondence, trade, technical, and business schools

1   Less than two years of college

3   More than two but less than four years of college

G   One college degree

GM   Two or more college degrees

4   Nursing

Occupation

1   Professional

2   Semiprofessional

3   Clerical

4   Sales

5   Service

6   Skilled

7   Unskilled

8   Farm

The tenth tenth is the highest ability group; the first is the lowest. The numbers in parentheses immediately below the major entries in the tables are the sample sizes associated with the entries. If there are no individuals in a cell, a footnote so indicates. It should be noted that in the text V and M are always combined and denoted V. The detailed description of these occupational categories is given in Table B-14.

TABLE B-1
*Median salaries
of Illinois,
Minnesota, and
Rochester, N.Y.,
males who had
different
post-high school
education, by
rank in high
school
graduating class
(in dollars)*

	Education after high school graduation			
Percentile rank in high school class (1)	*None** (2)	*Technical schools†* (3)	*Some college‡* (4)	*One college degree or more§* (5)
91–100	$4,600	$5,000	$5,600	$7,100
	(33)	(80)	(106)	(452)
81–90	4,600	4,900	5,400	6,300
	(54)	(82)	(125)	(321)
71–80	4,500	4,900	5,300	6,500
	(51)	(61)	(107)	(201)
61–70	4,600	5,000	5,700	5,700
	(45)	(50)	(85)	(127)
1–60	4,600	4,700	5,300	5,700
	(154)	(195)	(211)	(219)

*H + M
†V
‡1 + 3
§G + GM
NOTE: Sample sizes are given in parentheses beneath the dollar amounts.
SOURCE: Wolfle & Smith (1956).

TABLE B-2					
Median salaries of Minnesota males who had different post-high school education, with intelligence scores held constant (in dollars)			*Education after high school graduation*		
	Intelligence-test score (1)	None* (2)	Technical schools† (3)	Some college‡ (4)	One college degree or more§ (5)
	Highest 30 percent	$4,000	$4,900	$5,300	$6,300
		(9)	(15)	(49)	(171)
	Next 30 percent	4,500	4,400	5,200	6,100
		(33)	(55)	(107)	(197)
	Bottom 40 percent	4,300	4,400	5,100	5,200
		(57)	(106)	(159)	(191)

*H + M
†V
‡1 + 3
§G + GM

NOTE: Sample sizes are given in parentheses beneath the dollar amounts.
SOURCE: Wolfle & Smith (1956).

TABLE B-3					
Median salaries of Rochester, N.Y., males who had different post-high school education, with intelligence scores held constant (in dollars)			*Education after high school graduation*		
	IQ (1)	None* (2)	Technical schools† (3)	Some college‡ (4)	One college degree or more§ (5)
	Over 120	$5,500	$6,100	$6,100	$7,600
		(7)	(17)	(21)	(119)
	Under 120	5,000	5,100	5,700	7,400
		(33)	(68)	(65)	(190)

* H + M
†V
‡1 + 3
§G + GM

NOTE: Sample sizes are given in parentheses beneath the dollar amounts.
SOURCE: Wolfle & Smith (1956).

TABLE B-4 *Average salaries of Minnesota, Rochester, N.Y., and Illinois males, by rank in class and education (in dollars)*

Rank in high school class	Education						
	H	M	V	1	3	G	GM
1	$4,523	$4,800	$4,111	$3,667	$5,400	$8,056	$10,250
	(11)	(5)	(18)	(6)	(10)	(9)	(1)
2	6,354	7,938	4,145	5,938	6,850	7,692	8,400
	(12)	(8)	(19)	(8)	(5)	(13)	(5)
3	4,600	4,250	6,875	8,346	9,023	6,187	5,500
	(10)	(4)	(20)	(13)	(11)	(20)	(3)
4	5,383	4,250	5,019	5,200	6,962	6,667	5,300
	(15)	(4)	(26)	(20)	(13)	(24)	(5)
5	4,909	5,406	4,920	6,583	6,521	5,987	7,844
	(33)	(8)	(56)	(24)	(36)	(40)	(16)
6	6,222	5,437	4,969	5,300	7,231	8,970	7,030
	(36)	(8)	(56)	(35)	(40)	(58)	(25)
7	5,816	5,909	5,120	5,702	5,909	6,836	6,691
	(34)	(11)	(48)	(31)	(44)	(93)	(34)
8	4,964	4,672	5,033	6,065	6,778	8,079	7,278
	(35)	(16)	(61)	(46)	(63)	(139)	(62)
9	5,378	6,200	5,235	5,656	6,326	8,045	8,487
	(49)	(5)	(82)	(53)	(72)	(201)	(120)
10	5,379	6,937	5,437	6,526	5,899	8,571	9,607
	(33)	(4)	(80)	(49)	(57)	(234)	(218)

NOTE: Sample sizes are given in parentheses beneath the dollar amounts. Rank 1 is lowest.
SOURCE: Unpublished data from D. Wolfle.

TABLE B-5 *Average salaries of Minnesota males, by rank in class and education (in dollars)*

Rank in high school class	Education						
	H	M	V	1	3	G	GM
1	$5,125	$4,800	$4,083	$3,667	$5,667	$8,056	$10,250
	(6)	(5)	(12)	(6)	(6)	(9)	(1)
2	4,000	9,250	3,475	6,125	7,313	8,350	11,333
	(3)	(5)	(10)	(4)	(4)	(10)	(3)
3	4,500	5,000	6,385	5,188	8,000	4,893	5,750
	(2)	(1)	(13)	(8)	(5)	(14)	(2)
4	4,900	4,000	4,636	5,083	5,250	5,341	4,000
	(5)	(1)	(11)	(12)	(8)	(11)	(2)
5	4,031	3,500	4,929	5,250	5,867	5,087	9,571
	(8)	(2)	(21)	(8)	(15)	(20)	(7)
6	4,682	5,625	4,103	5,059	7,571	7,150	7,025
	(11)	(4)	(17)	(17)	(14)	(25)	(10)
7	4,800	7,125	4,908	5,583	5,310	5,743	6,176
	(5)	(2)	(19)	(18)	(21)	(36)	(17)
8	4,615	3,594	4,268	5,528	6,464	6,623	7,054
	(13)	(8)	(28)	(27)	(35)	(71)	(28)
9	3,909	7,500	4,481	5,604	6,423	6,535	7,568
	(1)	(1)	(26)	(24)	(42)	(101)	(44)
10	4,606	5,006	5,118	5,033	5,327	7,770	7,522
	(5)	(1)	(19)	(15)	(26)	(87)	(69)

NOTE: Sample sizes are given in parentheses beneath the dollar amounts.
SOURCE: Unpublished data from D. Wolfle.

TABLE B-6 *Average salaries of Minnesota males, by ACE decile and education (in dollars)*

Rank on American College Entrance Examination	Education						
	H	M	V	1	3	G	GM
1	$4,000	$4,750	$4,094	$5,477	$4,521	$6,170	$9,219
	(13)	(1)	(24)	(11)	(12)	(22)	(8)
2	4,600	4,125	4,625	4,778	5,828	5,985	5,125
	(5)	(4)	(20)	(9)	(16)	(33)	(14)
3	4,382	5,792	4,560	5,056	6,803	5,395	6,750
	(17)	(6)	(46)	(36)	(38)	(62)	(25)
4	3,500	5,812	4,687	4,631	7,187	5,911	7,857
	(4)	(4)	(16)	(21)	(16)	(28)	(7)
5	5,256	5,000	4,391	4,870	6,190	7,384	7,431
	(10)	(3)	(23)	(23)	(25)	(58)	(18)
6	4,450	4,500	5,800	6,146	8,000	6,596	7,137
	(5)	(4)	(15)	(12)	(10)	(40)	(20)
7	5,028	14,000	4,809	5,442	6,083	6,672	8,250
	(9)	(2)	(17)	(13)	(24)	(45)	(16)
8	3,667		5,139	7,100	5,750	7,555	6,595
	(3)	*	(9)	(5)	(16)	(32)	(21)
9	4,000	5,000	4,200	6,571	5,250	6,407	7,275
	(1)	(1)	(5)	(7)	(11)	(43)	(20)
10	5,750	2,375	5,000	8,125	4,219	8,238	8,640
	(2)	(2)	(1)	(2)	(8)	(21)	(34)

No observations.

NOTE: Sample sizes are given in parentheses beneath the dollar amounts. Rank 1 is lowest.
SOURCE: Unpublished data from D. Wolfle.

TABLE B-7 *Average salaries of Illinois males, by rank in class and education (in dollars)*

Rank in high school class	Education						
	H	M	V	1	3	G	GM
1	$3,800		$4,167		$5,000		
	(5)	*	(6)	*	(4)	*	*
2	7,139	$5,750	4,889	$5,750	5,000	$5,500	$4,000
	(9)	(3)	(9)	(4)	(1)	(3)	(2)
3	4,625	4,000	7,786	13,400	9,875	9,208	5,000
	(8)	(3)	(7)	(5)	(6)	(6)	(1)
4	5,625	4,333	5,143	5,375	9,700	8,021	6,167
	(10)	(3)	(14)	(8)	(5)	(12)	(3)
5	5,190	6,042	4,891	7,250	6,988	6,887	6,500
	(25)	(6)	(32)	(16)	(21)	(20)	(9)
6	7,152	5,333	5,364	5,533	6,288	10,520	7,000
	(23)	(3)	(33)	(15)	(13)	(25)	(14)
7	4,606	5,639	5,167	5,865	6,162	7,622	7,406
	(26)	(9)	(21)	(13)	(17)	(45)	(16)
8	5,355	5,857	6,538	5,958	7,974	9,257	7,670
	(19)	(7)	(13)	(12)	(19)	(34)	(22)
9	5,333	6,250	5,761	5,250	6,083	9,651	8,294
	(12)	(2)	(22)	(10)	(18)	(43)	(34)
10	5,179		4,117	9,028	6,029	8,953	9,884
	(7)	*	(15)	(9)	(17)	(59)	(54)

*No observations.
NOTE: Sample sizes are given in parentheses beneath the dollar amounts. Rank 1 is lowest.
SOURCE: Unpublished data from D. Wolfle.

TABLE B-8 *Average salaries of Rochester, N.Y. males,* by rank in class and education (in dollars)*

Rank in high school class	Education						
	H	M	V	1	3	G	GM
6	$ 4,000	$5,000	$5,250	$5,500	$7,804	$9,813	$ 7,500
	(2)	(1)	(6)	(3)	(13)	(8)	(1)
7	18,000		5,500		7,292	7,167	4,000
	(3)	†	(8)	†	(6)	(12)	(1)
8	4,000	5,000	5,125	8,321	5,472	9,941	7,083
	(3)	(1)	(20)	(7)	(9)	(34)	(12)
9	6,019	5,500	5,471	5,934	6,354	9,509	9,607
	(26)	(2)	(34)	(19)	(12)	(57)	(42)
10	5,631	7,583	6,000	6,520	6,804	9,105	10,963
	(21)	(3)	(46)	(25)	(14)	(88)	(95)

*The five persons in ranks 1 through 5 have been omitted.
†No observations.
NOTE: Sample sizes are given in parentheses beneath the dollar amounts. Rank 10 is highest.
SOURCE: Unpublished data from D. Wolfle.

TABLE B-9 *Distribution of Minnesota males, by occupation, for various levels of ability and education*

	Occupation				
Education	1	2 + 4	6	3 + 5 + 7 + 8	Number of observations
A. First through fourth ability tenths					
H	.12	.22	.24	.42	50
M + V + 1 + 3	.29	.30	.19	.21	315
G	.71	.22	.01	.05	156
GM	.92	.03	.02	.03	59
B. Fifth through ninth ability tenths					
H	.19	.22	.08	.50	36
M + V + 1 + 3	.39	.31	.13	.17	249
G	.75	.18	.01	.06	233
GM	.91	.07	.00	.02	112
C. Tenth ability tenth					
H	.50	.00	.00	.50	2
M + V + 1 + 3	.13	.53	.00	.33	15
G	.80	.12	.00	.08	25
GM	.89	.11	.00	.00	36

NOTE: "Ability" is based on ACE scores. Rank 1 is lowest.
SOURCE: Unpublished data from D. Wolfle.

TABLE B-10
Average salaries of Minnesota males, by occupation and ability (in dollars)

Rank on American College Entrance Examination	Occupation			
	1	2 + 4	6	3 + 5 + 7 + 8
1–4	$6,212	$5,300	$4,592	$4,071
	(257)	(135)	(86)	(80)
5–9	6,765	6,236	5,022	4,034
	(356)	(129)	(44)	(59)
10	7,890	7,267	5,000	3,972
	(50)	(14)	(1)	(9)

NOTE: Sample sizes are given in parentheses beneath the dollar amounts. Rank 1 is lowest.
SOURCE: Unpublished data from D. Wolfle.

TABLE B-11 *Average salaries of Minnesota females,* by ACE decile and education (in dollars)*

Rank on American College Entrance Examination	Education						
	H	V	1	3	4	G	GM
1	$1,993	$2,302	$3,100	$2,500	$2,268	$2,797	
	(34)	(53)	(10)	(23)	(28)	(16)	†
2	2,206	2,360	2,316	2,580	2,527	3,011	$ 4,000
	(34)	(43)	(19)	(25)	(28)	(22)	(1)
3	2,161	1,894	2,229	2,350	2,206	3,100	3,000
	(14)	(33)	(12)	(25)	(34)	(30)	(2)
4	1,800	2,211	2,250	2,167	2,314	2,755	3,458
	(30)	(58)	(16)	(33)	(39)	(48)	(6)
5	2,300	2,432	2,833	2,200	2,635	3,015	3,679
	(20)	(37)	(12)	(30)	(39)	(34)	(7)
6	1,982	2,239	2,389	2,577	2,437	3,030	4,714
	(14)	(22)	(9)	(13)	(20)	(33)	(7)
7	2,000	2,500	2,292	2,357	2,050	3,062	5,000
	(11)	(11)	(6)	(7)	(15)	(36)	(2)
8	1,750	3,125	1,850	2,250	2,062	3,921	10,000
	(8)	(8)	(10)	(4)	(20)	(19)	(4)
9	2,250	2,179	2,437	2,281	2,434	2,707	3,250
	(3)	(21)	(24)	(8)	(19)	(41)	(2)
10	2,000	2,292	2,350	2,500	2,179	2,711	3,679
	(1)	(6)	(5)	(2)	(7)	(32)	(11)

* The five persons with Armed Forces and company school training have been omitted.

† No observations

NOTE: Sample sizes are given in parentheses below dollar amounts.

SOURCE: Unpublished data from D. Wolfle.

TABLE B-12 *Distribution of Minnesota males by ability (ACE decile), education, and occupation*

ACE decile	Sample	Occupation						
		1	*2*	*3*	*4*	*5*	*6*	*7*
A. High school								
1	15		0.0667	0.2000	0.1333	0.0667	0.3333	0.2000
2	7	0.1429	0.1429		0.1429	0.1429	0.1429	0.2857
3	6	0.3333			0.1667		0.1667	0.3333
4	22	0.1364	0.2273	0.0455		0.0455	0.2273	0.3182
5	14	0.1429	0.2143	0.2857	0.0714			0.2857
6	6	0.3333	0.3333					0.3333
7	12	0.2500	0.1667	0.1667			0.1667	0.2500
8	3						0.3333	0.6667
9	1			1.0000				
10	2	0.5000		0.5000				
B. Vocational and military schools								
1	32	0.1250	0.1875	0.2500	0.1250	0.0313	0.1875	0.0938
2	27	0.2222	0.2963	0.0370	0.0741		0.2963	0.0741
3	24	0.1667	0.2083	0.0417	0.1250	0.0417	0.2917	0.1250
4	57	0.1930	0.2456	0.0526	0.0526	0.1053	0.2632	0.0877
5	28	0.3571	0.2143	0.0357	0.0714	0.0714	0.2143	0.0357
6	24	0.2500	0.2917	0.1250	0.0833		0.1250	0.1250
7	21	0.3333	0.1429	0.0952	0.0952	0.0476	0.2381	0.0476
8	11	0.1818	0.1818	0.0909	0.1818		0.1818	0.0909
9	7	0.2857	0.1429	0.1429	0.1429		0.1429	0.1429
10	4		0.5000			0.2500		0.2500
C. Less than two years of college								
1	13	0.1538	0.3077	0.0769			0.3077	0.1538
2	10	0.4000		0.1000	0.1000	0.1000	0.3000	
3	22	0.1818	0.1818	0.2273	0.0455	0.0455	0.2727	0.0455
4	43	0.3488	0.1860	0.0698	0.0698	0.0465	0.0698	0.1628
5	26	0.3462	0.2308	0.1923	0.0385		0.0769	0.0769
6	13	0.2308	0.3077	0.0769			0.3846	
7	15	0.4000	0.2667			0.0667	0.1333	0.1333
8	6	0.5000			0.1667			0.1667
9	7	0.2857	0.2857	0.1429	0.1429		0.1429	
10	2		0.5000					0.5000

TABLE B-12 *(continued)*

ACE decile	Sample	Occupation 1	2	3	4	5	6	7
D. At least two years of college but no degree								
1	12	0.3333	0.1667		0.2500		0.2500	
2	16	0.3750	0.2500	0.1250			0.2500	
3	18	0.5000	0.2778	0.0556	0.0556	0.0556	0.0556	
4	41	0.5366	0.2683	0.0732	0.0976		0.0244	
5	28	0.5714	0.2500	0.0357	0.0357		0.0714	0.0357
6	11	0.4545		0.0909	0.2727	0.0909		0.0909
7	26	0.5000	0.3077	0.0385	0.0385		0.0769	0.0385
8	18	0.3333	0.3333	0.1667	0.0556		0.1111	
9	11	0.6364	0.1818		0.0909			
10	9	0.2222	0.5556					0.2222
E. One college degree								
1	22	0.5455	0.2273	0.0909	0.1364			
2	35	0.6571	0.1714	0.0571	0.0571			0.0286
3	31	0.6774	0.1935	0.0323	0.0645			
4	70	0.7857	0.0714	0.0143	0.0857		0.0286	0.0143
5	62	0.7419	0.1452	0.0323	0.0484		0.0161	0.0161
6	44	0.7273	0.1591	0.0227		0.0227	0.0455	
7	51	0.7059	0.1765	0.0392	0.0588			0.0196
8	36	0.6667	0.1111		0.1111	0.0556		0.0556
9	45	0.8000	0.1111	0.0222	0.0667			
10	25	0.8000	0.1200	0.0400				0.0400
F. More than one college degree								
1	9	1.0000						
2	15	0.8667			0.0667			
3	8	1.0000						
4	27	0.8889	0.0370	0.0370			0.0370	
5	24	0.7500	0.1250	0.0833	0.0417			
6	24	0.9167	0.0833					
7	19	1.0000						
8	22	1.0000						
9	24	0.8750	0.0833					
10	36	0.8889	0.0833		0.0278			

NOTE: The table gives, for any ability-education cell, the fraction of persons in each occupation. Although occupation 8 (unskilled) is included in the total, the details are omitted because it includes only four persons. Occupation 9 (housewives) is omitted for obvious reasons. Rank 1 is lowest.

TABLE B-13 *Average salaries of Minnesota males, by occupation and ACE decile (in dollars)*

ACE decile	Occupation						
	1	2	3	4	5	6	7
1	$5,856	$4,726	$4,067	$5,231	$4,500	$4,413	$3,917
	(33)	(21)	(15)	(13)	(2)	(23)	(3)
2	5,705	4,958	4,571	6,867	3,500	4,368	5,000
	(50)	(18)	(7)	(6)	(2)	(19)	(1)
3	6,500	5,044	4,000	4,643	4,667	4,844	2,875
	(47)	(17)	(8)	(7)	(3)	(16)	(2)
4	6,281	5,191	4,143	6,484	4,550	4,750	3,175
	(127)	(34)	(14)	(19)	(10)	(28)	(10)
5	6,779	5,810	4,344	5,639	3,500	4,900	3,667
	(95)	(29)	(16)	(9)	(2)	(15)	(6)
6	6,287	8,190	4,250	6,417	3,500	5,773	1,875
	(61)	(21)	(8)	(6)	(2)	(11)	(2)
7	6,997	5,823	4,000	5,250	2,500	4,583	10,250
	(78)	(24)	(7)	(6)	(2)	(12)	(1)
8	7,110	5,861	3,750	5,812	4,750	5,000	3,500
	(57)	(9)	(4)	(8)	(2)	(4)	(2)
9	6,615	6,318	4,500	5,792		4,500	
	(65)	(11)	(4)	(6)	*	(2)	*
10	7,890	7,519	4,000	4,000	750	5,000	4,600
	(50)	(13)	(3)	(1)	(1)	(1)	(5)

*No observations.

NOTE: Sample sizes are given in parentheses beneath the dollar amounts. Rank 1 is lowest.

SOURCE: Unpublished data from D. Wolfle.

TABLE B-14 *Description of occupational categories*

The detailed occupations included in our nine broad occupational categories are listed below.

1. *Professional*

   Humanities and arts

   Natural science

   Psychology

   Social science

   Engineering

   Applied biological science

   Health fields

   Business—managerial II (executives)

   Education (including school administrators)

   Other professions

2. *Semiprofessional-managerial*

   N.e.c.*

   Professional II (except school administrators)

   Semiprofessional

   Managerial I (owners)

   Managerial III (supervisors)

3. *Clerical*

   N.e.c.

   Stenographers, typists, secretaries, receptionists

   Bookkeepers

   Clerks, cashiers

   Mail carriers

   Telephone and telegraph operators

4. *Sales*

   N.e.c.

   Insurance, real estate, stocks and bonds, advertising

   Industrial sales

   Direct consumer sales

   Store sales (department, drug, grocery, etc.)

5. *Service*

   N.e.c.

   Government employees (police, firemen, etc.)

   Cosmeticians (barbers, beauty operators, etc.)

   Food work (waiters, cooks)

   Armed Forces (enlisted)

   Domestic (housekeepers, maids)

   Cleaning (janitors, charwomen, porters)

6. *Skilled*

   N.e.c.

   With supervisory duties, including foremen

   Manual skills (welders, painters, etc.)

   Service, skilled (truck drivers, bus drivers, etc.)

7. *Farm*

   N.e.c.

   Farm owners

   Farm managers

   Farm lessees, all types

8. *Unskilled*

   N.e.c.

   Salaried workers

   Day laborers

9. *Housewife*

   N.e.c.

   Never worked or not given

   Worked or working part time—professional

   Worked part time—clerical

   Worked part time—service, skilled

   Worked full time—clerical

   Worked full time—sales

   Worked full time—service, skilled

* Not elsewhere classified.

Appendix G: Estimation of the Mean Income for the Open-Ended Class

Wolfle's cross tabulations contain the number of people in the following annual-income classes:

1 Less than $1,500

2 $1,500 to $2,500

3 $2,500 to $3,500

4 $3,500 to $4,500

5 $4,500 to $5,500

6 $5,500 to $6,500

7 $6,500 to $8,500

8 $8,500 to $12,000

9 Over $12,000

For the first eight groups, we used the midpoint of the class as the average income in the interval.[1] In order to estimate the mean in the ninth class, we assumed that the upper tail of the income distribution follows the Pareto distribution. The validity of this assumption has been discussed in such studies as Klein (1962). Other investigators of the returns to education have estimated the mean of the open-ended class by using the Pareto distribution (see, for example, Becker, 1964). If the tail of the distribution is Pareto, the mean of the open-ended class $(\overline{Y}_o)$ can be expressed as

$$\overline{Y}_o = Y_L \frac{\alpha}{1 - \alpha}$$

[1]We used $750 for the first class.

where Y_L is the lower limit of the open-ended class (that is, $12,000 in this instance), and where α is estimated from the data. Since the Pareto is relevant only in the upper tail of the income distribution, we made two estimates, assuming first that the tail began in the $4,500 to $5,500 class, and then that it began in the $5,500 to $6,500 interval. For all three states (Illinois, Minnesota, and New York), only the professional, semiprofessional, and sales occupations contained people in the open-ended category.[2] Because of limitations in sample size, one estimate of α was made for all three states combined for each of the sales and semiprofessional occupations. A separate α was estimated in each of the three areas for professionals.

TABLE C-1
Estimated α and mean income of males for the open-ended class

	α_1	$\overline{Y}_1$	α_2	$\overline{Y}_2$
Professional, Minnesota	2.3	$ 21,000	2.2	$22,000
Professional, Illinois	2.2	22,200	1.7	29,000
Professional, Rochester, N.Y.	1.01	1,212,000	1.6	32,000
Semiprofessional	2.4	20,600	2.2	22,000
Sales	2.0	24,000	2.3	21,000

The estimates obtained when the upper tail was assumed to begin with the $4,500 to $5,500 class are denoted by the subscript 1; the estimates based on the data beginning with the $5,500 to $6,500 interval are denoted by the subscript 2. Except for professionals from Rochester, New York, the differences implied by the estimates are not large. In our computations we used the estimates given in the $\overline{Y}_2$ column.

In some calculations, we required the mean income for people in all occupations. We combined the above data to obtain an estimate of $25,000, which was used for all three areas. We also made some computations based on $20,000. The regressions reported in Chapter 3 indicate that the use of $20,000 rather than $25,000 did not result in substantial changes in the coefficients.

[2]In fact, for Rochester, New York, and Illinois nearly all cases were for professionals.

Appendix D: Grouping

The information contained in the cross tabulations in Appendix B can be used to estimate the effects of education and mental ability on income in the following manner. Suppose the equation to be estimated is

$$Y = XB + u \qquad \text{(D-1)}$$

where Y = a vector of wage and salary income

X = a matrix of independent variables, one of which is mental ability A

u = a random-disturbance term

Assume that observations are on individuals and that the data are ordered by the value of A, divided into groups such as tenths, and averaged. These averaged data may then be expressed in terms of a grouping matrix G applied to Eq. (D-1) after ordering by A.[1] That is,

$$GY = GXB + Gu \qquad \text{(D-2)}$$

The elements in GY, GX, and Gu are the mean values in each of the cells. As is well known, efficient estimation of such grouped data requires weighted regressions, with weights equal to the

---

[1] For example, with three groups involving three observations in the first group, and two observations in the others,

$$G = \begin{bmatrix} 1/n_1 & 1/n_1 & 1/n_1 & 0 & 0 & 0 & 0 \\ 0 & 0 & 0 & 1/n_2 & 1/n_2 & 0 & 0 \\ 0 & 0 & 0 & 0 & 0 & 1/n_3 & 1/n_3 \end{bmatrix}$$

square root of the number of observations in each group.[2] We can therefore obtain unbiased estimates of the coefficients in Eq. (D-1) by collapsing the information on the distribution of income (and the other variables) in each ability class into average values for each ability class.

As noted earlier, the data are available cross-classified by ability *and* occupation. The analysis of grouping just discussed also applies to this more detailed breakdown. We have disaggregated our data into occupation-IQ groups for several reasons. First, this disaggregation should increase the efficiency of our estimators by providing more dispersion in the independent variables. Second, this method substantially increases the number of observations to be used in the regressions—from 10 to about 70 for Minnesota males. Because for some purposes we wish to use five education variables and five or more ability variables, the larger sample size is very valuable. Finally, and perhaps most importantly, we wish to examine the effects of education within occupations. By using the data cross-classified by occupation and ability, we can explore some of the questions raised in earlier chapters. Note, however, that if occupation is correlated with the other independent variables as well as income, then dummy variables for occupations must be included as independent variables in order to obtain unbiased estimates of the parameters.

[2] If the grouping variable is correlated with the other X's, then unbiased estimates of the coefficients require the grouping variable to be one of the independent variables.

Appendix E: Response Bias, Test Scores, and Factor-Analysis

The usefulness of any sample depends in part on the accuracy of its information. In this appendix we explore this issue, discuss the construction of the ability measures, and examine the 1969 respondents to determine the extent of "response" and success biases. We begin our discussion by comparing the educational responses of 1955 and 1969. It is useful to compare the accuracy of the two answers as an indication of the accuracy both of the respondent's memory and of the education data. Also, it is of some interest to observe how much additional education was undertaken a decade after the end of World War II.

In each row in Table E-1 we present the distribution of 1969 educational responses (by the 1955 response) for each person who answered the questionnaire in 1969 and for whom we had a 1955 response.[1] Several features of the table are immediately apparent. First, the largest element in each row always occurs in the 1969 category that corresponds to the 1955 answer, that is, on the diagonal. For all but the high school and some-graduate-work groups, over 70 percent of the people gave the same answer in both years.

Second, most of the differences between the 1969 and 1955 answers indicate higher educational achievement in 1969. This difference could be expected for two reasons other than response error. First, in the 1955 sample, those who completed their education before 1946 were counted as having only a high school education, while in 1969 their correct education could be given.[2] Second, individuals could have achieved more education after 1955.

---

[1]Unfortunately, some of the 1955 questionnaires had been misplaced and were not available to us.

[2]This would, of course, be a measurement error in the 1955 data.

TABLE E-1 *Comparison of education reported for 1955 and 1969 by those responding in 1969*

Education as reported in 1955*	Education as reported in 1969					
	High school	Some college	Under-graduate degree	Some graduate work†	Master's‡	Ph.D.§
High school	.57	.34	.078	.005	.007	.003
	842	500	116	8	10	5
Some college	.14	.71	.10	.03	.01	.01
	88	463	65	21	9	7
Undergraduate degree	.01	.05	.79	.09	.05	.01
	15	57	941	107	61	10
Some graduate work†	.00	.09	.19	.40	.24	.08
	0	19	38	81	48	16
Master's‡	.01	.01	.04	.02	.78	.15
	2	4	11	6	242	45
Ph.D.§	.00	.01	.02	.01	.02	.94
	0	1	4	3	6	229

*Excludes those from whom education was not reported in 1955.

†Includes those with some graduate course work but no degree.

‡Includes those with an LL.B. or a J.D. and those with more credit than a master's but less than a Ph.D.

§Includes all graduates from a graduate program of three years or more.

NOTE: The upper entry in each cell is the percentage of the row sum. The lower entry is the number of people in the cell.

To determine what percentage of the greater educational achievement reported in 1969 is due respectively to missing information in 1955, to response errors, and to post-1955 education, we separated the items in each cell to the right of the diagonal into three groups of education completed: prior to 1946, from 1946 through 1955, and after 1955.[3] The results, which are given in Table E-2, indicate quite clearly that the response error is rather small. That is, approximately 80 percent of all individuals counted as high school graduates in 1955 but with higher reported education in 1969 can be accounted for by the lack of

[3] These categories are not quite perfect, since, for example, "some college" completed after 1955 could have been begun before 1955; and since a Ph.D. could be completed after 1955, the 1955 response in Thorndike and Hagen could still be in error.

TABLE E-2
Distribution of those with more education reported in 1969 than in 1955, by date of last year attended school

Education as reported in:		Last year attended school		
1955	*1969*	*Before 1946*	*1946–1955*	*After 1955*
High school	Some college	.828	.078	.094
		414	39	47
	Undergraduate degree	.759	.129	.112
		88	15	13
	Some graduate work	.500	.000	.500
		4	0	4
	Master's	.200	.100	.700
		2	1	7
	Ph.D.	.400	.200	.400
		2	1	2
Some college	Undergraduate degree	.138	.492	.369
		9	32	24
	Some graduate work	.095	.381	.524
		2	8	11
	Master's	.000	.111	.889
		0	1	8
	Ph.D.	.143	.571	.286
		1	4	2
Undergraduate degree	Some graduate work	.000	.477	.523
		0	51	56
	Master's	.016	.098	.885
		1	6	54
	Ph.D.	.000	.200	.800
		0	2	8
Some graduate work	Master's	.000	.229	.771
		0	11	37
	Ph.D.	.000	.063	.938
		0	1	15
Master's	Ph.D.	.000	.089	.911
		0	4	41

pre-1946 data in the 1955 questionnaire.[4] An additional 12 percent had continued their education after 1955 (with most in the some-college group). Thus, only about 6 percent of the 973 individuals who reported a high school education in 1955 made a response error.[5] Much of the extra education in 1969 in the other 1955 groups also represents post-1955 achievement.

After eliminating all cases of post-1955 achievement, we find that the response errors as a percentage of all persons reporting a given education in 1955 are:

- High school   6
- Some college   20
- Undergraduate degree   11
- Some graduate work   35
- Master's   9
- Ph.D.   6

Sizable response errors occur only in the some-college and some-graduate-work cases. In these instances, a large number of people who reported some college or postgraduate work, respectively, in 1955 did not report this education in 1969. We suspect that these people had a minimal amount of college or graduate work and reported it in 1955 either because they anticipated continuing their education or because the short stay was recent enough to remember. By 1969, neither of these reasons would be operative. If this logic is correct, such response bias would not be important either in terms of the reliability of memory or in the computation of regressions, though some recent work by A. Haspel has indicated that slightly higher $\bar{R}^2$s can be obtained by substituting the 1969 response when there is a response error. Overall, we would judge the response error for educational achievement to be very small in the sample.[6]

---

[4]It is also encouraging to note that only 13 people with a 1955 education greater than high school and a 1969 educational level above that of 1955 reported completing their education before 1946. Such early education should not have been reported in the 1955 data.

[5]In calculating the response rate, we have not used the 508 people who had completed their education before World War II because the 1955 questionnaire did not ask for this information.

[6]Some of the differences between the 1955 and 1969 responses reflect coding and punching errors and not a response error.

However, the misclassification arising from the lack of pre-1946 education in the 1955 sample is important, and as shown in Appendix F, this misclassification significantly alters our estimates of the effect of education on income.

It is interesting to note how many people in the sample continued their education after 1955. Table E-2 indicates that 329 people advanced to a new educational plateau after 1955.[7] Of these, 47 achieved some college education, 37 an undergraduate degree, 71 some postgraduate training, 106 an M.A. or equivalent, and 68 a Ph.D. or equivalent.

In the above discussion, and in the analysis in our study, a person is considered to have had a college education if he listed any education other than vocational after high school. The coding of the names of schools was finished after this study was completed. As should be expected, the quality of the schools varies greatly.[8] Not only are there Princetons and Podunks but there are also a few instances of unaccredited schools and several mortuary and embalming colleges. The effect of different institutions on earnings is the subject of a separate study already under way and will be explored here only briefly.

The people in our sample are much more highly educated than veterans of World War II in general. For example, of those veterans aged 25 through 34 in 1952 who had at least a high school diploma, about 60 percent had a high school education only, 20 percent had some college, and 20 percent had at least one college degree.[9] On the other hand, only one-quarter of our sample had a high school education only, one-quarter had some college, and the rest had graduated with at least one degree (see Table E-3.)

We can also consider briefly the accuracy of the earnings and ability data. The individual tests are fairly reliable in the sense that comparable results are obtained when identical or similar tests are administered to the same people after the passage of time. For several reasons, we judge the earnings data reported

---

[7]Of course, others may have continued their education without changing education categories.

[8]By "quality" we mean ranking on the Gourman Index, which, like the College Boards, has a mean of 500 and a standard deviation of 100.

[9]See, for example, Miller (1960, p. 997). Although some of these people would have attained more education by 1955, the differences between those in our sample and World War II veterans in general would still be large. Moreover, no one in our sample had less than a high school diploma.

	High school	Some college	Under-graduate degree	Some graduate work	Master's	Ph.D., LL.B., and M.D.
(1)	.416	.165	.262	.043	.060	.054
(2)	.363	.160	.292	.050	.076	.060
(3)	.232	.256	.288	.054	.092	.076

NOTE: Row 1 is based on the entire 1955 sample except for those for whom there was no information on education.

Row 2 is based on those who responded in 1969, using the education reported in 1955.

Row 3 is based on those who responded in 1969, using the education reported in 1969.

in 1969 and 1955 for those years, respectively, to be reliable—at least in comparison with other studies. First, such items as interest and dividends, which are more irregular in amount and timing, do not have to be recalled. Second, except for six people whose earnings exceeded $100,000 in 1969 and for whom $99,999 was used, we recorded the actual dollar amounts, and do not have to use midpoints of classes or estimate the mean of open-ended classes. As customary in such samples, however, large numbers of people reported such round figures as $10,000. Third, we have already shown that the education response is accurate.

We next consider whether there is a bias in the response rate of the variously educated groups. To do this, we calculate the distribution by education for all those in the 1955 sample and for those who responded in 1969. Since we do not know the pre-1946 education of those who did not respond in 1969, we use the educational information as recorded in 1955 for this comparison.

Comparing the first two rows of Table E-3, it is clear that in 1969 there was a response bias, with the more educated tending to be more likely to respond, though this bias does not appear to be very large. In row 3 we have the actual education of the 1969 respondents. The difference between rows 2 and 3, which reflects primarily the education obtained before 1946 and after 1955, confirms the results in Table E-1.

We have scores on 17 different tests in the sample. A brief description of the tests, taken from Thorndike and Hagen (1959, pp. 9–12), indicates the types of material and abilities covered in each test.[10]

Reading Comprehension   A test of comprehension of rather technical passages. Primarily a measure of verbal comprehension, it also depended somewhat on mechanical experience and on general reasoning ability.

General Information–Navigator   An information or vocabulary test dealing with the terminology of such fields as astronomy, trigonometry, and science. The common factor measured was one of verbal ability, though the content suggests that the test also reflects technical and quantitative academic leanings.

Mathematics   A test of knowledge of advanced arithmetic, algebra in large amount, and trigonometry to some extent. Performance appeared to depend upon a complex of factors, including numerical fluency, verbal comprehension, background in school mathematics, and general reasoning ability. [This is referred to in the text as Mathematics A.]

Arithmetic Reasoning   A test composed of arithmetic word-problems of the sort that are common in the subtests of both scholastic aptitude and school achievement batteries, but cast in terms of planes and aviation. Numerical fluency, general reasoning, and verbal comprehension were the main factors identified in this test. [This is referred to in the text as Mathematics B.]

Numerical Operations I and II   These were two scores, obtained separately for scoring convenience, representing speed and accuracy in simple numerical computations. Test I included addition and multiplication, Test II subtraction and division. These were nearly pure tests of numerical fluency.

Dial and Table Reading   The first part of this test required the subject to determine the numerical value represented by the reading on one of a set of airplane instrument dials, whereas the second part required him to locate entries in rather complex numerical tables. The test involved a number of ability factors, primarily numerical fluency, spatial relations, and perceptual speed.

---

[10]For the convenience of the reader, we also include the description of the information in the biographical items. The pilot and navigator biography keys are *not* included in the factor analysis.

Speed of Identification   This was a speeded test requiring the matching of visual forms. It was a rather pure measure of speed of visual perception.

Spatial Orientation I   This was also a perceptual matching test. In this case, small excerpts from aerial photographs had to be matched against locations in the complete photographs. Perceptual speed was again the chief factor involved.

Spatial Orientation II   This test required the matching of sections of aerial photographs with the locations on aerial maps corresponding to the photographs. Perceptual speed was again a major factor, together with some dependence upon spatial visualizing and on social studies background.

Mechanical Principles   This test was patterned closely after Benett's Mechanical Principles Test, except that the items were cast in an aviation setting. Pictorial situations presented problems involving mechanical concepts and principles. Performance on this test depended primarily on factors of mechanical experience and of visualizing ability, but also to a slight degree on verbal comprehension and general reasoning.

Two-Hand Coordination   This was an individual apparatus test in which the examinee, by manipulating lathe-type controls, had to keep a pointer in contact with an irregularly moving target button. Performance on the test appeared to depend in part upon mechanical experience, in part upon spatial factors, and in part upon psychomotor coordination.

Biographical Data Blank—Pilot Key   The Biographical Data Blank was an assembly of questions about home and family background, school activities and successes, out-of-school activities and hobbies, work experience, and certain other items. The pilot key was an empirical keying of those items that were found to predict success in pilot training. The main factor represented in the pilot key was mechanical experience.

Complex Coordination   This test was an individual apparatus one in which the examinee manipulated stick and rudder controls similar to those encountered in a light airplane. By moving the controls appropriately, he could match patterns of stimulus lights presented to him. His task was to match as many of the stimulus patterns as he could in a limited test period. The test appeared to measure primarily factors of spatial relations and psychomotor coordination.

Rotary Pursuit with Divided Attention   The subject's basic task was to keep a metal stylus resting on a target button that rotated on a 78 rpm phonograph turntable. At the same time, with the other hand, he had to depress the response button corresponding to one of two signal lights. The test appeared to measure psychomotor coordination as well as some type of spatial factor.

Finger Dexterity   This was a peg-turning test in which the subject was required to remove each of a series of square pegs from its hole, rotate it through 180°, and reinsert it. He was scored in terms of the number of pegs turned in a series of brief trials. Common factors measured by the test included psychomotor coordination and precision, visualizing, and possibly a little perceptual speed.

Aiming Stress   Basically, this was a test of hand steadiness, in which the subject had to keep a stylus pointer in a target hole without touching the edges of the hole. Verbal heckling was introduced in some trials to try to add an element of emotional stress. However, the only common factor appearing in this test was one of psychomotor coordination, so it should be thought of primarily as a motor test.

General Information—Pilot   This test was made up of a rather heterogeneous collection of information items selected because they appeared to have validity for predicting success in pilot training. These included items about planes and flying, auto driving, sports, and hobbies. The test appeared quite heterogeneous, and involved factors of pilot interest, verbal comprehension, mechanical experience, and perceptual speed.

Discrimination Reaction Time   This test was an individual test of speed of reaction. The reaction was to a pattern of visual stimuli, and the subject was required to choose the correct one of four response switches. Stimulus patterns were presented one after another, at about four second intervals, and the subject had to respond as rapidly as possible to each as it occurred. The test measured a complex of different factors, including spatial relations, psychomotor precision, perceptual speed, and visualizing.

Biographical Data Blank—Navigator Key   A second empirical key was established for the Biographical Data Blank, weighting those items that were found to predict success in navigator training. The key seemed to provide primarily a measure of extent of mathematical background.

From the titles and the above descriptions, it is clear that many of the tests measure different facets of the same ability. Rather than use all the tests or any arbitrary subset, we decided to use factor analysis to obtain a measure of a few types of ability.[11] The actual factor analysis was conducted by A. Beaton.

The basic idea in factor analysis is that any test contains information on one or more general abilities and a test-specific content. That is,

$$SC = F + u$$

where S is the set of scores; F represents the set of general abilities; and u represents the test-specific components. Using the scores on each of the tests, it is possible to estimate C by imposing certain conditions on u. Estimates of F can then be found from SC where C is the factor loadings. Each F is, of course, just a weighted average of the test scores.[12] In some instances, however, the major weights in each average are attached to items that measure one type of attribute; this attribute is then used to describe the factor.

In the NBER-TH data, the factor loadings for each of four factors are as in Table E-4. Consider the second factor, in which Rotary Pursuit, Two-Hand Coordination, and Complex Coordination all have loadings in excess of .65. In addition, Finger Dexterity, Aiming Stress, Discrimination Reaction Time, and Mechanical Principles have weights in the range .35 to .54. Since the common element in all tests is coordination, we refer to this as the complex-coordination factor. For the fourth factor, the only important tests are Speed of Identification and the two Spatial Orientation tests. Given the description of the Speed of Identification test, it seems clear that the fourth factor measures spatial perception and, perhaps, abstract reasoning.

Both these factors are easy to interpret or identify. The first and third are somewhat more difficult, although the first is clearer. In the first factor, the most important items, with loadings of at least .69, are Numerical Operations, mathematics (Math A), arithmetic reasoning (Math B), and Dial and Table

---

[11]It is, of course, true that the factors are linear combinations of the test scores; thus the same results could be achieved by entering linearly all the scores in our regressions. However, we are interested in studying nonlinear effects of various ability measures and interactions of ability with education, as well as determining which types of ability influence earnings. For these purposes it is appropriate to use the factors.

[12]Because the original test scores are standardized and then manipulated as correlations, all weights have to lie between +1 and −1. The importance of each test in a factor is indicated by the absolute size of its loading coefficient.

TABLE E-4
Factor loadings

Ability test	Factor loadings			
	1	2	3	4
Reading Comprehension	0.4123	0.0700	0.7186	0.0136
Mechanical Principles	0.0149	0.3522	0.7210	0.0247
Dial and Table Reading	0.6990	0.2566	−0.0129	0.3260
Spatial Orientation II	0.0658	0.1042	0.3117	0.6420
Spatial Orientation I	0.2217	0.1379	0.0311	0.7642
Numerical Operations I and II	0.7822	0.0597	−0.2183	0.1030
Speed of Identification	0.0500	0.1008	0.0643	0.7831
General Information– Navigator	0.4842	−0.1199	0.5605	0.1495
General Information– Pilot	−0.0811	0.0329	0.5874	0.3567
Mathematics B	0.7444	−0.0104	0.3514	−0.0717
Mathematics A	0.7464	−0.0469	0.3060	0.5071
Rotary Pursuit	−0.0304	0.6772	0.0453	0.0396
Two-Hand Coordination	−0.0385	0.6870	0.2703	0.0572
Complex Coordination	0.1251	0.7026	0.1877	0.2028
Aiming Stress	−0.0111	0.4128	0.0009	0.0093
Discrimination Reaction Time	0.3891	0.3800	0.0940	0.2636
Finger Dexterity	0.1974	0.5438	−0.1664	0.1253

Reading. All these tests are concerned with mathematics and quantitative skills and primarily measure numerical fluency or speed and accuracy, but not necessarily problem-solving techniques. Secondary but still important weights (.48 to .39) are accorded to General Information–Navigator, Reading Comprehension, and Discrimination Reaction Time. The navigator test does emphasize mathematical material, but the other two items do not. Nevertheless, we treat this as a mathematical-ability test.

In the third factor, Reading Comprehension and Mechanical Principles have loadings in excess of .7. General Information–Pilot and General Information–Navigator have loadings of about .5, while Math B and A have loadings of .35 and .30, and Spatial Orientation II has a loading of .31. In general, these tests encompass verbal ability, mathematical skills, reasoning, *and mechanical principles.* The first three items would be found in standard verbal-IQ tests, but mechanical principles would not. We have chosen to call this third factor IQ.[13] It is important to note, however, that Thorndike has written us to say he believes that the first factor would correlate much more closely with an IQ measure and should be named as such, while the third factor tends toward mechanical principles. The reader should keep this caveat in mind when examining our remarks about the importance of the different types of ability and when comparing the NBER-TH results with those of Wolfle-Smith.

The tests were administered in 1943, whereas the primary earnings data are for 1955 and 1969. If tested in 1955 or 1969, a person would not score the same on each test (or achieve the same standing on a particular factor) because of post-1943 education, general maturation effects, and sampling error from any test. The test-retest validity on the tests used was fairly high, so we can ignore the last possibility. The effect of post-1943 education on particular cognitive skills can be captured by, or impounded in, the overall effect of education on earnings. The available evidence in, for example, Bloom (1964) would indicate that, on the average, maturation effects are small between the ages of 20 to 50, though this may not be true for soldiers in a war. However, in our analysis we only use a dummy variable indicating to which fifth of the distribution a person belonged. Thus, we merely need to assume that a person's relative ability position did not change enough over time to move him to a different fifth.

Finally, it might be asked if the differences in pretest education affect the test scores and, thus, the ability measure. In Chapter 5, we demonstrated that the differences in the quantity and regional quality of pretest education had little or no effect on the scores.

It is of some interest to study the response bias in terms of ability and biography measures.[14] If the 3,743 respondents in 1969 whom we study were a random drawing, there would be

---

[13]Of course, we have constructed the factors to be orthogonal (for the 9,700 people). Although IQ and mathematical tests in general are correlated, it would be possible to factor-analyze such tests to extract several factors.

[14]As discussed below, the biography variable represents a mixture of ability, education, and socioeconomic background factors.

about 748 people in each fifth.[15] The number of 1969 respondents in each fifth for the various factors, which are presented in Table E-5, clearly indicate a tendency for respondents to be in the higher ability ranges. This is very pronounced for the mathematical and IQ factors, but it is also true for the other two.

SUCCESS BIAS We turn now to the question of whether there is a success bias in the 1969 respondents. We assume that success persists over time, so that the successful in 1955 would also be successful in 1969, and vice versa.[16] The success bias implies that those with above-average earnings will be more likely to respond. This bias cannot be measured simply by comparing average income of 1969 nonrespondents with that of the 1969 respondents, since we know from the preceding analysis that the 1969 respondents have, on the average, more education and ability. But the existence of a success bias would imply that the equation for earnings in 1955 for the nonrespondents would be different from the corresponding equation for respondents. The details of these regressions are presented in Appendix F but we briefly summarize the important findings here. Holding various ability measures, education, and time on the job constant, we do not reject the null hypothesis that the respondents and nonrespondents are randomly drawn from the same population. Based on individual coefficients, the only category in which there may be

---

[15]Some of the initial 4,443 observations were eliminated because of missing data. The quintile points were calculated from the distribution of the 9,710 individuals in the 1955 sample.

[16]If Mincer's on-the-job-training argument is correct, the validity of this assumption is weakened, though not invalidated.

TABLE E-5
Number of 1969 respondents in 1955-sample fifths for four ability factors

	Fifths (low to high ability)				
	1	2	3	4	5
Factor 1 (mathematical)	640	688	737	803	875
Factor 2 (complex coordination)	724	724	732	775	788
Factor 3 (IQ)	672	704	738	776	853
Factor 4 (spatial)	694	688	763	780	818
Biography variable	732	732	702	747	830

a bias is the three-year graduate degree (Ph.D., LL.B., and M.D.). In this category, the less successful individuals appear to have responded more.

The tests for success bias and the examination of the effects of measurement error lead to the following conclusions. The 1969 respondents do not contain an overrepresentation of the successful in each of the education-ability cells; hence, leaving aside the advantages of a larger sample size, the 1969 respondents could be used to represent the whole Thorndike group. The error introduced by not using the correct pre-1946 education data, however, has serious consequences for studying the returns to education. Thus, unless the advantages of the larger sample outweigh the disadvantages of the measurement error, we should use the 1969 respondents. For most of our purposes, a sample of about 4,000 is nearly as good as one of 8,000. In addition, we have collected other data in 1969 that are important determinants of income. For these reasons we use the smaller but more accurate sample in our analysis.

Appendix F: Success and Other Biases

In this appendix we will examine the data to determine both if the people who responded in 1969 were more successful than those who did not and if the omission of the pre-1946 education data in the Thorndike files seriously affects our estimates of the effect of education on ability.

We begin our analysis with the data retained by Thorndike. After eliminating instances in which questionnaires were misplaced and in which income was zero, we have about 7,600 usable observations.[1] First, we consider the importance of the success response bias and the omission of the pre-1946 education information.[2]

The test to determine if there is a success bias in the 1969 sample follows. First, we assume that success generally persists over time, so that the successful in 1969 were also successful in 1955. Under the null hypothesis that there is no such bias, both the 1969 respondents and nonrespondents should represent random drawings from the same populations and should yield equations that are not significantly different. Chow's F test can be used to test the proposition that the two samples are drawn from the same population. Alternatively, since our equations use dummy variables to represent various levels of education and ability, our regressions yield an estimate of the mean (and standard deviation of) income in each category. We can use

[1]The zero-income responses represent mostly "no answer," although there are approximately 70 students and 60 unemployed persons. Substantial numbers of medical doctors, managers, and farmers failed to report their income in 1955, although the zero-income respondents within a group were not related to education, except for M.D.'s, for whom there is only one education category.

[2]As noted earlier, the data retained by Thorndike do not contain information on those who terminated post-high school education prior to joining the Army.

standard tests to determine if the mean 1955 incomes in a given cell in the respondent and nonrespondent samples are significantly different. Since for the nonrespondents the only education information available is that retained by Thorndike, we use the 1955 education response for both groups. While this involves using data with a measurement error, there is no reason to expect the error (and the association bias) to be different for the two groups.

In Table F-1, we present an equation relating 1955 income to its determinants for all respondents in 1955, 1969 respondents, and 1969 nonrespondents.[3] The Chow F test for the equation as a whole is less than 1; hence, we cannot reject the null hypothesis that the same relationship holds for the 1969 respondents and nonrespondents. We conclude, therefore, that there is no overall success bias. On the other hand, there may be a suc-

---

[3]We discuss in detail below the interpretation of, and conclusions to be drawn from, the estimates of the coefficients.

TABLE F-1
Equations to test for success bias and importance of pre-1946 education with 1955 income data: monthly income (in dollars)

		Constant	*Some college*	*Undergraduate degree*	*Some graduate work*
(1)	All 1955 respondents*	$336.1	$19.1	$46.2	$ 37.0
		(17.2)	(2.0)	(5.0)	(2.2)
(2)	Nonrespondents in 1969*	333.8	19.0	51.7	15.0
		(11.9)	(1.4)	(3.8)	(.6)
(3)	Respondents in 1969, E as given in 1955	337.3	16.3	38.7	53.5
		(12.3)	(1.2)	(3.1)	(2.5)
(4)	Respondents in 1969, E in 1955 but corrected for pre-1946	290.1	61.9	90.4	103.5
		(10.7)	(4.9)	(6.8)	(4.7)

*Excludes those with zero income or missing questionnaires.
†Includes M.D.'s.

NOTE: In each equation the quintiles for the four factors and the biography variables were included, but the coefficients are not presented. Figures in parentheses are t statistics. Mean incomes for each education cell are calculated by adding the constant and the coefficient on the dummy together and then adjusting for different time-on-the-job coefficients.

cess bias associated with a particular level of education, which we test for by comparing mean incomes in the education groups (holding ability constant). Our tests indicate a significantly lower mean income for three-year-graduate-degree respondents than for nonrespondents, indicating a tendency for the less successful Ph.D.'s and LL.B's to respond. This may be due to successful Ph.D. holders' being difficult to locate because of high mobility.

We turn next to the effect of the measurement error that arises because the questionnaires retained by Thorndike did not contain pre-1946 education.[4] Of course, in the Thorndike-Hagen data, we cannot distinguish between people who completed their post-high school education prior to 1946 and those who were just high school graduates. We can correct the 1955 responses on the basis of the information available in the

[4]The data were available to Thorndike and Hagen in Air Corps records that are no longer extant.

Master's	*Ph.D and LL.B.†*	*M.D.*	*Teacher*	*Time on job*	*Sample size*	*$\bar{R}^2$/S.E.*
$46.2	$106.0	$208.6	$-148.2	$13.8	7,618	.055
(2.9)	(6.0)	(6.1)	(8.2)	(7.7)		279
51.0	155.9	79.7	129.8	13.4	3,873	.035
(1.9)	(5.7)	(1.4)	(4.2)	(5.1)		241
38.5	59.6	302.6	155.9	14.8	3,743	.080
(1.9)	(2.5)	(7.2)	(7.1)	(5.9)		266
87.7	112.0	298.2	-163.4	17.2	3,743	.090
(4.2)	(4.7)	(7.1)	(7.5)	(7.0)		264

1969–1970 reinterview of the 500 people for whom post-high school education was completed before 1946.[5] In equation 4 of Table F-1, we present the results for the 1969 respondents using such an adjusted education measure. The effects of the missing education data are quite large. One not unexpected result is that the $\bar{R}^2$ in equation 4 is higher—by .01—than that in equation 3. Of more interest are changes in the mean-income estimates as presented in Table F-2. The constant term, which is an estimate of the income earned by a high school graduate in the lowest fifth of ability and biography and zero years on the job, declines by $47 per month when the correct education data are used. The average income for the other education groups for zero time on the job is almost unchanged except for a $22 per month increase at the Ph.D. level. However, a more meaningful comparison

[5]It is not possible to use the 1969 education responses directly in estimating the equation for 1955 income because some education was completed after 1955, and for those cases it is not currently possible to determine education obtained prior to 1955.

TABLE F-2
Average monthly earnings in 1955 for the lowest fifth before and after correcting for pre-1946 education (in dollars)

	Pre-1946 education data missing		Pre-1946 education data used	
	Time on job = 0	*Average age = 33*	*Time on job = 0*	*Average age = 33*
High school	337	470	290	444
Some college	353	471	352	490
College degree	375	479	380	501
Some graduate work	386	475	393	506
Master's	375	464	378	481
Ph.D. and LL.B.	380	454	402	488
Teacher with college degree	219	323	217	338
M.D.	683	756	685	786

NOTE: The time-on-the-job variable used in these regressions was based on postwar experience. Many people in the sample who were 33 in 1955 had college training before the war. Thus, we used the following figures for time on the job: high school, nine years; some college, eight; college degree, seven; some graduate work and master's, six; and Ph.D., five. Changing these years by one or two would not affect the comparisons across rows, though it obviously would affect the between-row comparisons. Better estimates are derived in Chapter 5.

SOURCE: Equations 3 and 4, Table F-1.

requires the inclusion of the effect of differences in time on the job due to education. We find that those with a high school education only have an average monthly income of $26 less when we take account of the pre-1946 education, while average earnings rise by about $20 in the other education categories. Because of the decrease in high school incomes and the increase in other incomes, the return to education is greater and more significant (in equation 4, Table F-1) when we use the pre-1946 information. Except for time on the job, the other coefficients are nearly the same.

As indicated in the text, these tests indicate that is is better to base our analysis solely on the people who responded in 1969.

Appendix G: Questionnaires

This appendix contains the questionnaires sent out by Thorndike and Hagen in 1955 and by the NBER in 1969.

Do not write in this column

Survey of Post-War Education and Employment

1. Name _____

2. Present Address _____

3. (a) What schooling have you had since your first separation from the Armed Forces? If none, check here. _____

Place	Major Subject	Dates Attended From	To	Degree, Certificate or Diploma Earned
Example: **University of Maryland**	**Mathematics**	**Sept. 1946**	**June 1950**	**B. A.**

   (b) Have you had any on-the-job training since you were separated from the Armed Forces? Yes _____ No _____ If yes, what kind? _____

   (c) If your schooling or on-the-job training was taken under the GI Bill, under what public law did you receive education benefits? PL 16 (for disabled veterans) _____ PL 346 (other veterans) _____

4. What jobs have you had since your separation from the Armed Forces? (Please list your present job first, the one before that next, etc.)

Title of Job	Dates Starting	Ending	Kind of Business or Industry	Last Monthly Salary (Confidential)
Examples:				
a. **Welder**	**Feb. 1949**	**Present**	**Aircraft Factory**	**$290**
b. **Sheet Metal Worker**	**June 1947**	**Feb. 1949**	**Automobile Factory**	**$270**
1.				
2.				
3.				
4.				
5.				

5. (a) Describe what you do in your present job _____

   (b) How many employees do you supervise? _____

   (c) How well do you think you are performing in your present work? (Check one box)
   Barely Satisfactory ☐   About as well as average ☐   Better than average ☐   Outstandingly Successful ☐

   (d) How well do you like the type of work you are now doing? (Check one box)
   Dislike it ☐   O.K. It's a job ☐   Like it very much ☐   Better than any other ☐

6. Do you have a license or have you passed a certifying examination of any kind? (Example—Master Plumber License, CPA, Licensed Electrician, Teacher, etc.) Yes _____ No _____ If yes, what kind? _____

7. (a) When were you first separated from the Armed Forces? _____
      Month   Year

   (b) Have you had any tours of extended active duty since your first separation from the Armed Forces? (Do not count short tours of duty for reserve training.) Yes _____ No _____ If yes, please give dates:
      1. From _____ to _____
      2. From _____ to _____

8. Did you ever receive vocational counseling through the Veterans Administration? Yes _____ No _____

9. Please give your Social Security number if it is readily available _____

(Use the other side of the blank for any comments that you think will give us a better picture of your post-World War II career.)

Questionnaire sent to all men in survey sample.

A TWENTY-FIVE YEAR FOLLOW-UP SURVEY
Sponsored by the National Bureau of Economic Research, New York, New York

We plan to begin tabulations by July 1, and would appreciate your returning the questionnaire as soon as possible.

Identification

Disregard the small numbers to the right of the boxes; they are for tabulation purposes.

GENERAL INFORMATION

1. What is your age (last birthday)? . . . . years. 6-7

2. Please check X below to indicate your marital status.
   - Single . . . . ☐ 8-1
   - Married . . . . ☐ -2 . . . . 19 . . . . Date 9-10
   - Divorced . . . . ☐ -3
   - Widower . . . . ☐ -4
   - Other . . . . ☐ -5

3. How many children do you have?
   - None . . . . ☐ 15-1
   - 1 . . . . ☐ -2
   - 2 . . . . ☐ -3
   - 3 . . . . ☐ -4
   - 4 . . . . ☐ -5
   - 5 . . . . ☐ -6
   - 6 or more . . . . ☐ -7

4. Do you own your own home or co-operative apartment?
   - Yes—house . . . . ☐ 16-1
   - Yes—apartment . . . . ☐ -2
   - No . . . . ☐ -3

5. What is the state of your general health?
   - Excellent . . . . ☐ 28-1
   - Good . . . . ☐ -2
   - Fair . . . . ☐ -3
   - Poor . . . . ☐ -4

6. What is your approximate height?
   . . . . ft. . . . . inches 29-31

7. What is your approximate weight?
   . . . . lbs. 32-34

EDUCATIONAL BACKGROUND

1. Please fill in the following form. We have included an illustrative set of responses in dark type.

SCHOOLS ATTENDED	DATES ATTENDED	GRADUATED (X if yes)	TYPE OF DEGREE RECEIVED	DATE DEGREE RECEIVED
HIGH SCHOOL				
Locust Valley, Pennsylvania	1938-42	X		
. . . .	. . . .			
. . . .	 17-18	☐ 19-1		
VOCATIONAL TRAINING				
Automotive Repair School	1946	X		
. . . .	. . . .	☐ 20-1		
UNDERGRADUATE COLLEGE OR UNIVERSITY				
U. of Colorado, Boulder	1943, 45-48	X	B.A.	1948
. . . .	. . . .			
. . . .	. . . .	☐ 21-1	. . . . 22-1 -2	 23-24
GRADUATE SCHOOL				
. . . .	. . . .	☐	. . . .	. . . .
. . . .	. . . .	☐ 25-1	. . . .	 26-27

2. Please indicate the highest grade of schooling completed by each of the following family members: (High school graduate would be 12, college graduate 16, etc.):

	Highest Grade Completed	
Wife	. . . . yrs.	61-62
Your father	. . . . yrs.	63-64
Wife's father	. . . . yrs.	65-66

3. Based on your own personal experience, what do you think high schools and colleges should concentrate on? Indicate your choice by circling the appropriate number on the scale from 5 (very great importance) to 1 (very little importance).

	Great importance ◄				► Little importance	
Basic skills (reading, mathematics, etc.)	5	4	3	2	1	67
General knowledge (history, literature, science, etc.)	5	4	3	2	1	68
Career preparation (vocational, professional, etc.)	5	4	3	2	1	69
Activities (school clubs, newspapers, sports, etc.)	5	4	3	2	1	70
Social awareness (current social problems, community action, etc.)	5	4	3	2	1	71

WORK EXPERIENCE, EARNINGS, AND INCOME

1. We would like you to describe your work experience below, starting with your present job. An illustrative set of responses have been included in dark type.

For the earnings information, even very rough estimates will be helpful. If you are self-employed, mark column 1 as self-employed and interpret the salary columns as total income. If you have more than one job, please report salary on main job only.

Card II

	Position Held	Years Worked	Beginning Salary	Ending Salary (Annual full time)	Pension Plan (X if yes)	Average Weekly Hours During Last Year Main Job	Other Jobs
	Foreman	1961-69	$7,500	$9,600	X	42	4
PRESENT JOB	....	....	....	....	☐	....	....
PREVIOUS JOBS	....	....	....	....	☐		
	....	....	....	....	☐	Office Use	
	....	....	....	....	☐	 6-10	
	....	....	....	....	☐	 11-15	
	....	....	....	....	☐	 16-17	
	....	....	....	....	☐	 18-19	
	....	....	....	....	☐	 20-21	
FIRST JOB (Full-time, after finishing school)	....	....	....	....	☐	 22-1	

2. For the past year, please indicate the number of weeks spent doing each of the following:

Card III

	Number of Weeks	
Full-time work (or both full and part-time)...	....	6-7
Part-time work	....	8-9
Paid vacation	....	10-11
Out of work or on layoff	....	12-13
Check ☐ if seasonal		14-1
Unable to work due to illness	....	15-16
Other (please specify)	....	17-18
Total	**52**	

3. Please indicate your total household income for the following years. If your income was unusually high or low in these years, please indicate the average for surrounding years (e.g. 1967-68-69).

YEAR	YOUR TOTAL EARNINGS	TOTAL EARNINGS OF OTHER HOUSEHOLD MEMBERS	OTHER INCOME (dividends, capital gains, etc.)	TOTAL FAMILY INCOME
1968	$..........	$..........	$..........	$..........
1958	$..........	$..........	$..........	$..........
		19-40		
		41-62		

OCCUPATIONAL INFORMATION

A number of job descriptions are listed below. Please indicate X which of these best describes your own job (A), and which best describes the type of job held by your father (B), and your wife's father (C) during most of their working lives.

Card IV

JOB DESCRIPTION	A Your Own Job	B Father's Job	C Wife's Father's Job
Business Proprietor (owner)	☐ 6-1	☐ 8-1	☐ 10-1
Check X if farm operator			
A ☐ 12-1 B ☐ 13-1 C ☐ 14-1			
Managerial (executive, office manager, etc.)	☐ -2	☐ -2	☐ -2
Professional (Doctor, lawyer, accountant, teacher, etc.)			
Self-employed	☐ -3	☐ -3	☐ -3
Salaried	☐ -4	☐ -4	☐ -4
Check X if teacher			
A ☐ 15-1 B ☐ 16-1 C ☐ 17-1			
Technical, (draftsman, surveyor, medical, etc.)	☐ -5	☐ -5	☐ -5
Office worker	☐ -6	☐ -6	☐ -6
Salesman	☐ -7	☐ -7	☐ -7
Service worker	☐ -8	☐ -8	☐ -8
Protective (policeman, etc.)	☐	☐	☐
Retail or wholesale trade	☐	☐	☐
Other	☐	☐	☐
"Blue-collar" employee			
Foreman or supervisor	☐ 7-1	☐ 9-1	☐ 11-1
Skilled	☐ -2	☐ -2	☐ -2
Semi-skilled	☐ -3	☐ -3	☐ -3
Unskilled	☐ -4	☐ -4	☐ -4
Other (please specify)	☐ -5	☐ -5	☐ -5
Don't know	☐ -6	☐ -6	☐ -6
Not applicable	☐ -7	☐ -7	☐ -7

ATTITUDE TOWARD JOB

In this section we want to find out how people feel about their work. Just circle the number that best describes your own evaluation. The numbers constitute a scale ranging from five (highest, best, etc.) to one (lowest, worst, etc.)

	High				Low	
Do you enjoy your work?	5	4	3	2	1	18
Does your work provide a challenge?	5	4	3	2	1	19
Is your work interesting?	5	4	3	2	1	20

For the items listed below, how does your total work experience to date compare with what you expected when you first started? (3 = about as expected)

Financial compensation	5	4	3	2	1	21
Requirement for independent judgment	5	4	3	2	1	22
Responsibility	5	4	3	2	1	23
Prospects for advancement	5	4	3	2	1	24

Below is a list of possible requirements for achieving success in a particular job or profession. Indicate on the scale where your own type of work should be ranked. That is, to what degree does success in your work depend on: (3 = average importance for success)

Your own performance	5	4	3	2	1	25
Having the right connections	5	4	3	2	1	26
Being able to get along with people	5	4	3	2	1	27
Being lucky or unlucky	5	4	3	2	1	28
Having a college diploma	5	4	3	2	1	29
Working hard	5	4	3	2	1	30

ACTIVITIES

In this section we would like you to indicate X the extent of your participation in social, civic, religious, and other similar activities.

1. Which of the following types of groups, if any, do you devote some amount of time to, either as a member, an active participant, or an officer.

	Membership	Active Participant	Leadership	No. of Hours During Last Month
Service organizations (Rotary, Chamber of Commerce, etc.)	☐ 31-1	☐ -2	☐ -3	 32-33
Youth organizations (scouting, Little League, etc.)	☐ 34-1	☐ -2	☐ -3	 35-36
Veterans' organizations	☐ 37-1	☐ -2	☐ -3	 38-39
Professional and trade associations	☐ 40-1	☐ -2	☐ -3	 41-42
Political organizations.	☐ 43-1	☐ -2	☐ -3	 44-45
Educational organizations (PTA, etc.)	☐ 46-1	☐ -2	☐ -4	 47-48
Church or church related organizations				
Religious activity ...	☐ 49-1	☐ -2	☐ -3	 50-51
Educational activity.	☐ 52-1	☐ -2	☐ -3	 53-54
Social action	☐ 55-1	☐ -2	☐ -3	 56-57
Community and social action groups	☐ 58-1	☐ -2	☐ -3	 59-60
Organized volunteer work (hospital, etc.) ...	☐ 61-1	☐ -2	☐ -3	 62-63
Fund raising	☐ 64-1	☐ -2	☐ -3	 65-66
Personal service ...	☐ 67-1	☐ -2	☐ -3	 68-69
Informal helping out— friends, neighbors, or relatives		☐ 70-2		 71-72
Household tasks		☐ 73-2		 74-75

2. Please check X below to indicate your religious preference.

		Card V
Protestant	☐	50-1
Catholic	☐	-2
Jewish	☐	-3
Other	☐	-4
None	☐	-5

3. Please indicate X which of the following best describes your voting habits:

Always vote in local, state, and national elections	☐	51-1
Always vote in national elections, sometimes in state and local ones	☐	-2
Usually vote in national elections	☐	-3
Sometimes vote in national elections	☐	-4
Seldom vote in any elections	☐	-5

4. Do you think of yourself as politically conservative or liberal?

Very conservative	☐	52-1
Moderately conservative	☐	-2
Sometimes conservative, sometimes liberal	☐	-3
Moderately liberal	☐	-4
Very liberal	☐	-5

SOCIAL, ECONOMIC, AND POLITICAL ATTITUDES

In this section we would like you to indicate your attitude about various social and economic problems. Please check X the appropriate box, and feel free to add additional explanation where necessary.

1. Do you feel that young people today have too much freedom, too little, or about the right amount?

Too much ... ☐ 53-3   About right ... ☐ 53-2   Too little ... ☐ 53-1

2. Do you feel that people today are too much concerned with financial security, too little, or what?

Too much ... ☐ 54-3   About right ... ☐ 54-2   Too little ... ☐ 54-1

3. During the past ten years or so, do you think that the pace of racial integration has been too fast, too slow, or about right—considering the welfare of the country as a whole?

Too fast ... ☐ 55-3   About right ... ☐ 55-2   Too slow ... ☐ 55-1

4. Assuming you thought that the financial possibilities were about the same, would you prefer to work for yourself or for somebody else?

Prefer self-employment .... ☐ 56-3
No preference .... ☐ -2
Prefer salaried employment .... ☐ -1

5. Suppose you thought that the financial advantages were, on the average, slightly favorable if you worked for yourself rather than for someone else. Would you then prefer:

Self-employment .... ☐ 57-3
No preference .... ☐ -2
Salaried employment .... ☐ -1

ASSETS, DEBTS, SAVINGS, AND PURCHASES—OPTIONAL

The following questions are of considerable interest to us, but we know that some people regard financial information of this sort as very personal. If that is your feeling, just skip this section. Please return the form, since the other information will be of great help in the study. Once again, let us note that all replies will be treated with the strictest confidence.

1. Please check X to indicate the approximate amount of your household's assets or debts in each of the following categories:

Card V

APPROXIMATE AMOUNT (dollars)

	DON'T HAVE	Under $1,000	$1,000-2,000	$2,000-5,000	$5,000-10,000	$10,000-20,000	$20,000-40,000	$40,000-80,000	Over $80,000
Checking accounts	☐ 6-1	☐ -2	☐ -3	☐ -4	☐ -5	☐ -6	☐ -7	☐ -8	☐ -9
Savings accounts and government savings bonds	☐ 7-1	☐ -2	☐ -3	☐ -4	☐ -5	☐ -6	☐ -7	☐ -8	☐ -9
Common stock, mutual funds, other marketable securities (current market value)	☐ 8-1	☐ -2	☐ -3	☐ -4	☐ -5	☐ -6	☐ -7	☐ -8	☐ -9
Value of your home (what it would currently sell for)	☐ 10-1	☐ -2	☐ -3	☐ -4	☐ -5	☐ -6	☐ -7	☐ -8	☐ -9
Equity in annuities and life insurance (cash surrender value)	☐ 11-1	☐ -2	☐ -3	☐ -4	☐ -5	☐ -6	☐ -7	☐ -8	☐ -9
Equity in pension plan (other than Social Security)	☐ 12-1	☐ -2	☐ -3	☐ -4	☐ -5	☐ -6	☐ -7	☐ -8	☐ -9
Other assets (own business, real estate)	☐ 13-1	☐ -2	☐ -3	☐ -4	☐ -5	☐ -6	☐ -7	☐ -8	☐ -9
Mortgage on your home	☐ 14-1	☐ -2	☐ -3	☐ -4	☐ -5	☐ -6	☐ -7	☐ -8	☐ -9
Other personal debt (installment, etc.)	☐ 15-1	☐ -2	☐ -3	☐ -4	☐ -5	☐ -6	☐ -7	☐ -8	☐ -9

2. Please indicate the approximate **change** (either increase or decrease) over the past 12 months in each of the following:

	Amount of DECREASE				No Change	Amount of INCREASE			
	Over $2,000	$1,000-2,000	$500-1,000	Under $500		Under $500	$500-1,000	$1,000-2,000	Over $2,000
Checking and savings accounts, government bonds	☐ 16-1	☐ -2	☐ -3	☐ -4	☐ -5	☐ -6	☐ -7	☐ -8	☐ -9
Common stock, mutual funds, other marketable securities (count only net new money put in or taken out)	☐ 17-1	☐ -2	☐ -3	☐ -4	☐ -5	☐ -6	☐ -7	☐ -8	☐ -9
Equity in annuities and life insurance (cash surrender value)	☐ 19-1	☐ -2	☐ -3	☐ -4	☐ -5	☐ -6	☐ -7	☐ -8	☐ -9
Equity in pension plan (other than Social Security)	☐ 20-1	☐ -2	☐ -3	☐ -4	☐ -5	☐ -6	☐ -7	☐ -8	☐ -9
Other assets (count only net purchases or sales)	☐ 21-1	☐ -2	☐ -3	☐ -4	☐ -5	☐ -6	☐ -7	☐ -8	☐ -9
Mortgage balance outstanding	☐ 22-1	☐ -2	☐ -3	☐ -4	☐ -5	☐ -6	☐ -7	☐ -8	☐ -9
Installment and other debts outstanding	☐ 23-1	☐ -2	☐ -3	☐ -4	☐ -5	☐ -6	☐ -7	☐ -8	☐ -9

3. During the past 12 months, have you

	Yes	No	If yes, Approximate Cost	
Purchased a home	☐ 24-1	☐ -2	$............	25-29
Purchased a car	☐ 30-1	☐ -2	$............	31-35
Purchased major durables, appliances, or furniture	☐ 36-1	☐ -2	$............	37-41
Made major alterations or repairs on your home	☐ 42-1	☐ -2	$............	43-47

Thank you very much for your cooperation in filling out this questionnaire. If you would like to receive a summary of the results when the study is completed, indicate by X.

☐ Would like summary

Appendix H: Data on Earnings in 1968 and 1958

Before examining the results for 1968, it is necessary to point
out differences between the 1968 and 1969 data. As explained
earlier, the 1969 questionnaire asked for salary only on the
primary job if a person had two or more positions; in the same
questionnaire, total earnings for 1968 were requested. While the
effect on average earnings was shown to be small, this difference in itself would make 1968 a better income concept for
our purposes. There are, however, two offsetting considerations. First, since the questionnaires were mailed late in 1969,
there could be some response error because of the passage of
one year.[1] Second, in 1968 about 200 fewer people than in 1969
answered the earnings question.[2]

Since the results for 1968 are fairly similar to those for 1969,
we present only the important equations and make brief comments. From equations 12 and 13 in Table H-1, we observe that,
as in 1969, all interactions of graduate education with the first
ability factor are positive, but that only the Q_4 coefficient is significant. In equation 11 we find the same general pattern of
results as we did in 1969 except that the middle fifth in ability,
the second and third fifths in biography, and "father attended
college" are no longer significant at the 5 percent level (although
they are almost significant). Health and marital status as
measured in 1969 are quite important, but it should be expected
that the 1968 measurements on these variables would be very
highly correlated with the 1969 measurements.

---

[1] For one study dealing with the size and randomness of response error in a one-
year recall of income, see Summers (1956).

[2] Also, we have used the education as recorded in 1969. There may be a few instances in which people finished their education in 1969, but we doubt that this
is a serious problem.

TABLE H-1 *Regressions for salary, 1958 and 1968: 1969 respondents (in dollars per month)*

	Constant	Some college	Under-graduate degree	Some graduate work	Master's	Ph.D. and LL.B.	Doctor
(1) Y_{58}	$ 676.1	$100.6	$ 97.1	117.1	$ 10.1	$302.7	
	(43.3)	(4.7)	(4.8)	(3.2)	(0.3)	(8.8)	
(2) Y_{58}	493.5	101.6	102.4	121.3	13.2	307.6	
	(4.4)	(4.7)	(4.9)	(3.3)	(0.4)	(8.9)	
(3) Y_{58}	477.7	102.4	108.8	141.1	84.3	221.7	$403.2
	(4.3)	(4.8)	(5.3)	(3.9)	(2.5)	(6.0)	(6.2)
(4) Y_{58}	518.1	64.6	48.2	84.7	24.3	157.8	399.9
	(4.6)	(3.0)	(2.3)	(2.3)	(0.7)	(4.2)	(6.3)
(5) Y_{58}	519.4	65.4	50.1	62.4	1.8	132.2	399.4
	(4.6)	(3.1)	(2.3)	(1.5)	(0.0)	(3.0)	(6.3)
(6) Y_{58}	526.8	65.3	50.5	2.9	−55.9	72.2	399.5
	(4.6)	(3.1)	(2.4)	(0.9)	(0.9)	(1.1)	(6.3)
(7) Y_{58}	532.3	67.0	59.2	97.3	37.1	174.5	396.6
	(4.7)	(3.1)	(2.8)	(2.7)	(1.1)	(4.7)	(6.2)
(8) Y_{68}	1,162.0	248.4	425.3	348.4	283.7	825.5	
	(34.2)	(5.3)	(9.4)	(4.6)	(4.6)	(12.3)	
(9) Y_{68}	1,412.4	246.9	420.0	343.6	280.4	820.3	
	(4.6)	(5.3)	(9.2)	(4.5)	(4.5)	(12.2)	
(10) Y_{68}	1,366.1	250.1	425.1	393.7	503.4	767.5	462.7
	(4.4)	(5.4)	(9.4)	(5.2)	(7.2)	(10.8)	(3.4)
(11) Y_{68}	1,438.9	157.8	272.8	245.6	328.5	599.4	460.9
	(4.7)	(3.4)	(5.8)	(3.2)	(4.6)	(8.3)	(3.4)
(12) Y_{68}	1,442.7	160.5	279.4	188.5	259.5	529.5	456.3
	(4.7)	(3.4)	(5.9)	(2.3)	(3.2)	(6.4)	(3.4)
(13) Y_{68}	1,458.0	161.2	281.3	96.7	169.8	436.3	453.8
	(4.7)	(3.5)	(5.9)	(0.8)	(1.4)	(3.5)	(3.4)
(14) Y_{68}	1,522.1	170.9	320.4	292.4	388.8	661.1	454.3
	(5.0)	(3.7)	(6.9)	(5.9)	(5.5)	(9.3)	(3.4)

NOTE: Figures in parentheses are *t* statistics.

Teacher	Age	Ability				Interaction of graduate education with:			
		Q_2	Q_3	Q_4	Q_5	Q_2	Q_3	Q_4	Q_5
	$5.0								
	(1.6)								
$-209.8	5.5								
(5.5)	(1.8)								
-183.6	5.5	$10.7	$ 3.9	$ 25.3	$ 68.0				
(4.9)	(1.8)	(0.4)	(0.2)	(1.1)	(2.8)				
-182.6	5.5	11.3	5.4	16.8	61.3			$ 49.9	$ 38.5
(4.9)	(1.8)	(0.5)	(0.2)	(0.7)	(2.4)			(1.1)	(0.9)
-184.0	5.4	-0.9	-1.9	10.3	54.7	$100.6	$ 63.4	109.1	97.7
(4.9)	(1.8)	(0.0)	(0.1)	(0.4)	(2.1)	(1.3)	(0.9)	(1.6)	(1.5)
-190.0	5.5								
(5.1)	(1.8)								
	-5.4								
	(0.8)								
-571.4	-4.4								
(6.8)	(0.7)								
-506.0	-3.5	66.3	88.6	135.2	278.1				
(6.1)	(0.5)	(1.2)	(1.7)	(2.6)	(5.4)				
-494.2	-3.5	68.0	92.2	99.1	259.2			174.6	92.6
(5.9)	(0.5)	(1.3)	(1.8)	(1.8)	(4.5)			(1.8)	(1.0)
-496.5	-3.6	50.2	68.8	85.0	244.8	114.4	136.8	267.7	185.8
(5.9)	(0.6)	(0.9)	(1.2)	(1.5)	(4.2)	(0.8)	(1.0)	(2.0)	(1.5)
-534.3	-3.5								
(6.4)	(0.5)								

TABLE H-1 *(continued)*

	Health	Single	Father attended high school	Father attended college	Biography Q_2	Q_3	Q_4	Q_5
(1) Y_{58}								
(2) Y_{58}								
(3) Y_{58}								
(4) Y_{58}	\$ −65.5	\$−133.5	\$ 64.0	\$62.2	\$ −2.3	\$24.3	\$ 67.5	\$100.0
	(5.2)	(2.6)	(3.8)	(3.0)	(0.1)	(1.0)	(2.8)	(4.2)
(5) Y_{58}	−65.2	−134.9	63.6	61.7	−2.1	23.8	67.6	100.0
	(5.2)	(2.6)	(3.8)	(3.0)	(0.1)	(1.0)	(2.8)	(4.2)
(6) Y_{58}	−65.3	−132.9	63.6	61.8	−1.5	24.7	68.3	100.2
	(5.2)	(2.6)	(3.8)	(3.0)	(0.1)	(1.0)	(2.9)	(4.2)
(7) Y_{58}	−66.8	−130.2	66.1	68.1	−0.6	26.8	70.6	107.4
	(5.3)	(2.5)	(3.9)	(3.3)	(0.0)	(1.1)	(3.0)	(4.6)
(8) Y_{68}								
(9) Y_{68}								
(10) Y_{68}								
(11) Y_{68}	−203.9	−282.1	115.8	80.6	97.3	79.7	167.4	198.3
	(7.5)	(2.5)	(3.2)	(1.8)	(1.9)	(1.5)	(3.3)	(3.9)
(12) Y_{68}	−202.7	−287.8	115.2	79.4	97.8	80.3	168.1	198.3
	(7.5)	(2.5)	(3.2)	(1.8)	(1.9)	(1.6)	(3.3)	(3.9)
(13) Y_{68}	−202.4	−286.5	115.4	80.5	98.7	81.5	168.9	197.0
	(7.5)	(2.5)	(3.2)	(1.8)	(1.9)	(1.6)	(3.3)	(3.9)
(14) Y_{68}	−208.8	−266.6	123.9	99.1	102.9	87.9	176.8	226.9
	(7.7)	(2.3)	(3.4)	(2.2)	(2.0)	(1.7)	(3.4)	(4.4)

Ability factor	$\bar{R}^2$/S.E.
	.026
	434
	.027
	434
	.047
	429
Factor 1	.079
	423
Factor 1	.079
	423
Factor 1	.080
	423
	.075
	423
	.049
	959
	.049
	959
	.064
	952
Factor 1	.102
	934
Factor 1	.103
	934
Factor 1	.103
	934
	.094
	938

The returns to education given in Table H-2 are about 15 percent lower than those for 1969 (Table 5-8, page 100); for example, some college is 14 rather than 17 percent and Ph.D. is 52 rather than 61 percent. There is no reason not to expect either the memory lapse or the small increase in nonresponses to affect income at all education levels proportionately. Thus, it might be suspected that the 1969 restriction to primary earnings affected our estimate of the return to education. We doubt that this is the explanation, since (as explained above) when we calculated the income differentials due to education in 1968 and 1969 from

TABLE H-2 Percentage increase in 1958 and 1968 earnings, by education level	*Percentage by which earnings in each education level exceed:*	
	Earnings of average high school graduate	*Earnings of average member of preceding education level*
1958		
Some college	10	10
Undergraduate degree	7	−2
Some graduate work	13	5
Master's	4	−8
Ph.D. and LL.B.	23	19
M.D.	85	
Undergraduate degree (teacher)	−20	
Master's (teacher)	−24	
1968		
Some college	14	14
Undergraduate degree	23	9
Some graduate work	21	−2
Master's	28	6
Ph.D. and LL.B.	52	18
M.D.	91	
Undergraduate degree (teacher)	−20	
Master's (teacher)	−15	

SOURCES: 1958: Incomes of average person in each education class from equation 3, Table H-1; absolute increases from equation 4, Table H-1. Average age, 36. 1968: Incomes of average person in each education class from equation 10, Table H-1; absolute increases from equation 11, Table H-1. Average age, 46.

mean incomes of those with only one job in 1969, the returns were about $1^1/_2$ percent higher.[3] Thus, either because of general economic conditions or because of an age-income profile that is declining more rapidly, high school graduates in this sample did relatively worse in 1969 than in 1968.

The effect of ability is about the same as in 1969. Thus, the co-efficient on Q_5 of $278 is as great as that on the undergraduate-degree variable. When ability is omitted, the biases (although not recorded) are very slightly above the corresponding biases in Table 5-9, (page 103). Thus, the average lower-bound bias is 11 percent compated with 10 percent in 1969.

RETURNS TO EDUCATION IN 1958 For most of the respondents, information was collected in 1969 on 1958 income. The analysis of these data is beset by two problems. First, it is reasonable to expect that the measurement error of income is greater here than in the other years because of the longer lapse in reporting an event that, unlike the first job, would not be of particular psychological importance.[4] Second, the edited information currently available does not readily per-mit us to adjust for education obtained between 1955 and 1958. We have shown that about 19 percent of those in the sample finished their education after 1955 and much of this probably occurred soon after 1955; hence, education variables used in the 1958 analysis contain more measurement error.

Equations 5 and 6 in Table H-1 again indicate that the effect of ability is insignificantly greater at the graduate, compared with the nongraduate, level. When mathematical ability is used in equation 4, only the fifth fifth is significant, and only the fourth and fifth fifths of the biography variable are significant. In other years, the top three fifths of both variables were signifi-cant. In light of the fact that in 1955 the second through fourth fifths added no more than $600 a year to income, it is quite pos-sible that these differences are obscured by improper recall of 1958 information.

Response error also seems involved in the returns to educa-

---

[3]The mean incomes were not calculated holding constant the other determinants of income, but this should not greatly change the ratio of the returns in the two years.

[4]Rogers (1967), however, concluded after an interesting experiment that the re-sponse errors on income earned both five and ten years earlier were no greater than for current income.

tion reported in Table H-2. Holding ability, background, age, and biography constant, the extra income due to education is about 10 and 13 percent for those with some college and some graduate work, 7 and 4 percent for those with undergraduate and master's degrees who are not teachers, and 23 and 85 percent for Ph.D.'s and M.D.'s, respectively. The increase for Ph.D.'s and M.D.'s over 1955 is plausible, since in 1955 they would only recently have graduated and entered on the steepest portion of their age-income profile. But both the magnitude of the very small returns to the undergraduate-degree and master's-degree holders and their drop from 1955 levels seems strange. Before completely disregarding the returns at lower levels, one possible explanation can be offered. The period after 1955 witnessed some extremely large wage-rate increases. Although 1958 was a recession year, the high school graduates who were skilled workers would have had seniority and would probably have had skills needed to be good workers; hence, they would suffer less from layoffs than other union members. The college graduates, on the other hand, may have received smaller wage increases and bonuses because of the profit declines beginning in 1957. All in all, however, we attribute these strange results to measurement error and do not spend more time with the 1958 data.

Appendix I: Characteristics of the Residuals

In this appendix we examine some of the properties of the observed residuals (e_i) as an aid to evaluating our regression results. Any of our equations may be written in matrix form as $y = XB + u$, with the least-squares estimate of B denoted as b. Assuming that $E(b) = B$, then b is also the most efficient (linear unbiased) estimator of B, provided $E(uu') = \sigma^2 I$.[1] If, in addition, the individual elements u_i are normally distributed with a mean zero and variance σ^2, the least-squares estimates of B and σ are also the maximum-likelihood estimates, and the assumptions necessary to use the standard t and F tests (used in Chapter 5) are met. In the following analysis, we use the estimated errors to determine first if $E(uu') = \sigma^2 I$ and then if the u_i's are normally distributed.

In a general sense, heteroscedasticity exists whenever $E(uu') = \Omega \neq \sigma^2 I$. However, there is no reason to suppose in our case the $E(u_i u_j) \neq 0$, since we are considering unrelated individuals in a cross section. Therefore, we test the null hypothesis that $E(u_i^2) = \sigma^2$ for all i, against the alternative $E(u_i^2) = \sigma_i^2$, $\sigma_i^2 \neq \sigma_j^2$. Since we have repeated observations on X_i, that is, a number of people with the same X_i, we could develop an unbiased estimate of σ_i^2 from $e_i' e_i$. Of course, we would have to restrict ourselves to instances in which all the X_i's were the same for a group of people large enough to obtain reliable estimates of σ_i^2. We decided instead to use the entire sample in the following way. We divide the data into four education groups (with all graduate students combined) and five ability groups. Within each of the 20 possible cells, we compute $(\Sigma \bar{e}_i^2 - N_i \bar{e}_i^2)/(N_i - K)$

---

[1] The observed residuals cannot be used to test for bias because a property of least-squares residuals is that $(X'X)^{-1} X'e = 0$.

= 1, where K is the number of parameters in the equations and $\bar{e}$ is the mean error in the cell.[2] We also make this calculation for aggregated education cells, that is, for each education level after summing over all ability groups, and for aggregated ability cells.[3] In Tables I-1 and I-2 we present these estimates for 1955 and 1969.

All cells contain a large number of observations (see section A of both tables). In both 1955 and 1969, only two cells have less

[2] Estimates of $\bar{e}$ are obtained from equation 5 in Table 5-3 (pp. 82–85) and equation 5 in Table 5-7 (pp. 97–99).

[3] Of course, since the *b*s are estimated from the whole sample, the errors in the different cells are not independent; however, following the usual procedure as described in footnote 1 (of this chapter), we shall ignore such nonindependence.

TABLE I-1
Estimated variance by education and ability, 1955

	Ability: Y_{55}					
	Q_1	Q_2	Q_3	Q_4	Q_5	Total
A. Number						
High school	238	221	174	151	102	886
Some college	201	199	193	211	170	974
College degree	128	179	240	270	378	1,195
Some graduate	78	89	130	171	225	688
Total	640	588	737	803	875	3,743
B. Average Error $=\bar{e}$						
High school	15	1	18	−16	1	5
Some college	−13	33	−9	−17	21	2
College degree	18	−10	−6	14	10	5
Some graduate	−27	14	33	26	−19	5
Total	2	9	6	2	4	4
C. Variance (in thousands of dollars) $=(\Sigma e_i^2 - N_i\bar{e}_i^2)/N_i - K)$						
High school	53	53	65	52	51	51
Some college	68	141	71	65	207	98
College degree	57	51	49	109	84	70
Some graduate	43	68	78	74	65	60
Total	52	73	58	74	93	70

than 100 people.[4] The average errors vary widely across cells.[5] Although $\bar{e}$ must be zero (except for rounding) over the whole sample, there is no such restriction within each ability-education cell. However, if any $\bar{e}$ were significantly different from zero, then in our regression analysis we would have found an interaction between the education and ability levels corresponding to the cell.[6] None of the $\bar{e}$s is significantly different

[4] The reader is reminded that education changed between 1955 and 1969 and that there were different numbers of zero-income respondents who were dropped in the two years.

[5] Because of the sample size, we were not able to obtain residuals concurrent with the regression estimates. In the subsequent calculations of the residuals, we rounded all coefficients to one decimal, which created a small average rounding error of \$5.5 and \$-2.4 in 1955 and 1969, respectively.

[6] If the errors are normally and independently distributed, then the sum of T items would be distributed as $N(0,\sigma^2/T)$. A t test can be used to determine if any $\bar{e}$ is significantly different from zero.

| | | Ability: $\log Y_{55}$ | | | | | | Ability: Y_{55} with Q variable | | | |
Q_1	Q_2	Q_3	Q_4	Q_5	Total	Q_1	Q_2	Q_3	Q_4	Q_5	Total
238	221	174	151	102	886	212	200	158	136	970	803
201	199	193	211	170	974	183	177	177	199	159	895
128	179	240	270	378	1,195	123	169	226	253	364	1,135
73	89	130	171	225	688	70	84	122	160	213	649
640	688	737	803	875	3,743	588	630	683	748	833	348
.009	−.010	.025	−.028	.011	.001	21	−5	23	−1	10	10
−.022	.010	−.009	−.020	.011	−.007	−8	24	5	6	22	9
.022	−.011	−.019	.009	.003	−.0004	18	1	−8	31	11	11
−.049	.016	.033	.034	−.024	.003	4	17	31	26	−15	10
−.005	−.001	.003	−.0004	−.002	−.001	10	8	9	17	6	10
.136	.134	.150	.138	.148	.127	36	36	44	53	32	36
.150	.288	.146	.155	.176	.167	51	84	44	40	17	68
.144	.110	.121	.145	.149	.127	42	47	41	89	61	55
.154	.151	.131	.130	.167	.130	43	47	59	64	53	48
.130	.159	.125	.132	.147	.136	38	48	41	59	70	52

TABLE I-2 *Estimated variance by education and ability, 1969*

	Ability: Y_{69}					
	Q_1	Q_2	Q_3	Q_4	Q_5	*Total*
A. Number						
High school	219	214	162	152	92	839
Some college	202	179	208	208	162	959
College degree	124	160	216	263	352	1,115
Some graduate	98	121	161	195	285	860
Total	643	674	747	818	891	3,773
B. Average Error $= \bar{e}_i$						
High school	−47	12	39	15	−31	−2
Some college	65	11	−89	−24	39	−2
College degree	65	−6	66	−58	−24	−2
Some graduate	−125	43	−2	83	11	−2
Total	−2	−2	−2	−2	−2	−2
C. Variance (in ten thousands of dollars) $= (\Sigma e_i^2 - N_i \bar{e}_i^2)/(N_i - K)$						
High school	28	75	95	107	70	64
Some college	131	92	61	76	187	97
College degree	151	83	135	89	101	100
Some graduate	40	73	89	111	124	90
Total	78	73	88	87	112	87

from zero, although in 1969 they are almost significant in several of the graduate-ability cells.[7]

It is instructive to examine the general pattern of the variances. In 1955, the estimated variances of monthly earnings in the 20 cells range from a low of $43,000 to a high of $207,000, with only three estimates above $100,000. In 1969, the low is $280,000 and the high is $1,868,000, with only four lying outside the range of $1,000,000 ± $300,000. A clearer picture of the relationship of the variance to ability and education is obtained by considering the "total" row and columns. In 1955, as ability

---

[7] The dummy variables in equations 13 and 14 in Table 5-7 indicate that the graduate–high-ability cells are significantly different from the graduate—low-ability and the high-ability—other education cells. This result merely confirms what we discussed in the text.

		Ability: $\log Y_{69}$			
Q_1	Q_2	Q_3	Q_4	Q_5	*Total*
219	214	162	152	92	839
202	179	208	208	162	959
124	160	216	263	352	1,115
98	121	161	195	285	860
643	674	747	818	891	3,773
−.069	−.006	−.039	−.002	.137	.003
−.036	−.012	−.023	−.012	.104	.0002
−.087	−.027	.018	−.063	.074	−.002
−.138	−.047	−.026	−.001	.076	−.002
−.073	−.020	−.002	−.024	−.087	.0003
.178	.229	.272	.279	.298	.218
.283	.257	.210	.239	.327	.239
.346	.209	.236	.228	.232	.226
$.168n$	.188	.206	.212	.208	.186
.218	.204	.211	.218	.229	.215

increases from Q_1 to Q_5, the variance increases from \$52,000 to \$93,000, although not monotonically. The highest variance in the education column is for the some-college group, while the lowest is in the highest education group. In 1969, variances increase with ability from \$78,000 to \$1,112,000, while with regard to education only the high school category is far from the average. In general, then, there does appear to be some relationship between the variance and education and ability.

We use a chi-square test developed by Bartlett (1937) to test the null hypothesis that the variances in all the cells are drawn from the same population.[8] The results of this test are given in

[8] The test statistic is $Z = (A \ln v - \Sigma a_i \ln v_i/C$ where $C = 1 + [\Sigma(1/a_i) - 1(A)/3 (k - 1)]$; $A = a_i$; $v = a_i v_i/A$; v_i is the estimated variance in the ith cell; and a_i is the degrees of freedom in the ith cell. Z is distributed approximately as chi-square with $k - 1$ degrees of freedom.

TABLE I-2 (*continued*)

	Q_1	Q_2	Q_3	Q_4	Q_5	*Total*
			Ability: Y_{69} with Q variable			
A. Number						
High school	203	202	141	133	890	768
Some college	179	170	193	195	151	888
College degree	115	150	204	243	328	1,040
Some graduate	910	108	145	177	265	786
Total	588	630	683	748	833	3,482
B. Average Error $= \bar{e}_i$						
High school	-52	31	-19	93	60	0
Some college	58	-38	56	25	38	3
College degree	11	8	94	48	39	-2
Some graduate	-22	-27	-22	55	-13	-3
Total	-2	-4	3	20	-18	0
C. Variance (in ten thousands of dollars) $= (\Sigma e_i^2 - N_i \bar{e}_i^2 / N_i^2 / N_i - K)$						
High school	22	53	34	96	41	42
Some college	70	55	38	45	147	61
College degree	89	74	108	62	70	72
Some graduate	33	58	71	96	105	74
Total	46	53	59	65	85	62

Table I-3. In 1955, the test statistic for all cells is 252. For 19 degrees of freedom, the chi-square value that will be exceeded only 10 percent of the time (if all the variances are *drawn from the same population*) is 27.2.[9] Thus, we reject the null hypothesis of homoscedasticity for all education and ability cells. Further, performing this test for the education cells (after summing over ability) or ability cells (after summing over education) we still reject the hypothesis of homoscedasticity. Indeed, in 1955 (using equation 5 in Table I-3) we accept the null hypothesis only for the Q_1 column entries and the high school and graduate row entries.

In 1969, the test statistic over all cells is 244, which also exceeds the chi-square value at the 10 percent level. We reject

[9]The 5 percent level is 30.1.

the null hypothesis for the education cells and ability cells (after summing over ability and education respectively), although the test statistics are smaller than in 1955. The only instance in which we would accept the null hypothesis is for the variances in the Q_2 column in Table I-2.

Since the equations on which most of our analysis is based do not meet the necessary conditions for our estimates to be most efficient, it is necessary to consider whether alternative, more efficient estimates can be developed or, in other words, whether the heteroscedasticity has important implications for our results.

One common way to eliminate heteroscedasticity is to assume that the proper specifications of the equations is $\ln Y = \delta \ln X + v$, where v is normally distributed. The variances by education and ability for log equations are also given in Tables I-1 and I-2 and are tested for homoscedasticity in Table I-3.[10] In the log equations the results in Table I-3 are more favorable in both 1955 and 1969 to the null hypothesis than in the earlier equations, in that nearly all the test statistics are smaller. Even with these equations, however, we reject the null hypothesis over all cells, since the statistics of 46 and 67 exceed 27.2. In 1955 and 1969, we also reject the null hypothesis when testing the education cells, but we do not reject the null hypothesis when testing the corresponding ability cells in 1969. For the individual ability and education columns and rows, we reject the null hypothesis at the 10 percent level five out of nine times in 1969 and two out of nine times in 1955. Thus, while the log equations improve matters, the variances are still heteroscedastic.

Is it worthwhile, then, to analyze in detail the log equations, which are somewhat better in an efficiency sense than the ones in the text?[11] The following reasoning suggests that such a substitution is not worthwhile. The log equations yield estimates of the difference in log Y arising from education, ability, and so on. When Y varies over individuals, the average of the sum of the changes in the log of Y is not equal to the log of the differences in average income at the two education levels. Thus,

---

[10] Actually, we took only the log of Y. Since nearly all the other variables are zero-one dummies, logs of the independent variables are not necessary.

[11] Since nearly all our variables are entered in dummy-variable form and since we have tested for interactions, our equations with Y are as nonlinear as those with log Y.

TABLE I-3 *Test of equal variance in ability-education cells in 1955 and 1969*

Groups tested	Y_{55} Degrees of freedom	Y_{55} Test statistic	$\ln Y_{55}$ Degrees of freedom	$\ln Y_{55}$ Test statistic	Y_{55} with Q variable Degrees of freedom	Y_{55} with Q variable Test statistic
(1) All cells	19	252	19	67	19	249
(2) Education over all ability	3	108	3	27	3	84
(3) Ability over all education	4	74	4	14	4	88
(4) Education in Q_1	3	5*	3	1*	3	5*
(5) Education in Q_2	3	66	3	48	3	32
(6) Education in Q_3	3	10	3	3*	3	5*
(7) Education in Q_4	3	81	3	1*	3	33
(8) Education in Q_5	3	108	3	2*	3	101
(9) Ability in high school	4	3*	4	1*	4	10
(10) Ability in some college	4	97	4	31	4	121
(11) Ability in undergraduate	4	54	4	7*	4	43
(12) Ability in graduate	4	6*	4	4*	4	4*

*The null hypothesis is not rejected at the 10 percent level.
NOTE: At the 10 percent significance level, the value of the chi-square is 6.3, 7.8, and 27.2 for 3, 4, and 19 degrees of freedom.

we would have to convert the log of the geometric income differences to the arithmetic income differences. This conversion can be done in two ways. First, for every individual we could (1) add on to the log of his actual income the difference in log Y arising from education, (2) take the antilog of the new income, (3) find the difference in income, and (4) average over all individuals in a given beginning education level. Although this method would yield the correct answer for this sample, it need not be suitable for generalization to the census and other samples with different income distributions. Alternatively, if e^v is distributed log normally, it can be shown that $AM = GM exp$ $(-\sigma^2/2)$, where AM and GM are the arithmetic and geometric means of income respectively. Unfortunately, as shown below, the distribution of e^v is not log normal, and we only have es-

Y_{69}		*ln* Y_{69}		Y_{69} *with* Q *variable*	
Degrees of freedom	*Test statistic*	*Degrees of freedom*	*Test statistic*	*Degrees of freedom*	*Test statistic*
19	244	19	46	19	296
3	29	3	15	3	72
4	44	4	3*	4	76
3	141	3	23	3	81
3	2*	3	3*	3	5*
3	39	3	4*	3	70
3	8	3	11	3	31
3	49	3	15	3	47
4	81	4	13	4	85
4	65	4	9	4	92
4	36	4	2*	4	19
4	44	4	3*	4	37

timates of σ_v^2; hence, the variances in our log equations would not give valid estimates of the variance associated with the arithmetic mean.

The results on heteroscedasticity based on equation 5, Table 5-3 (pp. 82–85), and equation 5, Table 5-7 (pp. 97–99), need not hold once we introduce the Q variable (the individual's residual from the other cross section). That is, suppose that there is an unobservable variable P that has a common mean but different variance in each ability-education cell. Assuming that P is a determinant of income in each year, our Q variable will eliminate at least part of its effect and the remaining error could be distributed homoscedastically. Unfortunately, as indicated in Table I-3, we still reject the null hypothesis of homoscedasticity except for four instances in 1969 and 1955.

All these tests suggest the existence of heteroscedasticity, and indeed we can explain to some extent why it is found in our sample. In Chapter 8 we presented estimates of the variance of the *e*s by occupation and education level. These variances differ by occupation and, to some extent, by education. But education and occupation, as well as IQ and occupation, are correlated. This suggests that we could reduce heteroscedasticity by including occupational dummies, but the inclusion of such variables will yield education coefficients inappropriate for the (direct) determination of the return to education.[12] Now let us turn to the implications of heteroscedasticity. As noted earlier, the existence of heteroscedasticity means that our estimating technique is inefficient. Since we are using regression analysis to accomplish a form of variance analysis, however, the inefficiency aspect is not as severe as usual. That is, in variance analysis, we are interested in the means of items in various cells. Suppose we only had two education classes; then even if the variance in the two classes were different, we would calculate the mean income in each cell as $(1/N) \Sigma Y_i$. Our regression analysis with dummy variables makes exactly the same calculation for mean income or differences in means except, of course, that we eliminate the effects of ability (and other) variables. Since these variables are not orthogonal to the education variables and since the effects of ability need not be the same in each education level, our estimates of mean income need not be efficient.

We did experiment with a generalized least-squares estimate to eliminate heteroscedasticity. For equation 5 in Tables 5-3 and 5-7, we weighted each observation by the reciprocal of the standard error of the ability-education cell in which the observation falls. As reported in Chapter 5, the 1955 coefficients are about the same, while their standard errors are smaller. In 1969, some of the coefficients changed slightly, but our basic conclusions remained unaltered.

The second general question to consider is whether the distribution of the errors is normal. To examine this question, we arrayed the errors monotonically and tabulated the number of

---

[12]See Chapter 2 for a discussion of this proposition.

residuals that fell within successive intervals of length $\sigma/2$.[13] The results for various equations are presented in Table I-4 for 1969 for the various ability and education cells. In both 1969 and 1955 the log equation has a median and mode less than zero and a large right-hand tail. In addition, the equation without Q has its median and mode less than zero. The right-hand tails reflect the fact that none of our equations will predict the earnings of those whose income is over $40,000. We also studied the distribution by ability and by education of those individuals whose residual exceeded 3.5σ. Generally, the educational and ability distribution of those individuals is about the same as in the sample; hence, being very successful is not a function of education or mental ability. Moreover, as shown in Table I-4, the tail and skewness can be found in each ability and education cell.

Finally, the information in Tables I-1 and I-2 can be used, albeit in a nonrigorous fashion, to discuss one other problem. There is some evidence in the literature that the income distribution (above some minimum income level) follows a Pareto distribution in which the *expected* value of the variance of income is infinite.[14] Even if the distribution of income is Pareto, the distribution of the error term, u, could be normal. However, if the distribution of the error term is also Pareto, then ordinary least squares is not an efficient estimating technique.

We believe that the above evidence strongly suggests that the error term is not distributed as Pareto. That is, if we took random drawings of the us and computed σ^2, we should not find the estimates converging to a single value as we increased our sample size, nor should we find the σ^2s of a given set of drawings following a particular pattern. As we increase the sample sizes by summing over the rows and columns in Tables I-1 and I-2, however, the estimates do converge. Moreover, the differences that remain follow the same pattern in 1955 and 1969 and are explainable by the occupational variations.

---

[13] We calculated the percentages in intervals of $0 \pm (k/2\sigma)$ and $^1/_4 \pm (k\sigma/2)$, where $k = 0, 1, \ldots$.

[14] Of course, in any finite sample, the formula for a variance could be used to obtain finite value.

TABLE I-4 *Distribution of errors for* Y_{55} *and* Y_{69}

	Ph.D.	Master's	Some graduate work	B.A.	Some college	No college	Q_5	Q_4	Q_3	Q_2	Q_1
Number in cell											
log Y_{55}	293	360	206	1,115	959	839	891	818	747	674	643
Range of σ											
$-2\frac{1}{2}$ to -2	.003	.000	.000	.000	.000	.000	.001	.000	.000	.000	.000
-2 to $-1\frac{1}{2}$	.017	.000	.000	.002	.000	.000	.004	.001	.001	.001	.000
$-1\frac{1}{2}$ to -1	.102	.027	.028	.047	.025	.004	.081	.026	.020	.012	.014
-1 to $-\frac{1}{2}$	.268	.159	.269	.280	.303	.177	.245	.282	.273	.230	.217
$-\frac{1}{2}$ to 0	.230	.387	.368	.342	.332	.505	.319	.363	.365	.405	.433
0 to $\frac{1}{2}$	.139	.258	.170	.144	.168	.176	.149	.151	.174	.199	.186
$\frac{1}{2}$ to 1	.088	.056	.090	.072	.073	.058	.082	.065	.068	.062	.074
1 to $1\frac{1}{2}$	.078	.016	.042	.044	.033	.032	.050	.034	.037	.044	.022
$1\frac{1}{2}$ to 2	.017	.021	.009	.025	.023	.019	.026	.027	.021	.015	.016
2 to $2\frac{1}{2}$	.030	.005	.014	.011	.008	.009	.009	.018	.009	.006	.012
$2\frac{1}{2}$ to 3	.003	.005	.009	.014	.011	.007	.010	.016	.008	.007	.006
3 to $3\frac{1}{2}$	.007	.003	.000	.010	.009	.008	.007	.008	.011	.007	.006
$3\frac{1}{2}$ to 4	.003	.000	.000	.002	.000	.000	.006	.000	.000	.001	.003
4 to $4\frac{1}{2}$	.003	.000	.000	.004	.002	.001	.002	.000	.003	.001	.000
$4\frac{1}{2}$ to 5	.003	.005	.005	.000	.002	.000	.001	.001	.001	.003	.000
5 to $5\frac{1}{2}$	.000	.000	.000	.002	.001	.001	.000	.001	.001	.000	.002
$5\frac{1}{2}$ to 6	.000	.000	.000	.002	.001	.000	.000	.002	.001	.001	.000
6 to $6\frac{1}{2}$	.000	.000	.000	.001	.000	.000	.001	.000	.000	.000	.000
$6\frac{1}{2}$ to 7	.007	.003	.000	.001	.002	.000	.003	.001	.001	.000	.002
7 to $7\frac{1}{2}$	.000	.000	.009	.003	.004	.001	.003	.000	.004	.003	.005
$7\frac{1}{2}$ to 8	.000	.000	.000	.000	.000	.002	.000	.001	.000	.000	.000

log Y₆₉

Range of σ

Range of σ											
-4 to $-3^1/_2$	.000	.000	.000	.001	.000	.000	.001	.000	.000	.000	.000
$-3^1/_2$ to -3	.003	.000	.000	.001	.001	.000	.001	.000	.001	.000	.002
-3 to $-2^1/_2$	.007	.003	.005	.003	.000	.005	.001	.006	.000	.001	.000
$-2^1/_2$ to -2	.010	.006	.005	.013	.008	.002	.014	.008	.001	.006	.009
-2 to $-1^1/_2$	.050	.014	.028	.030	.030	.017	.042	.021	.029	.028	.012
$-1^1/_2$ to -1	.060	.066	.056	.085	.113	.085	.081	.090	.088	.082	.093
-1 to $-^1/_2$	.147	.141	.225	.175	.198	.147	.155	.191	.209	.188	.174
$-^1/_2$ to 0	.260	.302	.263	.257	.212	.291	.258	.255	.239	.261	.263
0 to $^1/_2$	.197	.251	.164	.176	.166	.175	.182	.172	.179	.188	.185
$^1/_2$ to 1	.130	.144	.141	.103	.115	.086	.116	.105	.107	.113	.110
1 to $1^1/_2$	.097	.046	.052	.073	.075	.058	.077	.066	.065	.055	.078
$1^1/_2$ to 2	.030	.023	.033	.038	.036	.039	.032	.038	.040	.044	.022
2 to $2^1/_2$	.013	.006	.014	.024	.020	.019	.020	.027	.013	.010	.022
$2^1/_2$ to 3	.007	.006	.005	.011	.015	.015	.009	.011	.012	.012	.016
3 to $3^1/_2$	.003	.003	.000	.004	.003	.006	.003	.004	.007	.006	.000
$3^1/_2$ to 4	.003	.003	.005	.004	.006	.001	.007	.002	.003	.003	.005
4 to $4^1/_2$	.000	.000	.005	.000	.002	.002	.000	.000	.003	.001	.003
$4^1/_2$ to 5	.000	.000	.000	.000	.000	.001	.000	.001	.000	.000	.000

Appendix J: Interpolation Methods

EX POST
PROFILES In Table 6-1 (p. 115) we presented estimates of the mean income earned by education level in the years 1955, 1968, and 1969.[1] In addition, in Table 5-10 (pp. 108–109) we presented estimates of starting salary by year and education level. For such purposes as computing rates of return, we need a complete profile through age 65 for a person 24 years old in 1946 who had no higher education before the war.[2] The purpose of this section is to describe the various interpolation procedures used. To make maximum use of the data available, we used different interpolation devices for the periods 1946–1950, 1950–1955, 1955–1969, and after 1969.

Consider first the period 1946–1950. We have estimates on starting salary by education level during this interval. Some of the sample sizes are too small to be reliable, but the estimates for those with an undergraduate degree are large for 1947 to 1950 and reasonable in 1946. For those with some college we have large samples from 1946 through 1949, for high school graduates only the 1946 sample has more than 100 people, and for those with graduate training we have large samples from 1948 through 1951.

For the large samples, we use average initial salary as a starting point. The numbers after 1946 must be adjusted because those who began work in 1946 received lower salaries than those beginning work later. In our analysis of 1955 data, we estimated the effect of both age and postwar time-on-the-job vari-

---

[1] We presented estimates based both on the average ability and background characteristics of each education level and on the average high school graduate.

[2] We shall indicate below how to convert the profile to apply to an individual who was 18 years old in 1946.

ables. The latter seemed more appropriate for adjusting initial salaries. After correcting the coefficient estimated in 1955 for inflation, we determined that each year on the job after 1946 added about $112 to income.[3]

Since we are interested in the profile of a person deciding on higher education in 1946, we do not need college-graduate incomes until 1950.[4] However, we interpolate the income of high school graduates using incomes of college graduates. In Table J-1, we give the adjusted incomes of the college graduates. (The unadjusted estimates are in parentheses.) Next, we compute G for 1946 and 1955 from $Y_{HS} = Y_{BA}/(1 + G)$, where Y_{HS} and Y_{BA} are the incomes of high school graduates and college graduates. From 1946 to 1955, G rose from 1.5 to 12 percent. We judge this change to be a valid representation of the real world for two reasons. First, the low value in 1946 is confirmed by the ratios that can be calculated from the much smaller samples of 1945, 1947, and 1948. Second, most theoretical and empirical work would suggest that the age-income profiles of the more educated are steeper. We then interpolated G linearly and estimated high school incomes by applying the above formula to the adjusted Y_{BA} in the years 1947 to 1950.

For the period 1951–1954, there are no directly relevant data. Rather than interpolate college-graduate income linearly, however, we based our estimates on the percentage change in the median income of white males in each year relative to the total percentage change in this median income from 1950 to 1955. Then we applied $Y_{BA}/(1 + G)$ to these estimates.

Our income figures are, of course, only estimates, but we would expect these to be accurate enough for our purposes. The B.A. income figures from 1947 to 1950 are in each year based on more than 100 observations, while the time-on-the-job effect is close to that estimated from Miller (1960). Our estimates of G between 1946 and 1955 are interpolations, but the errors introduced here should not be great. For example, if in 1953 G were 5 percent rather than 10 percent, our estimate of the high

[3]The data presented in Miller (1960) yield estimates of the same magnitude for 1946.

[4]Following Becker (1964), we set their part-time earnings to one-quarter of the average high school graduate's earnings.

[5]Constant-dollar figures are given in U.S. Bureau of the Census (1966). To the percentage change implied by these figures we added the percentage change in the Consumer Price Index.

	Earnings of those with undergraduate degrees— adjusted for time on the			Earnings of high school
Year	job		G	graduates
1946	$3,433		1.5%	$3,342
1947	3,576		2.7	3,480
1948	3,970		3.9	3,820
1949	3,850		5.1	3,660
1950	4,250	(3,800)	6.3	4,000
1951	5,471	(5,271)	7.5	5,089
1952	5,935	(5,835)	8.7	5,460
1953	6,277	(6,233)	9.9	5,711
1954	6,228	(6,188)	11.1	5,605
1955	6,720	(6,720)	12.0	6,000

TABLE J-1 Estimates of yearly earnings of high school and college graduates, 1946–1955 (in dollars)

NOTE: Unadjusted estimates are in parentheses.

school graduate's income would be 5 percent higher. Random errors of this magnitude have little effect on our computations discussed on pages 123 to 131. The interpolations for the average college graduate's income between 1951 and 1954 are crude, but since we primarily use differences in income, much of the error in the levels is not crucial.

For those with some college, we used the sample information from 1946 to 1949 and then interpolated through 1955 on the basis of median wage incomes. The results are given in Table J-4, in which the whole profile is presented. The estimate for those with graduate training is taken from the sample information in 1952, and in other years the estimates are set at the 1950 estimate of 94 percent of earnings of those with college degrees.

Beginning in 1956, we have more information that we use in a different interpolation scheme. The U.S. Bureau of the Census has published periodically since 1955 mean incomes of males in various age and education groups.[6] Using the mean age in our

[6] The estimates are in *Current Population Reports* (U.S. Bureau of the Census, 1968). The data are available for 1956, 1958, 1961, 1963, 1964, 1966, and 1968. In all these years, it is possible to obtain data on high school graduates, those with one through three years of college, and those with four years of college. After 1956, separate estimates are available for those with four years of college and those with four or more years. We assume that from 1956 to 1958 both these categories grew at the same rate as the group with four or more years of college.

TABLE J-2 *Mean income and earnings for 33- and 48-year-olds in 1955 and 1968:* Current Population Reports *(income) and NBER-TH (earnings) (in dollars)*

	High school	Some college	College degree	Some graduate work	Master's	Ph.D.	LL.B.
Current Population Reports							
(1) 1955	4,680	5,400	5,985		7,200		
(2) 1968	9,106	11,072	14,281		17,223		
NBER-TH*							
(3) 1955	6,000	6,600	6,720	6,900	6,612	6,140	7,150
(4) 1968	13,968	15,852	17,232	16,908	17,906	16,715	24,189
1955 ratio (3)/(1)†	1.28	1.23	1.12	.96	.92	.85	.99
1968 ratio (4)/(2)†	1.53	1.43	1.21	.98	1.04	.97	1.40

*Calculated at the characteristics of the average high school graduate.

†For the graduate levels, each item in (3) and (4) is divided by the income figures for all graduates given in (1) and (2).

sample, we estimate mean income for the years available from the corresponding age group in the census or, where necessary, from the average of two age groups. In order to compare our sample with the census, we need data from both for the same year. This information is available in 1968 and can be estimated for 1955 by adjusting the 1956 census estimate to match the change from 1955 to 1956 in median money wages of white males. These estimates and their ratios are given in Table J-2.

In each instance, our series grew faster than the census series. Since our sample consisted of high-ability people and since we have already shown that the income of the more able grew faster than that of the less able, this increase in the ratio seems reasonable (though, of course, the 1955 estimate is not as good as that for 1968, since no appropriate *Current Population Reports* were available for 1955).[7] Therefore, we spread the difference in the ratios evenly from 1955 to 1968. Note that since the difference in the ratio for 1955 and 1968 is not large in any education category, the differences in income across education

[7]Given the high average ability in our sample, our high school graduates should be relatively more able—compared to the population—than the more educated in the sample; thus, it is encouraging to find the ratio decreasing as educational attainment increases.

groups are approximately the same as if the 1968 ratios had been used.

Finally, we filled in the missing years from the *Current Population Reports* on the basis of movements in median income of white males. The data from the *Current Population Reports* and our estimate for all years are given in Table J-3. In Table J-4, we present the entire ex post age-income profiles (through 1969) for the different education categories.

The above profiles were derived for people who were 24 in 1946. While this is the average age in our sample, most rates of return are calculated for 18-year-old high school graduates. It is necessary, therefore, to convert the profile for a 24-year-old to one for an 18-year-old. The basic hypothesis is that employers will pay nothing for skills learned during World War II. With this assumption, the initial salary of an 18-year-old high school graduate would be the same as that of the 24-year-old in our sample, while in 1950 the starting salaries of undergraduate-degree holders would be the same for 28-year-old veterans and for 22-year-old nonveterans. Assuming, then, that the effects of

TABLE J-3
Nationwide mean earnings of age groups over time, by education level (in dollars)

Age in our sample	Year	High school	Some college	Under-graduate degree	Graduate degree (s)
33	1955	$4,680	$ 5,400	$ 5,985	$ 7,200
34	1956	5,200	6,000	6,650	8,000
35	1957	5,250	6,150	6,900	8,300
36	1958	5,300	6,300	7,150	8,650
37	1959	6,000	7,500	9,000	10,200
38	1960	6,200	7,800	9,500	10,600
39	1961	6,411	8,100	10,000	11,000
40	1962	6,900	8,200	10,350	11,200
41	1963	7,200	8,300	10,700	11,300
42	1964	7,300	8,600	10,900	12,400
43	1965	7,800	9,400	12,000	13,700
44	1966	8,250	10,200	13,000	15,000
45	1967	8,700	10,600	13,500	16,000
46	1968	9,106	11,072	14,200	17,200

SOURCE: U.S. Bureau of the Census (1968, 1969) and interpolations described in Chapter 6.

TABLE J-4 *Ex post age-income profiles, 1946–1969 (in dollars)*

	High school	Some college	Under-graduate degree	Some graduate work	Master's	Ph.D and LL.B.
1946	3,392					
1947	3,480					
1948	3,820	4,377				
1949	3,660	4,240				
1950	4,000	5,207	3,800			
1951	5,089	5,798	5,271	4,223	4,223	
1952	5,460	6,104	5,835	5,213	5,103	
1953	5,711	6,317	6,233	5,909	5,722	
1954	5,605	6,293	6,188	5,829	5,650	5,814
1955	6,000	6,600	6,700	6,900	6,612	6,732
1956	6,767	7,492	7,533	7,724	7,466	7,713
1957	6,734	7,773	7,885	8,071	7,869	8,245
1958	7,102	8,058	8,243	8,473	8,331	8,845
1959	8,156	9,708	10,466	10,063	9,975	10,726
1960	8,547	10,215	11,144	10,532	10,812	11,456
1961	8,963	10,731	11,830	11,008	11,086	12,210
1962	9,780	10,989	12,348	11,287	11,454	12,758
1963	10,344	11,249	12,873	11,468	11,725	13,202
1964	10,629	11,787	13,223	12,671	13,051	14,848
1965	11,508	13,027	14,678	14,097	14,624	16,805
1966	12,332	14,292	16,031	15,541	16,235	18,836
1967	13,171	15,014	16,534	16,220	17,062	19,980
1968	13,961	15,851	17,232	16,908	17,906	21,157
1969	13,212	15,423	17,280	16,635	17,402	21,230

experience on income also do not depend on military service, we can use the same age-income profile for an 18-year-old as for our 24-year-old veteran, except that we must add six more years at the end. This hypothesis, of course, need not be correct. In particular, we would expect some vocational training in the Air Corps to be of value in civilian life. Hence, we would expect 18-year-olds to earn somewhat less than the people in our sample at all education levels, at least until the 1960s.[8] If the age-in-

[8] This would be particularly true of pilots in our sample.

come profile reflects aging as well as experience, however, we would expect the income profile of the 18-year-olds to reach a peak after the incomes of those in our sample reach a peak. We judge the net effect of these changes to have a small impact on the rate of return.

CROSS-SECTION PROFILES The basic data on income by age and education are taken from Miller (1960) for 1946 and 1949 and from the *Current Population Reports* for 1968. These data provide estimates of the income differences due to education at the average ages of 30, 40, 50, and 60. These differences are biased upward because no account has been taken of ability and background factors. We correct these estimates of income differences on the basis of the ratios of our returns to education after correcting for age, ability, biography, and background to our estimates with only age held constant. These ratios, which we calculated from our 1955 and 1969 equations, are given in Section A of Table J-5.[9] We

[9]These corrections differ from those in Chapter 5 because all background and ability variables are omitted.

TABLE J-5 *Bias corrections by age and education level, 1946, 1949, and 1968*

A. Bias from omitting ability and background as a percentage of unadjusted return to education

Age	Some college	B.A. plus Graduate	B.A.	Graduate
33	32	43	44	43
47	30	30	32	30

B. Change in bias by cohort because of shifts in δ where $A = \delta_0 + \delta ED$

Average date of high school graduation of cohort	δ
1957	.52
1947	.52
1937	1.0
1927	1.0
1917	.43
1907	.43

NOTE: *ED* is the percentage of high school graduates who enter college. *A* is the percentage rank on an IQ test.
SOURCE: Taubman and Wales (1972).

used these two bias corrections for ages 30 and 50 and obtained the biases at 40 and 60 by linear extension.

These corrections assume that the relationship between ability and education is the same in each cohort as in our sample. Even assuming that this is the case for the whole cohort aged 33 in 1955, evidence in an earlier paper of ours (Taubman & Wales, 1972) suggests that this would not be true for other cohorts. Thus we have adjusted the bias by the ratios given in Section B of Table J-5. Also, as discussed in Chapter 7, we adjusted these profiles for technical change in calculating ex ante rates of return.

Appendix K: Estimating Private and Social Costs of Higher Education

The purpose of this appendix is to describe briefly the procedure followed in estimating the private and social costs of higher education used in calculating the ex ante and ex post rates of return. The two main components of social costs are current expenditures by institutions of higher learning and a return on capital used by such institutions.[1] We assume a 12 percent return before depreciation on this capital and, following Becker, that taxes on such institutions, if they were not tax-exempt, would have been 1.5 percent of the value of the capital. We assume further that 71 percent of the business of higher institutions is educational (rather than research-oriented). Consequently, we estimate the social cost per student as

$$0.71 \; [(0.12 + 0.015) \; xP + E]/N$$

where P is the value of plant and plant funds, E is current expenditures, and N is resident enrollment in institutions of higher learning.[2] Data are available to make these estimates for 1946, 1948, 1950, 1952, and 1954, and we have interpolated linearly to obtain the intervening years. These estimates are presented in Table K-1.

According to Becker, private tuition costs were $228, $209, and $242 in 1949, 1956, and 1958, respectively. We have used the value of $228 in 1949 and have adjusted this figure by the Consumer Price Index to obtain estimates for 1946, 1947, and

[1] The basic data used in calculating social costs are taken from various editions of the *Statistical Abstract of the United States* (U.S. Bureau of the Census, 1965–1969).

[2] Although these data for plant are in historical dollars, our estimates agree with the more systematic estimates provided in Becker (1964).

1948. For the period 1950–1954, we approximate tuition costs by assuming they do not change from their 1949 value of $228. Finally, we increase each of these figures by 53 percent for such education-related expenses as travel, books, and so on. Our estimates appear in Table K-1.

TABLE K-1
Estimated social and private costs of higher education, 1946–1954 (in dollars)

Year	Social cost	Private cost
1946	619	273
1947	640	326
1948	658	349
1949	724	349
1950	790	349
1951	917	349
1952	1,044	349
1953	1,082	349
1954	1,119	349

Appendix L: The Effects of Education on Incomes of the Successful: Evidence from the Lewellen Data

W. G. Lewellen (1968) has recently estimated and analyzed the after-tax incomes—including in "income" the value of the various deferred-compensation schemes such as pension plans and stock options—for the first up to the fifth highest-ranking executives of 50 of the 70 largest manufacturing firms in the United States in the period 1940–1963.[1] Professor Lewellen has generously made available his data for our use.

Despite its obvious special nature, this sample is of interest for several reasons. First, contrary to the situation with other cross-section studies in general and high-income samples in particular, this sample has an accurate earned-income measure. Second, it is useful to see whether education differences are important for successful people, especially since it may be possible to compare the results with the Terman sample of geniuses.

We have attempted to obtain relevant demographic characteristics from various sources for each of the executives.[2] We have determined the education attainment, undergraduate and graduate school attended (if any), and age for about 350 of the 500 individuals in the Lewellen sample. Consequently, we can estimate the relationship between after-tax income, education, and years on the job. Unfortunately, except for academic

---

[1] The Securities and Exchange Commission requires the basic information on annual company reports.

[2] These are *Who's Who in America* (1950); *Who's Who in Commerce and Industry* (1940 and 1950); *World's Who's Who in Commerce and Industry* (1963); and *Poor's Register of Directors and Executives* (1940, 1950, and 1963). *Who's Who in Commerce and Industry* provided the most comprehensive data. This was the first source consulted. *Poor's Register* listed more names than did *Who's Who in Commerce and Industry*, but it was not nearly as comprehensive. *Poor's* listed college education only if a degree had been obtained, and in that case also listed the date the degree was received.

honors, no direct measure of ability is available. However, in view of the nature of the sample (very successful individuals in a narrowly defined occupation), we would expect the appropriately defined ability of almost everyone to be very high. Moreover, we would suspect that a measure of drive or ambition would be a more relevant variable than mental ability as measured by IQ. In addition, we do have information on the undergraduate college attended by each individual, and evidence exists that college quality is correlated with the mental ability of those attending.[3] The major disadvantage of the sample is that, since it is not typical, no conclusions of a general nature can be drawn from our findings.

CHARACTERISTICS OF THE SAMPLE Before considering our regression results, it is useful to consider the characteristics of the sample from 1940 to 1963. Perhaps the most interesting question is the distribution of educational attainment over time. In Table L-1 we present the percentage of people (for whom we have the data) in each of four educational classes. In this table we have combined the data for the five positions.

In 1940, approximately 23 percent of the top executives had not attended college, an additional 12 percent had not graduated from college, 44 percent had an undergraduate degree only, and 21 percent had received more than one degree. Throughout the sample period, there was a steady trend toward more and more education of the people in the top job positions; thus, in 1950 the corresponding figures were 14 percent, 10 percent, 51 percent, and 25 percent. By 1963, only 7 percent had not attended college (and nearly all these people had been in the sample since 1939), and 8 percent had attended college but had not received a degree. On the other hand, 55 percent of the people had received one degree and an additional 30 percent had more than one degree.

It is of some interest to compare these developments with educational achievement in general and with the educational composition of the managerial-executive class in particular. For population cohorts born from 1890 through 1905, less than 15 percent of employed males had attended college (Taubman &

---

[3] See, for example, Solmon (1969), who correlated the quality measure we used with mean SAT scores. See also Wolfle (1954).

	High school*	Some college	Under- graduate degree†	At least one graduate degree
1940	23	12	44	21
1941	21	12	44	23
1942	20	12	44	24
1943	20	10	45	25
1944	20	10	47	23
1945	20	09	48	23
1946	18	10	49	23
1947	16	09	52	24
1948	15	09	52	24
1949	14	11	51	23
1950	14	10	51	25
1951	12	10	53	25
1952	12	10	51	27
1953	12	10	52	26
1954	13	11	50	27
1955	12	11	50	27
1956	13	10	51	26
1957	12	10	53	25
1958	09	09	59	23
1959	08	08	57	27
1960	07	08	58	27
1961	07	07	58	28
1962	07	06	57	29
1963	07	08	55	30

TABLE L-1
Percentage distribution of top executives by education, 1940–1963

*One individual who did not graduate from high school is included in this group.
†A few people with some postgraduate work but no degree are included in this group.

Wales, 1972).[4] It is obvious, therefore, that top management had received much more education than the population as a whole.

It is also of interest to compare the education of top executives with the education of all executives in the same age group. The data that are more relevant (in ways described below) for

[4] The average age of the executives in our sample is about 50 in 1940 and 58 in 1960.

this comparison are not available. Some crude approximations obtained from the 1940, 1950, and 1960 censuses are given in Table L-2 for the category of nonfarm proprietors, managers, and officials 45 through 64 years of age. The distribution across the three education classes has shown little change over time. Educational upgrading has occurred, however: Those with *less* than a high school diploma in this occupation fell from about 60 percent of the total in 1940 to about 45 percent in 1960. For making comparisons with the Lewellen data, the data in Table L-2 are crude in several respects. The Lewellen sample involves executives of the largest manufacturing concerns. The census data include all types of companies of all sizes. In the 1960 census it is possible to obtain the educational distribution of salaried nonfarm managers and officials. This category should eliminate many of the owners of retail stores and small concerns. Although, as shown in the last row in Table L-2, there are fewer people in the high school and some-college groups, the distribution is still very different from that given in Table L-1. This difference could arise because reaching the top of the corporate ladder depends on ability, which is correlated with education. As shown in our earlier work (Taubman & Wales, 1972), even for the age cohorts being studied here, the more mentally able students would have, on the average, received more education. This may explain the high concentration of education in the Lewellen sample.

The above data certainly do not deny, and may even confirm, the proposition that more highly educated people have a better chance of reaching the highest-paying positions in American business. This sample can be used to answer several other interesting questions. First, we can determine the extent to which education affects the income of the successful by using the standard linear regression model, in which income is the dependent variable and education one of the independent vari-

TABLE L-2 Percentage distribution of nonfarm proprietors, managers, and officials, aged 45 to 64, with at least a high school education, 1940, 1950, and 1960	Description	*High school graduates*	*Some college*	*One or more college degrees*
	1940 census	51	26	22
	1950 census	50	27	24
	1960 census	47	29	24
	1960 census, salaried	43	28	29

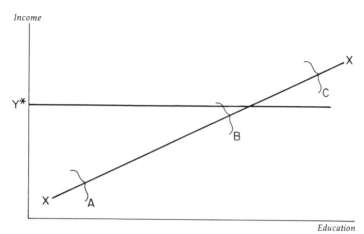

Figure L-1
Truncation of
sample
by income
level

ables. Second, we can attempt to determine the extent to which education affects earnings for the population (of executives) as a whole. But to use our sample for this purpose, we must determine if application of the usual regression model to our data yields the same result as it would when applied to random samples of executives.

In the discussion to follow, the "estimated education coefficient" is the one obtained using regression analysis on our sample, while the "true coefficient" is the relationship between education and earnings in the population. It can be shown that the estimated education coefficient will in fact be biased downward if its true value is positive, will be unbiased if it is zero, and will be biased upward if it is negative. The case of a positive education coefficient may be understood by considering Figure L-1.

Suppose the true relationship is given by the line *XX,* and that the representative distributions of income about its mean at each education level are given by *A, B,* and *C*. Suppose also that (after translating success into income levels) only levels of income above *Y** are used in the sample. Then, for education levels corresponding to *C,* the entire distribution of earnings is represented in the sample, while for education levels corresponding to *B,* only the highest income values in the distribution are included. The effect of this is clearly to underestimate the effect of education on income. Earnings and education values corresponding to *A* are irrelevant as they are not contained in the sample at all.

In his study, Lewellen derived estimates of earnings on an

after-tax basis, on a before-tax basis, and on an equivalent before-tax basis under the assumption that the after-tax earnings had all been wages and salaries. Although we could have used any of the measures as our dependent variable, we have used only the after-tax income. Our choice was based on several considerations. First, after-tax income is the appropriate concept for calculating the private return. Since the sample covered such a small and select group of people, it is not possible to generalize to all college graduates; hence, a social-return concept is not worth pursuing.

In addition, we would expect that for top executives the after-tax return is a reasonable measure of differences in productivity for the following reasons.[5] Suppose we ignore the fact that top management has a large say in the setting of its earnings and the composition of its pay package and assume that each firm tries to minimize costs by reducing its before-tax payments to executives while at the same time increasing executives' after-tax earnings by altering their compensation package. If firms do not pay managers their marginal product, other firms could afford to hire them away (unless the executives' skills were company-specific) and, consequently, firms will have to set the after-tax pay package equal to the marginal product of each person. Since firms should tailor the components of the package to the wishes of their managers, after-tax earnings for a given tax structure will probably differ from before-tax earnings by a factor that is reasonably constant for all individuals in a given year. Years in which tax laws differ, however, cannot be combined if there is a lag in the adjustment to the tax provisions.

A few other details concerning the income data should be noted. First, the marginal-productivity theory is expressed in terms of real wages. Within any year we can treat prices as the same for the members of the cross section, but in comparing results for different years or in combining data from different years, we must deflate the income measure. The deflator we have used in regressions with different years combined is the Consumer Price Index (CPI) with 1957–1959 equal to 100. We recognize that the CPI is not really appropriate for upper-income individuals, but no alternative is readily available. Since Lewellen used a CPI with 1940 as the base year, our real-income figures are about twice as large as his.

---

[5] We shall show that the after-tax earnings are equal to the marginal productivity times $(1 - t)$, where t is the average marginal tax rate.

The second point is that, while individuals must be employed when in our sample, their incomes are still subject to cyclical swings because of profit sharing, wage bonuses, and stock options valued on the basis of stock prices.[6] Within any cross section, it is reasonable to assume that the cyclical developments would affect people with different education equally. Over time, this need not be true, since the educational composition of our sample changes. Thus, when comparing cross sections, we included zero-one dummy variables for the various years.

RESULTS The data can be analyzed using regressions at many different levels of aggregation. First, for each year an equation can be estimated for each position. Second, for a given year the effects of the education variables on earnings can be assumed to be the same at all positions, although the level of income also depends on the position. In this case, we can have one equation for each year with dummy variables for the positions. Finally, the data can be combined for sets of years (after deflating the income variable), while including dummies for positions and/or years. Such pooling of the data assumes that the effects on earnings of the independent variables are constant over time as well as over positions.

Consider the question of whether the data should be combined by position. Assuming that individuals receive their marginal products, there is no reason to believe a priori that additional education will have different effects that depend on the individual's position in the firm.[7] On the other hand, it is clear

---

[6] See Chapter 4 in Lewellen (1968) for a discussion of this method of valuing stock options.

[7] We have some empirical evidence on the effect of education on income for different positions. We ran some preliminary regressions (using years of schooling as the education variable) designed to determine if, in fact, these differences exist. Cross-section regressions for 1940, 1950, and 1963 computed separately for the five positions do not suggest different effects of education on income. For 1940, the education coefficients for the third, fourth, and fifth positions are marginally significant and have almost identical values. The coefficients for the first two positions differ considerably, but have such high standard errors that little significance can be attached to the point estimates. For 1950, the education coefficients for the second and fourth positions are significant, and almost identical, while the others are insignificant. Although these results do not prove that the effects of education are the same at all positions, they at least provide no evidence of significant differences. Consequently, in the analysis to follow we pool the data for different positions, thus forcing the coefficients of the independent variables to be the same across positions.

that income differences that reflect the hierarchical nature of the firms' administrative setup will exist between individuals in different positions within firms, even though they have the same age and education. If the attainment of the higher positions is due to such factors as ability and drive, which are excluded from our model but which are correlated with education, then we should include dummy intercept variables for the positions in order to avoid attributing to education some of the income differences due to ability and other factors. It is conceivable, however, that education better equips a person to obtain the more senior positions. In this situation, the inclusion of dummy intercept variables for positions would eliminate part of the return to education.[8] It is likely that the return to education is bracketed by the estimates obtained through including, and then excluding, the dummies. Since it is not clear which interpretation is more accurate, we present our main results for both cases—that is, inclusion and exclusion of the intercept position dummies.

As noted earlier, it is possible to study each year separately or to combine all individuals for those years in which the tax structure was constant. We have made both calculations. Consider first the results for the period 1954–1963, which is the longest interval available.

$$\frac{Y_{it}}{P_t} = -66.7 - 40.1PBK + 2.97(Age - E) + 9.13Coll + 62.5CGrad$$
$$(2.6) \qquad (3.4) \qquad\qquad (7.7) \qquad\qquad (.7) \qquad\qquad (5.6)$$

$$+ 57.7PGrad \qquad\qquad\qquad\qquad \bar{R}^2 = .06 \quad \text{(L-1)}$$
$$(4.7)$$

$$\frac{Y_{it}}{P_t} = 62.7 - 25.3PBK + 1.89(Age - E) + .21Coll + 53.6CGrad$$
$$(2.5) \qquad (2.3) \qquad\qquad (5.1) \qquad\qquad (.01) \qquad\quad (5.2)$$

$$+ 51.2PGrad - 69.8D2 - 84.5D3 - 105.4D4 - 116.2D5$$
$$(4.4) \qquad\quad (8.8) \qquad (9.8) \qquad (11.4) \qquad\quad (11.9)$$

$$\bar{R}^2 = .19 \quad \text{(L-2)}$$

where Y_{it} = after-tax earnings of the ith individual in the tth

---

[8]Of course, if there is no correlation between educational attainment and positions, then the coefficient on the education variable will be the same.

year, measured in thousands of dollars

P = the Consumer Price Index, 1957–1959; equals 1.00

PBK = a dummy variable for honors in college; the categories included are Phi Beta Kappa, Sigma Chi, and graduated with academic honors[9]

Age = age of individual

E = years of schooling after high school[10]

$Coll$ = a dummy variable that equals 1 if the person attended but did not graduate from college

$CGrad$ = a dummy variable that equals 1 if a person graduated from college but did not receive a graduate degree

$PGrad$ = a dummy variable that equals 1 if the person received one or more graduate degrees (including any law degree)

$DJ, J = 2{-}5$ = a dummy for the position of the individual in his firm

In Eq. (L-1) we have included all individuals from the top to the fifth executive for whom we have the necessary educational information. In this equation there are several striking results, the most surprising of which is that the 20 or so people who achieved academic honors in college earn a statistically significant $40,000 less than their colleagues with the same education. As long as positional dummies are excluded in all our equations, the coefficient on PBK is always minus $40,000 to minus $45,000. As typified in Eq. (L-2), when position dummies are included, the PBK coefficient is still minus $25,000. Two tentative explanations for the negative effect of PBK are the following: (1) while those who earned the PBK have intellectual and other talents necessary to succeed in academic programs, the non-PBK people who graduated from college and who reached the top in the business have greater amounts of other nonacademically oriented talents than those with PBK, and these nonacademic talents are more valuable in performing managerial functions; (2) The non-PBK people took programs that bet-

[9]The individual is credited with PBK whether or not he has an advanced degree.

[10]Part-time college attendance was counted as two years, a college degree as four years, a master's degree or some postgraduate education as five years, and a Ph.D. or law degree as seven years.

ter prepared them for the business world, but these programs either did not give an honors award or gave one that was not considered worth listing in *Who's Who* or elsewhere. For those who are still suspicious of this result, it should be noted that when Eqs. (L-1) and (L-2) are rerun without *PBK*, the other coefficients are only very slightly changed.

For the period 1954–1963 the average age in the sample is close to 60, and the average income of a high school graduate in this sample is $112,000 (in 1957–1959 dollars). Eq. (L-1) indicates that each additional year of employment after completion of schooling adds $3,000 to income. Those who attended college but who did not graduate earned a mere (and statistically insignificant) $9,000, or 8 percent, more than high school graduates. Although just going to college did not add much to income, graduation (without *PBK*) adds $62,500, or 50 percent, to a person's income.[11] A graduate with a *PBK* earns only $20,000 more than a high school graduate.

That college graduates do so well is not so surprising, but it may seem unusual to find that those with graduate degrees earn less than those with just an undergraduate degree. Thus, while the average college graduate had an income of $175,000, the average advanced-degree holder had an income of only $170,000. Moreover, since college graduates have been working four years longer, they receive an additional $12,000 more than an advanced-degree holder of equal age. This pattern also occurs in the 1960 census data. For example, for nonfarm salaried managers, college graduates in the age group of 45 to 64 earn approximately 50 percent, and advanced-degree holders 46 percent, more than high school graduates. To find the same percentage in returns is surprising, because our sample includes only the successful managers, whereas the census data include some who have switched from a professional to a managerial position and have had less time to reach the top positions in their field.

The $\bar{R}^2$ in Eq. (L-1) is very low—.06—partly because we have included people from the top five positions in each firm without taking account of the wage structure within the firms. Eq. (L-2) enters dummy variables for the various positions.

[11]Of course, since the person has been on the job four years less than a person the same age who did not go to college, he would earn only $50,000 ($62,000 − $12,000) more than a high school graduate of the same age.

Before considering these results, we remind the reader that according to our previous discussion, if education aids in advancing to the top, the coefficient in this equation will understate the returns to education.

In Eq. (L-2), we see quite clearly the wage structure by position. The average company head with a college degree earns $225,000, and the corresponding person in the second position earns about $155,000. Those with a college degree in the third, fourth, and fifth positions earn $140,000, $120,000, and $110,000, respectively. Once we have held positions constant, the effects of education are somewhat smaller. Within each of the positions, college dropouts earn a minuscule $200 more, and college graduates and advanced-degree holders earn about $50,000 more, than high school graduates. Thus, holding positions constant in Eq. (L-2) reduces the coefficients on the various educational categories in Eq. (L-1) by $7,000 to $10,000. The *PBK* coefficient changes from minus $40,000 to minus $25,000. This indicates that those with *PBK* not only do not get as high up on the management ladder but also earn less on a given rung. As noted earlier, Eqs. (L-1) and (L-2), which yield similar education effects, should bracket the true coefficient. With the introduction of the position dummies, the $\bar{R}^2$ increases to .19.

We have reestimated both equations including yearly dummies. Compared with 1963, executives earned $40,000 more in 1955–1957, and $20,000 more in 1959–1962. Since these dummies had only minor effects on the education and time-on-the-job coefficients, we do not present the equations.

We also computed regressions in which we added a variable defined as $Q \times CGrad$ where Q is a measure of college quality and $CGrad$ is the same dummy variable as before. The measure of Q we used was the Gourman rating for 1955, the earliest one available.[12] While the quality ratings of schools change slowly, 1955 ratings may be too far removed from the dates at which people attended college, since even in 1963 most people in the sample had attended college more than 30 years earlier. Still, it is of some interest to use such a variable, since the best schools and worst schools do not change greatly over such time periods.

Since by construction $CGrad$ must be uncorrelated with all the

---

[12]See Gourman (1956). The Gourman rating is available for subsequent years but not earlier. The rating scheme, which we understand is not infallible, takes account of quality of students, faculty, and facilities.

variables except *PBK* and (*Age* − *E*) and since *Q* happens to be uncorrelated with these two variables, the coefficients on the other variables are unchanged when we introduce the new variable. The coefficient on *CGrad,* which indicates the income earned if *Q* were zero, is about $20,000. Each one-point increase in *Q* adds about $70 to income when position dummies are not included and $50 when they are included.[13] Since *Q* in our sample ranges from under 300 to 770, college quality differences could account for a range of about $35,000 in income, which is less than the difference between high school and college graduates. It should be noted that evidence in Wolfle (1954) and in Solmon (1969) indicates that average school quality and average IQ are correlated, but that within schools there is a wide range in individual abilities. Thus, the quality variable reflects both individual mental-ability differences and quality-of-schooling differences.[14]

The coefficients of (*Age* −*E*) from Eqs. (L-1) and (L-2) indicate that an additional year on the job adds about $3,000 to income if positions are not held constant and $2,000 if they are. That is, those who are successful and move to higher positions can expect to receive, on the average, a salary increase per year $1,000 higher than those who are not promoted.

We turn next to the equations obtained when each year is treated as a separate cross section. In these regressions, we have not deflated the income data; hence, in making year-to-year comparisons, it is necessary to deflate all the coefficients. In the following discussion, we shall ignore the results for the World War II years 1942 to 1945. Table L-3 contains the results when the position dummies are excluded, while Table L-4 presents the equations that include the position dummies.

Although the education coefficients in Table L-4 are generally lower than those in Table L-3 and although the positions dummies always have the correct signs and are statistically significant, the same qualitative pattern emerges in both tables. Therefore we will only discuss Table L-3. An intriguing pattern

---

[13]Both estimates are significant at the 5 percent level.

[14]We attempted to include a variable to account for nepotism based on a dummy variable with a value of 1 when the individual had the same surname as an older person who had been an officer of the company during the period 1940–1963 and in a few instances when a person was known to be related to the major stockholder.

emerges. For the period 1940–1941, the coefficient for some college is positive, significant, and somewhat greater than the coefficients for one degree or several degrees. Although in 1940 some of the people in the sample may have been the founders of the company, the same result emerges in Table L-3, in which positions are held constant. After World War II, the variable for some college is never significant. Between 1945 and 1958, *CGrad* and/or *PGrad* are generally significant, whereas after that, no education variable is significant. From 1956 to 1963, *CGrad* does not differ significantly from *PGrad*. *PBK* is positive until the late forties and insignificantly negative thereafter. The time-on-the-job variable is positive except in 1962 and significant until 1960 (1958 in Table L-4).

The consensus that emerges from these equations is that *PGrad* is never very different from *CGrad*, and that except in the early years, the income of those with some college does not add to the income of the top executives. These results are in conformity with the continuous cross-section results given above. The *PBK* results are in rough conformity, since the variable is negative in each of the years from 1954 to 1963.

CONCLUSION   We have studied the after-tax incomes of top corporate executives for the period 1940–1963. In the early part of this period, those who attended college but did not graduate received the most income. During the post-World War II era the following pattern emerges: When each year from 1950 to 1958 is analyzed separately, those with one or more degrees generally earn significantly more income than high school graduates. After 1958 there is no significant relationship between education and income. When the years 1954 to 1963 are combined, college-degree holders earn significantly more income than either high school graduates or college dropouts. In no case is there a significant difference between the incomes of those with one college degree and those with more than one college degree. In the postwar period, college dropouts earn approximately the same income as high school graduates. The above results hold whether or not the executive's position in the firm is held constant using dummy variables.

It is interesting to compare these results with others in the literature. For example, in a recent study, Shane J. Hunt (1963) finds a zero or negative rate of return for graduate education.

TABLE L-3 *Annual income-education regressions, 1940–1963*

	PBK	Time on the job	Coll	CGrad	PGrad	Constant	$\bar{R}^2$
1940	19.0	2.1	30.2	19.8	25.6	−61.9	.10
	(0.9)	(4.2)	(2.1)	(1.8)	(1.9)	(2.1)	
1941	9.8	2.3	47.4	18.1	24.4	−78.1	.12
	(0.5)	(4.2)	(3.0)	(1.5)	(1.7)	(2.4)	
1942	6.2	0.8	9.4	17.0	18.1	−13.0	.09
	(1.7)	(3.7)	(1.4)	(3.3)	(3.0)	(0.9)	
1943	10.8	.7	8.4	11.9	11.9	−3.9	.10
	(1.7)	(3.6)	(1.6)	(3.1)	(2.7)	(0.4)	
1944	0.4	1.5	4.1	13.9	28.5	−49.6	.18
	(0.0)	(5.8)	(0.5)	(2.5)	(4.3)	(3.1)	
1945	5.8	1.2	−1.2	4.3	11.0	−23.7	.09
	(0.6)	(4.3)	(0.1)	(0.8)	(1.6)	(1.4)	
1946	20.8	1.1	−4.1	4.7	9.1	14.7	.16
	(2.7)	(4.8)	(.6)	(.9)	(1.4)	(1.0)	
1947	−.5	1.5	−5.9	9.7	13.5	−34.0	.10
	(0)	(4.8)	(.5)	(1.2)	(1.5)	(1.8)	
1948	−2.5	2.0	−10.8	6.5	17.5	−41.2	.21
	(.2)	(6.7)	(1.0)	(.9)	(2.0)	(2.2)	
1949	−14.3	1.6	3.1	13.8	28.3	−27.9	.16
	(1.3)	(5.6)	(0.3)	(1.9)	(3.4)	(1.6)	
1950	−13.2	1.8	2.5	15.2	24.2	−29.2	.12
	(1.1)	(5.0)	(0.0)	(1.7)	(2.4)	(1.3)	
1951	−20.3	1.5	11.6	29.6	35.0	−24.0	.08
	(1.4)	(3.7)	(0.8)	(2.8)	(2.9)	(0.9)	

NOTE: Figures in parentheses are *t* statistics.

This result is substantiated by rough calculations using 1960 census data on the managerial occupation. Our findings suggest the same conclusion even for people working in a narrowly defined occupation who have proved to be successful. In addition, we find that those with one degree earn approximately 50 percent more income than high school graduates—an estimate once again roughly in accord with census calculations.

	PBK	Time on the job	Coll	CGrad	PGrad	Constant	$\bar{R}^2$
1952	−11.0	1.4	24.8	31.4	32.7	−17.6	.05
	(0.6)	(3.0)	(1.5)	(2.4)	(2.2)	(0.6)	
1953	− 4.0	2.0	31.9	37.1	38.9	−46.6	.06
	(0.2)	(3.6)	(1.5)	(2.3)	(2.1)	(1.3)	
1954	− 9.5	1.9	24.9	45.9	48.2	−42.3	.07
	(0.5)	(3.4)	(1.2)	(2.9)	(2.8)	(1.2)	
1955	−53.6	5.4	46.8	99.4	104.4	−226.4	.10
	(1.2)	(4.1)	(1.0)	(2.7)	(2.6)	(2.7)	
1956	−39.8	5.6	2.2	102.6	88.2	−217.3	.09
	(0.7)	(3.7)	(0.0)	(2.6)	(2.0)	(2.3)	
1957	−51.4	4.5	3.5	95.4	88.7	−161.0	.09
	(1.1)	(3.4)	(0.1)	(2.6)	(2.1)	(1.9)	
1958	−39.4	1.7	3.2	44.0	39.6	−6.0	.06
	(1.6)	(2.4)	(0.1)	(2.1)	(1.6)	(0.1)	
1959	−53.3	2.2	−18.1	33.1	27.8	3.2	.04
	(1.8)	(2.1)	(0.4)	(1.0)	(0.8)	(0.0)	
1960	−41.4	2.7	3.4	35.6	35.2	−25.2	.03
	(1.3)	(2.4)	(0.1)	(1.0)	(0.9)	(0.3)	
1961	−55.5	2.6	−15.7	44.9	43.9	−20.6	.02
	(1.4)	(1.8)	(0.3)	(1.0)	(0.9)	(0.2)	
1962	−58.6	−0.2	−0.5	43.7	20.2	145.7	−.009
	(1.4)	(0.1)	(0.0)	(0.9)	(0.4)	(1.3)	
1963	−28.3	0.4	−4.9	49.6	20.7	85.8	−.001
	(.08)	(0.3)	(0.1)	(1.2)	(0.5)	(0.9)	

TABLE L-4 *Annual income-education regressions (with positions held constant), 1940–1963*

	PBK	Time on the job	Coll	CGrad	PGrad
1940	21.9	1.6	22.3	17.7	18.8
	(1.2)	(3.3)	(1.6)	(1.8)	(1.5)
1941	14.8	1.9	38.7	14.1	18.2
	(0.8)	(3.6)	(2.5)	(1.2)	(1.4)
1942	8.5	0.7	3.2	13.4	13.9
	(1.1)	(3.5)	(0.5)	(2.9)	(2.6)
1943	11.6	4.9	29.0	8.8	8.9
	(2.2)	(3.1)	(0.7)	(2.7)	(2.3)
1944	−3.7	1.2	−2.5	10.0	22.1
	(0.0)	(4.6)	(0.4)	(2.0)	(3.6)
1945	4.2	0.9	−10.4	1.5	5.6
	(0.5)	(3.6)	(1.4)	(0.3)	(0.9)
1946	23.8	.9	−6.6	4.8	1.6
	(3.7)	(4.4)	(1.1)	(1.1)	(.3)
1947	4.6	1.1	−13.3	7.1	6.1
	(.4)	(3.8)	(1.3)	(1.0)	(.7)
1948	4.6	1.1	13.3	7.1	6.1
	(.4)	(3.8)	(1.3)	(1.0)	(.7)
1949	−4.0	1.2	−3.9	7.1	23.5
	(0.4)	(4.7)	(0.4)	(1.1)	(3.3)
1950	−3.6	1.3	−8.7	9.1	20.6
	(0.4)	(4.3)	(0.9)	(1.2)	(2.3)
1951	−7.5	1.0	−5.2	21.5	25.4
	(0.5)	(2.6)	(0.4)	(2.2)	(2.3)

NOTE: Figures in parentheses are *t* statistics.

Position 2	Position 3	Position 4	Position 5	Constant	$\bar{R}^2$
−43.8	−53.0	−54.4	−55.8	8.5	
(4.0)	(4.3)	(4.8)	(4.9)	(0.3)	.26
−27.0	−40.0	−43.6	−51.3	−24.7	
(2.2)	(3.1)	(3.3)	(4.1)	(−0.7)	.21
−13.8	−20.4	−25.7	−29.6	14.4	
(2.8)	(3.9)	(5.0)	(5.7)	(1.1)	.27
−13.6	−18.4	−22.9	−26.3	22.3	
(3.8)	(5.2)	(6.5)	(7.0)	(2.3)	.36
−16.5	−22.8	−27.4	−30.0	−8.6	
(3.0)	(4.1)	(4.7)	(5.0)	(0.5)	.31
−13.4	−24.4	−29.0	−29.2	11.0	
(2.5)	(4.2)	(5.2)	(4.5)	(0.6)	.25
−13.3	−26.1	−33.8	−35.8	20.4	
(2.9)	(5.5)	(7.0)	(7.3)	(1.6)	.43
−21.5	−34.2	−34.2	−39.3	12.4	
(3.0)	(4.3)	(4.3)	(5.4)	(.6)	.26
21.4	34.2	34.1	39.2	12.3	
(3.0)	(4.3)	(4.3)	(5.4)	(.6)	.42
−25.5	−27.8	−39.6	−51.9	26.1	
(4.4)	(4.5)	(6.5)	(7.7)	(1.6)	.41
−28.9	−34.0	−51.9	−60.0	32.0	
(3.9)	(4.3)	(7.1)	(7.3)	(1.6)	.37
−24.2	−39.1	−50.7	−47.8	40.2	
(2.8)	(4.3)	(7.1)	(7.3)	(1.6)	.25

TABLE L-4 (continued)

	PBK	Time on the job	Coll	CGrad	PGrad
1952	−5.1	1.0	8.0	25.5	30.3
	(0.3)	(2.3)	(0.4)	(2.0)	(2.2)
1953	2.0	1.3	12.7	28.9	31.8
	(0.1)	(2.3)	(0.6)	(1.8)	(1.8)
1954	−2.5	1.2	6.3	37.0	41.3
	(0.1)	(2.1)	(0.3)	(2.5)	(2.6)
1955	−43.0	3.5	20.3	80.8	81.4
	(1.0)	(2.7)	(0.4)	(2.3)	(2.1)
1956	−4.6	3.8	−15.2	89.7	78.2
	(0.1)	(2.5)	(0.3)	(2.4)	(1.9)
1957	−17.5	3.4	−6.8	83.7	88.0
	(0.4)	(2.7)	(0.2)	(2.4)	(2.2)
1958	−32.7	0.9	0.3	40.6	31.9
	(1.5)	(1.4)	(0.0)	(2.1)	(1.5)
1959	−45.1	1.2	−19.7	21.5	22.3
	(1.6)	(1.3)	(0.5)	(0.7)	(0.7)
1960	6.9	1.3	10.0	33.5	29.7
	(0.2)	(1.2)	(0.2)	(1.1)	(0.9)
1961	−43.1	1.9	−14.2	42.0	43.9
	(1.1)	(1.3)	(0.3)	(1.0)	(0.9)
1962	−38.3	−0.8	−13.3	46.5	23.0
	(1.0)	(0.5)	(0.2)	(1.0)	(0.4)
1963	−13.8	0.2	20.8	57.8	35.3
	(0.4)	(0.2)	(0.4)	(1.5)	(0.8)

Position 2	Position 3	Position 4	Position 5	Constant	$\bar{R}^2$
−29.7	−42.0	−50.4	−48.0	39.5	
(2.7)	(3.6)	(4.3)	(3.8)	(1.3)	.16
−34.4	−46.9	−54.9	−54.3	32.6	
(2.5)	(3.3)	(3.6)	(3.2)	(0.8)	.15
−30.9	−62.0	−53.4	−66.1	45.9	
(2.4)	(4.7)	(3.7)	(4.4)	(1.2)	.21
−83.9	−107.7	−111.4	−129.1	−28.9	
(2.8)	(3.4)	(3.3)	(3.7)	(0.3)	.19
−109.9	−116.7	−141.0	−133.6	−21.1	
(3.4)	(3.5)	(3.8)	(3.3)	(0.2)	.20
−91.5	−99.3	−138.2	−131.7	−10.9	
(3.2)	(3.1)	(4.0)	(3.8)	(0.1)	.21
−53.2	−57.2	−77.8	−103.5	90.7	
(3.7)	(3.6)	(4.9)	(5.5)	(2.0)	.27
−62.7	−61.3	−101.5	−122.5	124.5	
(3.0)	(2.6)	(4.3)	(5.1)	(1.9)	.21
−67.1	−100.0	−109.8	−122.3	118.5	
(3.1)	(4.0)	(4.6)	(4.7)	(1.7)	.21
−60.3	−68.1	−110.7	−99.7	72.7	
(2.2)	(2.1)	(3.1)	(2.9)	(10.7)	.09
−92.3	−86.4	−123.8	−149.4	241.9	
(3.0)	(2.5)	(3.2)	(3.4)	(2.2)	.11
−62.0	−66.4	−97.3	−123.6	134.1	
(2.5)	(2.5)	(2.9)	(3.0)	(1.5)	.10

References

Anderson, G. L., and T. J. Berning: "What Happens to Minnesota High School Graduates?" *Studies in Higher Education,* University of Minnesota Committee on Education Research, Biennial Report, 1938–1940, The University of Minnesota Press, Minneapolis, 1941, pp. 15–40.

Arrow, K.: *Higher Education as a Filter,* June 1972. (Mimeographed.)

Arrow, K., and R. Lind: "Uncertainty and Evaluation of Public Investment Decisions," *American Economic Review,* vol. 60, pp. 364–379, June 1970.

Ashenfelter, O., and J. D. Mooney: "Graduate Education, Ability and Earnings," *Review of Economics and Statistics,* vol. 50, pp. 78–86, February 1968.

Astin, A.: "Undergraduate Achievement and Institutional 'Excellence,'" *Science,* vol. 16, pp. 661–667, Aug. 16, 1968.

Bartlett, M.: "Properties of Sufficiency and Statistical Tests," *Proceedings of the Royal Statistical Society,* ser. A, p. 273, 1937.

Becker, G. S.: *Human Capital,* Columbia University Press for the National Bureau of Economic Research, Inc., New York, 1964.

Becker, G., and B. Chiswick: "Education and the Distribution of Earnings," *American Economic Review,* vol. 56, pp. 358–370, May 1966.

Berg, I.: *Education and Jobs: The Great Training Robbery,* Beacon Press, Boston, 1971.

Bergman, B.: "The Effect of White Incomes of Discrimination in Employment," *Journal of Political Economy,* vol. 79, pp. 294–314, March–April 1971.

Bloom, B. S.: *Stability and Change in Human Characteristics,* John Wiley & Sons, Inc., New York, 1964.

Bowles, S.: "Towards an Education Production Function," in W. L. Hansen (ed.), *Education, Income and Human Capital,* Studies in Income and Wealth, no. 35, National Bureau of Economic Research, Inc., New York, 1970, pp. 11–61.

Bowman, M.: "Costing of Human Resource Development," in International Economics Association, *The Economics of Education*, The Macmillan Company, New York, 1966.

Bridgman, D.: "Success in College and Business," *Personnel Journal*, vol. 9, pp. 1–19, June 1930.

Campbell, D. P.: *The Results of Counseling: Twenty-five Years Later*, W. B. Saunders Company, Philadelphia, 1965.

Cramer, J. S.: "Efficient Grouping, Regression and Correlation in Engel Curve Analysis," *Journal of the American Statistical Association*, vol. 59, pp. 233–250, March 1964.

Cutright, P.: *Achievement, Military Service, and Earnings*, U.S. Social Security Administration, Washington, May 20, 1969. (Mimeographed.)

Denison, E. F.: "Measuring the Contribution of Education (and the Residual) to Economic Growth," in E. Denison (ed.), *The Residual Factor and Economic Growth*, Organization for Economic Co-operation and Development, Paris, 1964, pp. 13–102.

Duncan, O. D., D. Featherman, and B. Duncan: *Socioeconomic Background and Occupational Achievement: Extensions of a Basic Model*, U.S. Department of Health, Education and Welfare, Office of Education, Bureau of Research, Washington, May 1968.

Feldman, K., and T. Newcombe: *The Impact of College on Students*, Jossey-Bass Publishers, Inc., San Francisco, 1969, vol. 1.

Folger, J. K., and C. B. Nam: *Education of the American Population*, a 1960 Census Monograph, U.S. Bureau of the Census, Washington, 1967.

Gintis, H.: "Education and the Characteristics of Worker Productivity," *American Economic Review*, vol. 61, pp. 266–280, May 1971.

Gourman, J.: *The Gourman Report*, The Continuing Education Institute, Phoenix, 1956.

Griliches, Z., and W. Mason: "Education, Income and Ability," *Journal of Political Economy*, vol. 80, pp. 74–104, May–June 1972.

Hanoch, G.: "An Economic Anaylsis of Earnings and Schooling," *Journal of Human Resources*, vol. 2, pp. 310–329, Summer 1967.

Hansen, W. L., B. A. Weisbrod, and W. J. Scanlon: "Schooling and Earnings of Low Achievers," *American Economic Review*, vol. 60, pp. 409–419, June 1970.

Hartman, R.: "The Rationale for Federal Support of Higher Education," in L. Solmon and P. Taubman (eds.), *Does College Matter?*, Academic Press, Inc., New York, 1973.

Hause, J.: "Earnings Profile of Ability and Schooling," *Journal of Political Economy*, vol. 80, pp. 108–138, May–June 1972.

Holt, C.: "Job Search, Phillips' Wage Relation, and Union Influence: Theory and Evidence," in E. S. Phelps (ed.), *Microeconomic Foundations of Employment and Inflation Theory*, W. W. Norton & Company, Inc., New York, 1970, pp. 53–123.

Hoyt, D. P.: *The Relationship Between College Grades and Adult Achievement: A Review of the Literature*, ACT Testing Program, Research and Development Division, Iowa City, Iowa, September 1965.

Hunt, Shane J.: "Income Determinants for College Graduates and the Return to Educational Investment," *Yale Economic Essays*, vol. 3, pp. 305–357, Fall 1963.

Husén, T.: "Talent, Opportunity and Career: A Twenty-six Year Follow-Up," *School Review*, vol. 76, pp. 190–209, June 1968.

Jencks, C., and David Riesman: *The Academic Revolution*, Doubleday & Company, Inc., Garden City, N.Y., 1968.

Juster, F. Thomas: "Introduction and Summary," in F. T. Juster (ed.), *Education, Income, and Human Behavior*, McGraw-Hill Book Company, New York, 1974.

Klein, L. R.: *An Introduction to Econometrics*, Prentice-Hall, Inc., Englewood Cliffs, N. J., 1962.

Lewellen, W. G.: *Executive Compensation in Large Industrial Corporations*, National Bureau of Economic Research, Inc., New York, 1968.

Lydall, H.: *The Structure of Earnings*, Oxford University Press, New York, 1969.

Lynch, M.: "Does the Level of Physicians' Incomes Indicate a Shortage?" University of Pennsylvania Discussion Paper no. 166, University of Pennsylvania Press, Philadelphia, 1968.

Miller, H.: "Annual and Lifetime Income in Relation to Education: 1939 to 1959," *American Economic Review*, vol. 5, pp. 962–986, December 1960.

Miller, S., and F. Reissman: "The Credential Trap," in S. Miller and F. Reissman (eds.), *Social Class and Social Policy*, Basic Books, Inc., New York, 1969.

Mincer, J.: "The Distribution of Labor Incomes: A Survey with Special References to the Human Capital Approach," *Journal of Economic Literature*, vol. 8, pp. 1–26, March 1970.

Morgan, J., and M. David: "Education and Income," *Quarterly Journal of Economics*, vol. 78, pp. 346–347, August 1963.

Phelps, E.: "The New View of Investment: A Neoclassical Analysis," *Quarterly Journal of Economics*, vol. 76, pp. 548–567, November 1962.

Project Talent: *The American High-School Student,* Cooperative Research Project no. 635, The University of Pittsburgh Press, Pittsburgh, 1964.

Rogers, D. D.: *"Private Rates of Return to Education in the United States: A Case Study,"* Ph.D. dissertation, Yale University, New Haven, Conn., 1967.

Schultz, T. W.: *The Economic Value of Education,* Columbia University Press, New York, 1963.

Sewell, W., W. Haller, and A. Portes: "The Educational and Early Occupational Attainment Process," *American Sociological Review,* vol. 34, pp. 82–92, February 1969.

Simon, B., and P. Ellison: "Does College Make a Person Healthy, Wealthy, and Wise?" in L. Solmon and P. Taubman (eds.), *Does College Matter?,* pp. 35–63, Academic Press, Inc. New York, 1973.

Solmon, L. C.: *The Meaning of Quality of Colleges and Universities,* National Bureau of Economic Research, Inc., New York, 1969. (Mimeographed.)

Solmon, L., and P. Taubman (eds.): *Does College Matter?,* Academic Press, Inc., New York, 1973.

Soloman, E. (ed.): *The Management of Corporate Capital,* The Free Press of Glencoe, Ill., New York, 1959.

Solow, R. M.: "On the Dynamics of the Income Distribution," Ph.D. dissertation, Harvard University, Cambridge, Mass., 1951.

Spence, M.: *Market Signalling,* Harvard University, Cambridge, Mass., 1972. (Mimeographed.)

Summers, R.: *An Econometric Investigation of the Size Distribution of Lifetime Average Annual Income,* Technical Report no. 31, Stanford University Press, Stanford, Calif., 1956.

Taubman, P., and T. Wales: "The Impact of Investment Subsidies in a Neoclassical Growth Model," *Review of Economics and Statistics,* vol. 51, pp. 287–298, August 1969.

Taubman, P., and T. Wales: *Mental Ability and Higher Educational Attainment in the Twentieth Century,* National Bureau of Economic Research, Inc., and Carnegie Commission on Higher Education, Berkeley, 1972.

Taubman, P., and T. Wales: "Higher Education, Mental Ability, and Screening," *Journal of Political Economy,* vol. 81, pp. 28–56, January–February 1973.

Terman, L. M., and M. Oden: *Genetic Studies of Genius,* vol. 4, *The Gifted Child Grows Up,* Stanford University Press, Stanford, Calif., 1947.

Theil, H.: *Economic Forecasts and Policy,* North-Holland Publishing Company, Amsterdam, 1961.

Thorndike, R., and E. Hagen: *Ten Thousand Careers,* John Wiley & Sons, Inc., New York, 1959.

Thurow, L., and R. E. B. Lucas: *The American Distribution of Income: A Structural Problem,* Joint Economic Committee, Washington, D.C., 1972.

Tobin, J.: "Liquidity Preference as Behavior Towards Risk," *Review of Economic Studies,* February 1968.

U.S. Bureau of the Census: *Statistical Abstract of the United States, 1965; 1966; 1967; 1968; and 1969; 1965–1969.*

U.S. Bureau of the Census: *Trends in the Income of Families and Persons in the United States: 1947–64,* Technical Paper no. 17, 1966.

U.S. Bureau of the Census: "Annual Mean Income and Educational Attainment of Men in the United States for Selected Years, 1956–1966," *Current Population Reports,* ser. P-60, no. 56, Aug. 14, 1968.

U.S. Bureau of the Census: "Income in 1968 of Families and Persons in the United States," *Current Population Reports,* ser. P-60, no. 66, Dec. 23, 1969.

Wales, T.: "The Effect of College Quality on Earnings: Results from the NBER-Thorndike Data," *Journal of Human Resources,* vol. 8, pp. 306–317, Summer 1973.

Weisbrod, B. A.: *External Benefits of Public Education,* Princeton University Press, Industrial Relations Section, Princeton, N.J., 1964.

Weisbrod, B., and P. Karpoff: "Monetary Returns to College Education, Student Ability and College Quality," *Review of Economics and Statistics,* vol. 50, pp. 491–497, November 1968.

Wolfle, D.: *America's Resources of Specialized Talent,* The Report of the Commission on Human Resources and Advanced Training, Harper & Brothers, New York, 1954.

Wolfle, D., and J. G. Smith: "The Occupational Value of Education for Superior High-School Graduates," *Journal of Higher Education,* vol. 27, pp. 201–213, April 1956.

Index

Spatial orientation test, 204 – 207
Spatial-perception ability, 79
 and income, 70, 104
 vs. response bias, 209
 and returns to education, 74
Spatial relations test, 203
Speed of identification test, 204, 206, 207
Spence, M., 155*n*.
Stanford University, 14
Starting salaries:
 and education, 108, 109, 111, 112
 and ability, 76, 110 – 112
 (*See also* Initial job)
Statistical theory, 89
Status and occupational choice, 165
Success bias:
 analysis of, 197 – 210
 of data, 209 – 215
 and education vs. income, 212, 213
Successful people, 255 – 274
Supply and demand:
 vs. education, 31
 vs. screening, 155, 156

Taubman, P., 19, 27*n*., 39, 42, 49, 50, 251*n*.,
  252, 256, 258
Teachers:
 earnings of: vs. education, 71, 86, 100,
  212 – 214, 228
 and salary regressions, 82, 83, 96, 97,
  224
 IQ of, 56
 nonmonetary rewards for, 86*n*.
 occupational regressions for, 144 – 146
Technical occupations:
 earnings for, 8
 and education, 66 – 68, 139 – 141, 164,
  170
 for occupations, 146
 for professions, 146
 occupational regressions for, 144 – 148
 vs. education, 144 – 146
Technical school education, 180, 181
Terman, L. M., 62, 255
Test scores:
 for air cadets, 4
 bias analysis for, 197–210
 and factor analysis, 203 – 209
 and IQ, 5*n*., 181

Tests:
 coordination, 204 – 207
 dexterity, 205 – 207
 prejob, 30
 for screening, 31
 (*See also* Intelligence-test scores; IQ
  scores; Test scores)
Thorndike, R., 3, 4, 5*n*., 6*n*., 8*n*., 12, 59 – 61,
  69, 74, 79, 93, 107*n*., 143, 157, 198*n*.,
  203, 208, 211 – 213, 217 – 222
Thorndike-Hagen questionnaire, 217 – 222
Thorndike-Hagan sample (*see* NBER-TH
  sample)
Thurow, L., 20
Time-on-the job (*see* Experience; Job experience; On-the-job training; Work
  experience)
Training (*see* Education; On-the-job training; Military training; Vocational
  training)

Undergraduate degrees:
 and abilities, 232 – 236
 and age, 92, 93, 248, 249
 and earnings, 90, 103, 115 – 119
 vs. age, 248, 249
 and mathematical ability, 92, 93
 vs. education, 116, 212 – 214
 by occupation, 139, 141
 and earnings increase, 7, 71, 86, 100, 117
 vs. education, 228
 and ex ante rates of returns to, 133
 and executives, distribution of, 257
 ex post age-income profiles for, 121, 250
 ex post rates of returns to, 126, 127
 vs. income-education regressions,
  268 – 273
 and initial salaries, 109
 and mathematical ability, 92, 93, 248, 249
 and nonfarm managers, 258
 by occupation vs. earnings, 139 – 141
 occupational regressions for, 144 – 146
 and regression analyses: vs. abilities,
  232 – 236
 vs. salaries, 82, 83, 96, 97, 224
 (*See also* B.A. degrees; B.S. degrees;
  College degrees)
Unskilled workers, 53, 187
 description of, 192